KLOP

KLOP

BRITAIN'S MOST INGENIOUS
SECRET AGENT

PETER DAY

Biteback Publishing

First published in Great Britain in 2014 by
Biteback Publishing Ltd
Westminster Tower
3 Albert Embankment
London SE1 7SP

ISBN 978-1-84954-693-5

10 9 8 7 6 5 4 3 2 1

A CIP catalogue record for this book is available from the British Library.

Set in Caslon by Soapbox
Printed and bound in Great Britain by
CPI Group (UK) Ltd, Croydon CR0 4YY

CONTENTS

ACKNOWLEDGEMENTS

What started out as a simple task – to turn the assorted reports of Klop Ustinov's espionage exploits into a coherent story – has escalated into an epic journey from the tropical heat of Ethiopia in the nineteenth century through the Russian Revolution and two World Wars to the icy tundra of the Cold War. As it grew in scale and complexity it became ever more difficult to keep track of the many characters that flitted in and out of the narrative, not to mention the incomprehensible military and intelligence acronyms. To aid navigation a glossary of principal characters and organisations has been included towards the end of this book.

Inevitably much of the preliminary research was done at the National Archives at Kew where the staff were, as ever, patient and knowledgeable. I relied heavily, too, on the resources of the London Library and the British Library and, to a lesser extent, on the Imperial War Museum, Churchill Archives and Cambridge University Library.

I was drawn to the United States by the meticulous investigations of Professor Richard Breitman and the Interagency Working Group who supervised the release of around ten million pages of documents under the 1998 Nazi War Crimes Disclosure Act and distilled them into a single volume of essays. Some former members of the team were among the enthusiastic research advisers and assistants who guided me through a couple of fruitful weeks at the US Archives at College Park, Maryland.

Despite the best endeavours of the language teachers at the Goethe Institute in London, my command of German would not have been adequate to the task without the generous time and effort of Günter Scheidemann and his colleagues in the reading room of the German Foreign Office archive in Berlin; and likewise Marco Birn and colleagues at the Baden-Württemberg state archive in Stuttgart. Thanks also to the licensing department of the archives in Stuttgart and Ludwigsburg for permission to reproduce photographs. Other photos were provided by The National Archives, the Imperial War Museum, Getty Images, Mrs Elizabeth Head, and under Crown copyright from government records. The publishers, Macmillan, authorised the use of extracts from *Klop and the Ustinov Family* by Nadia Benois.

My thanks to all those at Biteback who contributed to the book's publication, particularly commissioning editor Mick Smith and editors Hollie Teague, Olivia Beattie and Victoria Godden. Various individuals weighed in with advice and support during the research stage, among them Ustinov family friends Cathy Bazley, Emily Beanland, Owain Hughes, June Lewis-Jones and Liz Head, née Brousson, who was incredibly generous with her time and hospitality. Special thanks are due to Klop's grandson, Igor Ustinov, for permission to use previously unseen sketches from Nadia Benois's notebooks and for his encouragement and thoughtful insights.

All of these people have helped me get closer to the truth about an elusive subject but cannot be held responsible for errors and misapprehensions. It has always to be borne in mind that the original source for much of what follows was two world champion raconteurs, Klop and his son Peter, and they may, just occasionally, have been guilty of that failing so often attributed to journalists – not letting the facts get in the way of a good story.

CHAPTER 1: MAGDALENA

Nobody wants to be known as a bedbug. Except Klop Ustinov. The Russian diminutive was more fun than doleful Jona, the name his parents gave him. He looked the part: only 5ft 2in., his head slightly too big for his body; his protruding grape-green eyes shamelessly undressing any attractive woman who crossed his line of vision. What's more, he shared the tiny parasite's capacity to turn up, not exactly uninvited but quite surprisingly, in more than a few of their beds. He was a real-life spy with more lovers than James Bond. Like Bond, he was a man who appreciated fine food and wine. But he was no 007, licensed to kill. Codenamed U35, his mission was to beguile and confuse.

Bond's creator Ian Fleming and Klop Ustinov were contemporaries. Fleming masterminded subversion in Spain and Portugal for naval intelligence while Klop was intriguing with MI6 double agents in Lisbon during the Second World War.

Sir Dick White, the only man ever to be director of both MI5 and MI6, nurtured Klop's career from its earliest days. He described him as his best and most ingenious operator.[1] The problem is to explain how, and why, he earned such an accolade.

Several other countries had better claim to his loyalty. Money and notoriety were not his motives. He was never rich, usually lived beyond his means, and would rather die than cash in on the many secrets he harboured. He left no memoirs. Yet to all appearances he was neither especially secret nor even discreet. His battlegrounds were the social salons of Europe; his disguise the showman's talent to entertain and amuse; his most potent weapon the spellbinding art of the storyteller: all the qualities which shaped his more famous son Peter Ustinov as an actor, director and raconteur.

Klop's friend and fellow MI6 officer Nicholas Elliott might have been thinking of him when he described the attributes needed to succeed:

> They will be personalities in their own right; they will have humanity and a capacity for friendship; and they will have a sense of humour which will enable them to avoid the ridiculous mumbo-jumbo of over secrecy.[2]

He explained that it was all about gaining other people's confidence and occasionally persuading them to do things against their better judgment.

Peter Ustinov said of his father that he regarded life as a superficial exercise, an extent of thin ice to be skated on, for the execution of arabesques and figures of fun. Klop would have agreed with Cecil Rhodes that to be an Englishman meant that the first prize in the lottery of life had been won. Rhodes was a commanding figure of the British Empire. For Klop, the lottery of life had its origins in two other imperial dynasties – Russia and Ethiopia.

★

On a plateau 3,900ft above the Bechilo valley, the great brass cannon called Sebastopol gave out a roar that could be clearly heard two miles away. It was the most powerful weapon in the armoury of the Emperor Theodore, modelled on the Russian guns that faced the Charge of the Light Brigade at Balaclava.

The fearsome, unpredictable despot had conquered his rival tribes and ruled over all the fabulous lands of Abyssinia, better known now as Ethiopia. He was the latest embodiment of an uncertain lineage which traced its roots to the Biblical King Solomon and the Queen of Sheba. He had heard of that terrible slaughter in the Crimea and now believed that he, too, could strike fear in the red-coated soldiers of the British Army gathered on the plain before Magdala, his impregnable mountain fortress, towering 9,000ft above sea level.

In January 1868, 10,000 British and Indian soldiers and 30,000 support staff and hangers-on landed at Annesley Bay on the Red Sea. They were under the command of Lieutenant General Sir Robert Napier, veteran of the Sikh Wars, the Indian Mutiny, the North West Frontier and the second Anglo-Chinese War. He didn't stint on equipment. There were forty-four Indian elephants, 2,538 horses and 16,022 mules to carry his men plus 300,000 tons of arms and supplies. They built their own railway and negotiated safe passage with the emperor's enemies.

The vanguard of fighting men made an extraordinary forced march across 400 miles of uncompromising terrain. They crossed the Bechilo valley, labouring up the side of the ravine through intense heat with insufficient water, and now stood implacably before Magdala, come to right a tiny wrong. Theodore had insulted Queen Victoria, whose dominions extended beyond his imagination.

He had previously hoped to be friends with Her Majesty and made diplomatic overtures. She had responded with a gift of silver embossed pistols. But when the British Foreign Office failed to reply to his overtures with sufficient alacrity or respect he took their representative hostage. Charles Cameron spent more than four years in captivity. He was joined by the emissary sent to negotiate his release, Hormuz Rassam, and by missionaries, European artisans and adventurers, and various princelings of rival tribes. The princes were hostages against the continued subservience of their tribes. Their lives depended on Theodore's murderous black moods, often occasioned by strong drink. Among the European hostages was Moritz Hall, a former Polish soldier, a Jew who had converted to Christianity and an opportunist who had agreed, under duress, to build Theodore's great cannon.

Legend has it that Moritz was chained to the gun to prevent him escaping.[3] If so, he was lucky to survive: its barrel was flawed and eventually burst upon firing. Theodore took it as an ill-omen that his stronghold would fall to the mighty force of redcoats assembled by General Napier. And Magdala did fall. But only after Theodore, in a quite unexpected act of clemency, released all his European hostages; he had previously propelled his native captives to their deaths over a sheer cliff. He had already seen some of his best troops cut to pieces by rocket fire and new Snider-Enfield rifles, which were capable of firing ten rounds per minute. They were slaughtered as they hurtled down from their fortress in a hopeless spear charge on the British positions. Imperial pride would not countenance surrender. Theodore hoped that freedom for his prisoners and a peace offering of 1,000 cattle would suffice.

Down the mountain on the Easter Saturday of the year 1868 came 61 hostages, with 187 servants and 323 animals. Among them was the hapless royal armourer Moritz Hall with his wife Wayzaru Walatta Iyassus, otherwise known as Katarina, the daughter of a German artist and an Ethiopian princess. By Easter Sunday there was an addition to their ranks – Mrs Hall gave birth to a baby girl.

In the midst of such momentous events her birth might have passed unnoticed, but the celebrated American war correspondent Henry Morton Stanley recorded the new arrival for his readers. He had the child's name as Theodora, in tribute to the emperor. Maybe Morton was mistaken, maybe her parents pragmatically changed their minds, but eventually the child was christened Magdalena. At the age of twenty Magdalena would marry an aristocratic Russian-born Protestant, of German nationality, who was well over twice her age. Their eldest son was Jona Ustinov, otherwise known as Klop.

Stanley's attention was quickly diverted to the storming of the fortress, on Easter Monday. Drummer Michael Magner and Private James Bergin won the Victoria Cross for leading a heroic assault, cutting through the brushwood defences with their bayonets and leading the charge on the dispirited defenders. Theodore committed suicide, with one of Queen Victoria's pistols, rather than endure the humiliation of capture; the victorious troops discovered his liquor store and pretty soon ran riot, looting and pillaging until Napier eventually restored some sort of order.[4]

Theodore's fortress contained many religious and imperial treasures, some of which he himself had looted during his conquests. These were auctioned and carried back to Britain. A good few of them ended up in the British Museum, the Victoria and Albert Museum and the Royal Collection – the tangible legacy of a military adventure in which no territory was captured, no other tribute exacted and no trade links established. Theodore's son and heir, Prince Alemayehu, accompanied the retreating British Army, as did his mother until she succumbed to illness and died. Alemayehu was introduced to Queen Victoria at Osborne on the Isle of Wight, tutored by his guardian Captain Tristram Speedy and then given a traditional education for an English gentleman, Rugby public school and Sandhurst military college. He lived in Leeds until he died of pneumonia at the age of eighteen, a sad and disorientated figure. At Queen Victoria's insistence, he was buried in the crypt beside St George's Chapel at Windsor Castle. Moritz Hall, his wife and family, including the infant Magdalena, were part of that military procession back to the landing point on the Red Sea. Nobody knew it then, but Magdalena's destiny dictated that she, too, would become part of an enduring British legacy. Her family settled in Palestine, in the ancient city of Jaffa which now forms part of Tel Aviv in Israel. Her mother Katarina retained her links with Abyssinia, returning in 1902 to become a lady-in-waiting at the court of the Emperor Menilek and a close friend of his wife, Empress Taytu. Magdalena's brother, David, became a counsellor of state to the next emperor, Haile Selassie.[5]

Magdalena's father, Moritz Hall, was born in 1838 in the Polish city of Cracow, then part of a Russian protectorate. Two years later Magdalena's future husband, Platon Ustinov, or Oustinoff, was born in St Petersburg, the son of an extraordinarily dissolute father and an exceptionally beautiful mother. Their wealth dated back to the last years of the seventeenth century when Adrian Ustinov made a fortune in the Siberian salt trade. He had noble antecedents and a family crest that bore a salt press, an eagle's wing, a star and a bee buzzing across two blades of wheat.

Adrian's son, Mikhail, settled in Saratov in southern Russia on the lower reaches of the Volga River. Thanks to an imperial favour he acquired estates covering 240,000 hectares, employing 6,000 serfs. Mikhail in turn had five sons. The fifth, Grigori, installed his beautiful wife Maria in a St Petersburg town house while he set himself up in a separate property in the same street where he could give full rein to his debauched tastes. Breakfast consisted of a banquet of caviar, smoked salmon, suckling pig, hard-boiled eggs, anchovies, pickled herrings and salted cucumbers, washed down with vodka and supplemented with a bevy of teenage peasant girls, recruited from his country estates, whom he seduced, singly or several at a time, until lunch. After that he could repair to the Moscow English Club, where only aristocrats were admitted, for an evening of drinking and gambling. Confronted with such licentiousness, his youngest son Platon developed a puritan streak.

Platon had seemed destined for a career in the Chevalier Guards regiment of cavalry but at the age of twenty-one a fall from his horse left him temporarily paralysed and with lung damage. He travelled to the Mediterranean to convalesce, staying in a Protestant mission hostel in Palestine. There he succumbed to the preaching of a Protestant pastor from Germany, Peter Metzler, and the good looks of his daughter, Maria. He invested money in their mission and then invited Pastor Metzler and his family to return to Russia with him to manage his estates. Displaying a wilfulness and disregard of the consequences that characterised his life, Platon refused to take an oath of allegiance to the tsar, on the grounds that he had embraced the Protestant religion and could not simultaneously swear devotion to the Orthodox Church.

While his father Grigori's personal and private immorality was no bar to his social standing, Platon's public rejection of one of the pillars of the Russian state provoked a scandal. Exile and disgrace beckoned. He sold his share of the family estates and moved to the Germanic kingdom of Württemberg, which was an astute move. In 1846 King Karl V had married the tsar's daughter, Olga. Queen Olly, as she liked to be known, welcomed Platon and granted him citizenship. So, when Württemberg joined the confederation of states that formed the German Empire, in 1870, Platon became an accidental German.

Not that he spent much time in the fatherland that had adopted him. He married the pastor's daughter, Maria Metzler, and made the most distressing discovery, on his wedding night, that he was not her first lover. Most husbands of the time would have been scandalised by such a revelation; it was beyond forgiveness as far as the puritanical Platon was concerned. He disowned her immediately but for many years refused a divorce. In his outrage and shame he gravitated back to the Holy Land and created his own little Garden of Eden in Jaffa.[6]

Baron Platon von Ustinov still had considerable wealth, both in money and possessions, from the sale of his Russian estates. Not trusting banks, he carried it all with him wherever he went. He had a disdain for everyday transactions, washing his cash before handling it. But once settled in Jaffa he invested in property, in the form of a mansion in the German colony, a district dominated by the Temple Society, an evangelical Protestant denomination. Around his new home he created a botanical garden with 170 different kinds of flowers and a miniature zoo which became a haven of peace for tourists and settlers alike. He donated money to found a hospital, hospice and girls' school.

Moritz Hall had settled in the same neighbourhood and the two men became friends. Two of Hall's sons opened a hotel in the Baron's house. The Hotel du Parc soon became a recommended venue in Baedeker's and contemporary guide books. In 1898 Kaiser Wilhelm of Germany and the Empress Augusta stayed there during a visit to Palestine. The kaiser is recorded as having especially enjoyed the pure air of the garden at night and the view of the moon reflected on the Mediterranean.[7]

Platon took no part in the running of the hotel, preferring to shut himself in his private study with his books. He became expert in ancient languages, such as Amharic, Greek, Hebrew, and became a philanthropist, too. He allowed the congregation of the newly formed Immanuel Evangelical Church, among them Moritz Hall, to use a room in the Hotel du Parc and helped finance the building of the church which still stands in Beer Hofman Street. A fellow church benefactor, the German banker Johannes Frutiger, became a close friend. He had known Platon during his first visit to Jaffa from 1862 to 1867 and renewed their friendship when he returned to Palestine ten years later. His wife Maria and their children, Hermann, Adolf, Cornelia, Frederike and Bernhard spent holidays at the Hotel du Parc.

Platon had finally divorced Maria after discovering that she and her new lover were plotting to kill him so that they might remarry and start a new life in Australia. They had tampered with Platon's revolver, which he kept to deter burglars, with the intention that it should blow up in his face the next time he fired it.[8] New love, and marriage to Magdalena came late in life.

The stern, bearded, patriarchal figure made an incongruous picture alongside his dark, young, serious-looking new bride, who shared his deep religious convictions. At first they were not blessed with children. There were a series of miscarriages before Jona von Ustinov became Platon's firstborn son, on 2 December 1892. The father was fifty-six. Jona was born two months premature and weighing only two pounds, Platon fed him milk through the dropper of a Waterman's fountain pen.

Jona was named for the Biblical character who had been swallowed by a whale after setting out, against the Lord's bidding, on a ship sailing from Jaffa – where the Ustinovs now resided. The boy hated the name, and in later life was happy to be known by the nickname Klop bestowed on him by his Russian wife, Nadia Benois.

Childhood photographs give no clue to the man. His parents kept Jona's fair hair girlishly long. His pale green eyes are innocently wide; by his teens, though, they have a knowing intensity. He grew thoroughly spoilt, even though four siblings followed, indulged by a father who veered between strict insistence on completing all homework set by the German colony school to providing the Arab pony on which Jona galloped wildly along the sands, terrorising his neighbours.

Platon, short and broad with long flowing locks and full beard, led an austere lifestyle, largely vegetarian, often dressing from head to toe in white (except on the beach where he strode around stark naked). He eschewed medicine but would drink a whole bottle of champagne as a cure for flu.

He instructed his children in the ways of the world by reading aloud to them from his newspaper at the breakfast table. In this deeply religious household, Jona, who had inherited his father's gift for languages, first learned English from Moody and Sankey, publishers of a popular hymnbook. The children grew up with Russian nannies, Arab servants and guests who spoke French, German and English.[9]

He attended a high school in Jerusalem but when he reached the age of thirteen it was decided to send him away to the gymnasium in Düsseldorf to take his *Abitur*, the German equivalent of the International Baccalaureate. His younger brother Peter followed in his footsteps. Lodgings were obtained for Klop in the home of a retired *Hauptmann* (army captain) and his wife. According to Jona's later account, the captain was committed to an asylum after chasing him round the house brandishing a sabre, convinced that his young lodger was an incarnation of Mephistopheles. Given the boy's reputation for childish devilment it is possible there was some provocation. Platon had maintained his connections with Germany. Jona's godmother was Gräfin (Countess) von dem Bussche-Ippenburg, a member of one of the country's oldest aristocratic families, and as a young man he visited her on her estates near Osnabrück. School in Düsseldorf was followed by a spell at Yverdon in Switzerland, improving his French, and then Grenoble University.

Sexual awakening began early. We have only his word for this, surprisingly recorded in faithful and uncritical detail by his wife Nadia, whom he regaled with his many liaisons, youthful and adult. These stories seem neither confessional nor boastful; they are gleeful accounts of exploits to be savoured, entertainment almost.

She recounts how, as a boy, he peeped through neighbours' windows to watch girls undress. Returning by ship from school to Jaffa he would practise his flirtation techniques with girls on board and learned to appreciate the varying charms of their different nationalities. He was particularly taken with a Scottish redhead whom he pursued while she was attending finishing school in Yverdon, eventually keeping a tryst with her by scaling a high wall topped with glass and emerging bloody, with trousers torn, but triumphant. It was typical of Klop the storyteller that he should claim to have encountered the woman twenty-five years later, still beautiful and unmarried, at a society dinner in London. Such coincidences were not uncommon in Klop's retrospective accounts of his amorous adventures.

What he lacked in height he compensated for by close attendance to his appearance. The young man had groomed and pomaded hair, manicured nails, elegantly tailored clothes and a monocle – quite the dandy. And it worked. In Grenoble he pursued his fellow female students as well as the daughter of a wealthy chateau owner, Geneviève de la Motte. He seduced his landlady's daughter – a passionate year-long affair that only ended when the girl fell for an Italian count. Next came a Bulgarian student and Klop would claim that many years later he was introduced to a Bulgarian diplomat who turned out to be her son.

Yet, according to Nadia, he was cautious and suspicious of women, building a protective wall around his emotions and avoiding serious commitment. She wrote:

> He said that, in his opinion, far too much importance is attributed to sentiment in love. He believed in physical enjoyment garnished with light-hearted banter and sprinkled with touches of romance.[10]

Much later, Jona's son Peter, who was offended by what he regarded as his father's humiliation of his mother, offered what was, under the circumstances, a generous assessment that his father was not really a womaniser but was thrilled by the unpredictable, fleeting moments of flirtation. He lacked the secretive nature required for a serious affair. He was: 'a flitter from flower to flower, a grazer of bottoms rather than a pincher.'[11]

In Grenoble, aside from the female distractions, Klop had to turn his mind to earning a living. He already had the taste for travel, for socialising with colourful and interesting people and being at the centre of events. A diplomatic career beckoned and he took himself off to Berlin, intending to study law.

He scarcely had time to immerse himself in his studies when a family crisis summoned him home to Jaffa. Platon, too often the benefactor of good causes and needy relatives, was facing financial ruin. The solution, it was decided, was to sell his collection of antiquities to some wealthy Western institution. It included more than 1,500 items, dating from the end of the Iron Age onwards: sculptures, pottery, clay vessels, terracotta figurines, gems, scarabs, glass objects, coins and bronzes. Among its more significant finds was Palestinian pottery from the ancient port of Ashkelon. He had begun by collecting Phoenician inscriptions but then became motivated by a desire to protect Jewish and Christian art and antiques from being destroyed or defaced by the area's Muslim inhabitants. He had no scientific or archaeological training and shunned dealers, preferring to buy direct from poor peasants, believing that he was helping them financially.

The family left Palestine in 1913, pausing briefly to confirm Platon's German citizenship 'on account of his Protestant leanings' before settling in Shepherd's Bush in west London. Klop was appointed as salesman, attempting to arouse interest in the collection not only in London but in Paris and Berlin. A family friend, the Norwegian shipping magnate Sir Karl Knudsen, who had taken British nationality and settled in London, represented the family's interests with the British Museum. He had met Platon for the first time a year earlier, during a visit to Palestine, and considered the collection unique. It had attracted favourable attention from Middle East scholars and there was interest from the Louvre in Paris, but Platon wanted to keep the collection together and was advised that London was the best place to exhibit it and, if necessary, auction it. Knudsen arranged for it to be put on display at 59 Holland Park Avenue, the home of Julian D. Myers, a wealthy City of London clothes wholesaler.

Knudsen assured Arthur Hamilton Smith, keeper of the department of Greek and Roman antiquities at the museum, that he had no personal financial interest in the transaction and that Platon would not sell until all the interested parties had a chance to view it.

One of the British Museum's scholars, Wordsworth E. Jones, seems to have been quite bowled over by what he saw. He regarded it as unique, and a great pleasure, to find such material, including pristine Greek and Roman marbles, in Palestine, which previously had been barren ground for artefacts of this type. The Greek art included a torso of Alexander the Great, by the sculptor Lysippus, discovered at Tyre and thought to represent Alexander leading a seven-month siege of the city. Among other gems was an Egyptian scarab in green jade thought to have belonged to a pharaoh's daughter who married King Solomon. Jones had a word of praise, too, for the baroness, who had packed the hundreds of specimens herself so that when they arrived in London not one was broken. They amounted to 'almost a small museum and such as is rarely brought to London by one man'.[12]

He recommended it for acquisition but it seems Platon's asking price was too high. The collection was eventually bought by a consortium of wealthy and influential Norwegians. Most of it was put in storage but some of the more select items eventually found their way to the Norwegian National Gallery in Oslo.[13]

At this point, after about fifty years in exile, Platon decided it was time to regain his Russian nationality and wrote directly to Tsar Nicholas II for permission to return to the land of his birth. His application was supported by the Russian ambassador in London, Count Benckendorff, one of the architects of the Triple Entente that bound together Britain, France and Russia against the imperial designs of Kaiser Wilhelm II of Germany.

The sequel to that treaty, precipitated by the assassination of the Archduke Franz Ferdinand in Sarajevo on 28 June 1914, was the Great War that tore Europe asunder. It rent the Ustinov family in three conflicting directions. Their days in London before war was declared were the last they would spend together.

CHAPTER 2: GRENADIERS

Klop was the first to depart the Ustinov family home in London, accompanied by his brother Peter: like many young men they were caught up in the patriotic fervour of the moment, rushing to volunteer with little thought of the slaughter that awaited. But Klop and Peter were German; their duty lay with the kaiser on the Continent, not with Lord Kitchener and King George V.

Platon, meanwhile, got his wish and returned to Russia where, despite being seventy-three years old, he was still technically an officer of the Chevalier Guards. His wife Magdalena and daughter Tabitha, then aged fourteen, joined him soon after, heading for a country that they barely knew and where they would soon find themselves destitute. The two youngest children, Platon junior, aged eleven, and Gregory, seven, were left behind at boarding school in London. They were in the care of wealthy and influential friends, the shipping magnate Sir Karl Knudsen and his wife, and relatives of the banker Johannes Frutiger. Norwegian-born Sir Karl had taken British nationality and married a Scot, Anne Macarthur. He played a vital role during the war in liaising with Norwegian ship owners whose fleets helped keep Britain supplied.

Peter, who had been born in Tölz, in Bavaria, in 1895 and had been planning to study medicine, was first to enlist, on 7 August. Klop signed up three days later in the 123rd Grenadiers of the 5th King Karl of Württemberg infantry regiment. He gave his next of kin, rather grandly, as the Gräfin von dem Bussche. She at least had impressive German credentials compared with his relatives, who were scattered through lands which were now enemy territory. He began his career as a *Gefreite*, or lance corporal, but seems to have been marked out for rapid promotion and by March 1915 held the junior officer rank of *Leutnant*. The regiment had marched out from its headquarters at Ulm, anthems playing and flags fluttering in the breeze, advancing into Belgium. They followed the old Roman road down which Attila had led the Hunnish hordes in his assault on the empire of Valentinian III nearly 1,500 years earlier. Attila got to Orleans, west of Paris, before being driven back at the Battle of the Catalaunian Plains. The kaiser's army never got that far. By the winter of 1914 they were trapped in the primeval landscape of the forest of the Argonne east of Reims in northern France where even the place names were redolent of death. It was hard, attritional warfare. There was impenetrable undergrowth, gorse bushes and head high bracken growing between ancient oaks and beeches. The troops made shelters in the foliage and dug foxholes. Now they had to fight their way forward step by step through the forest and the trenches. A contemporary photograph shows Klop, with close-cropped hair and a steely gaze, in his ankle-length greatcoat on a snow-covered hillside. In January 1915 he had taken part in the storming of the Valley of Dieusson in the Bois de la Grurie. Recognition that he had been acting above his rank was signified by the promotion to *Leutnant* and the award of an Iron Cross, Second Class. The Dieusson attack cost the French about 3,000 men, roughly three times the German casualties. In the first three months of 1915, fighting mostly in the Argonne, the French Third Army lost nearly 30,000 men. The Germans, under General Bruno von Mudra, were gaining the upper hand. By summer they were able to muster concentrated artillery attacks; for the first time shells were delivering poison gas and a new design of hand grenade was available.[14] The Grenadiers were temporarily trapped under heavy artillery bombardment from the French and when it relented the kaiser visited them to present bravery awards. During the autumn Klop continued to attract attention in regimental records for his noteworthy actions. Hans Speidel was a platoon commander and singled out Klop as one of his fellow junior officers who forged an unbreakable comradeship with their men which helped to maintain their morale as they experienced the terror of mechanised warfare for the first time. They finally escaped the 'accursed forest' for the even greater hell-holes of the trenches of the Somme towards the end of the year. Behind them, in a grove of mighty oaks, they had buried their dead comrades, with a regimental memorial carved into one of the trees. To have fought in the Battle of the Argonne Forest became a badge of honour.[15]

Sir Arthur Conan Doyle visited the opposing French troops there in 1916, in his capacity as war correspondent of the *Daily Chronicle*, and wrote:

> The great forest consists of sturdy oaks and beeches and firs, with a thick tangle of undergrowth, mountain, valley, and plateau alternating. The soil is soft clay, admirably suited for entrenching, tunnelling, and mine warfare – when it is dry. As an outside observer, I do not see why the war in this area should not go on for a hundred years, without any decisive result. What is happening now is precisely what happened last year. The only difference is that the trenches are deeper, dug-outs better made, tunnels are longer, and the charges of explosives heavier.[16]

Klop had established an important and lifelong friendship with Speidel, who became a career soldier, later a general and chief of staff in France and on the Russian Front in the Second World War. Speidel was ashamed of Nazi racial policies and took part in the 1944 plot to assassinate Hitler. In the late 1950s he was appointed commander-in-chief of NATO forces in Central Europe.

For them the year 1916 began in Flanders, where their job was to cling on to the hard-won positions that they called *Der Bastion* and *Doppelhöhe 60*, known to the Allies as the notorious Hill 60. From there they could look out over the unattainable goals of St Martins Cathedral and the medieval Cloth Hall of Ypres, a town they occupied briefly at the start of the war but never recaptured. All around it both sides suffered terrible losses.

Hill 60 was not much more than an embankment, rising only a little over 60 metres above sea level, created artificially from the spoil of a nearby railway cutting. It had been captured by the Germans in 10 December 1914 and became the first scene of the underground warfare in which British engineers and miners tunnelled under the German lines in April 1915 to plant around 4,500kg of explosives. The blast that followed caused an enormous crater and flung debris 300ft in the air.

The British then suffered heavy casualties trying to defend the position – the Victoria Cross was awarded on four occasions in a single night's fighting – but in May 1915 the Germans recaptured the barely recognisable landmark with a lethal assault of poison gas.

The 123rd Grenadiers held on grimly to what was left of Hill 60 during the early months of 1916 but were beaten back from the nearby stronghold known as The Bastion at the beginning of March. They had sustained heavy losses in a night-time artillery barrage followed by an infantry advance at 4:30 a.m. on 2 March. British troops reported that many of the Germans they took prisoner had no weapons. The Grenadiers were withdrawn from the frontline after that reverse and given a couple of months leave in the peaceful surroundings of Bruges, Ghent and Ostend. Hill 60 was only recaptured by the Allies in June 1917 after they detonated 450,000kg of explosives under enemy lines at the start of the Battle of Messines, reputedly killing 10,000 German soldiers with a blast so loud that it was claimed it had been heard in London and Dublin.

The Grenadiers had by then long moved on to other scenes of slaughter. As the Battle of the Somme raged on throughout

1916 they were rushed in July to the defence of the villages of Guillemont and Combles. Once more they came under relentless bombardment. They were forced to exist in the ancient underground catacombs at Combles and when they were finally obliged to retreat during August they left many dead and dying comrades behind them in the caves.

They dug in once more, in front of High Wood near Guillemont where the German Army had a divisional headquarters. They were under constant attack by the British, led by officers on horseback and preceded by artillery assaults that reduced everything to dust and rubble. Probably the worst was on 17-18 August when the artillery barrage lasted twenty-six hours. The 2nd Argyll & Sutherland Highlanders attacked, accompanied by flame-throwers, but German machine-gun fire coupled with the British bombardment, which did not let up, even when their own troops reached the disputed ground, forced them back.[17] In that bleak landscape, a smouldering slag heap where no plant life survived, the Grenadiers were invited to surrender and refused, despite having lost three-quarters of their men, fighting on with only a few machine guns and precious little ammunition. They were finally withdrawn at the end of August, highly praised for their steadfastness, but it was in vain. Guillemont fell to the Allies a fortnight later.[18]

Klop's fastidious ways were hardly suited to the mud and filth of the trenches. It must have been a relief when he got a chance to train with the recently formed Luftstreitkräfte, the German Army's air force section. He and his brother Peter had not been fighting side by side. Peter had started with the 1st Württemberg Regiment, joined Klop in the 123rd Grenadiers in May 1915 and then joined the 127th in February 1917 but he was also taking part in flying training. Klop quickly found that the glamorous image of an aviator in uniform opened the way to conquests that were altogether more amenable than confronting the British Tommy in the trenches. As he later confided to his wife Nadia, 'he was able quite effortlessly to have any and every female he fancied'. He described to her how he and Peter contrived to be billeted in chateaux where the owner invariably had at least one beautiful daughter. Unblushingly, he told her he shared girlfriends with his brother and indulged in three-in-a-bed sessions with two sisters. In the officers' mess he was developing his skills as an entertainer, playing the piano, impersonating the singers of popular songs in English and French as well as German, making friends in high places who would serve him well in later life.

On the ground, the fighting was concentrated around Messine and Wytschaetebogen where the British began a massive seventeen-day bombardment around the middle of May. Klop was a witness.[19]

Aviation was still its infancy. Crashes were commonplace. Dogfights were becoming lethal with the development of cockpit-mounted machine guns that could fire through the propellers. Previously, enemy airmen fired at each other with pistols or threw missiles at each other. Klop claimed to have once escaped unscathed from a cockpit riddled with bullets, some of which had passed through his cap without causing injury. He liked to maintain that it was the Red Baron, Manfred von Richthofen, who had come to his rescue. By April 1917 Klop had qualified as an observer rather than a pilot. His duties involved spotting targets on the Western Front for the artillery and occasionally dropping bombs.

It was then that he and Peter were reunited in flying section A250. Their comradeship was to be short-lived. On the morning of Friday, 13 July 1917, Peter Ustinov sat on the end of his brother's bed and said farewell before taking off on a mercy mission. With white streamers attached to the wings of his plane, he was heading behind enemy lines to drop bags of mail from British prisoners of war to their loved ones back home. British anti-aircraft gunners failed to see the white streamers, and Peter Ustinov and his pilot Georg Fick met their deaths in no man's land at Hollebeke, just south of Ypres. For Klop, who led the search party to recover his body, it was a shattering experience. A month later Klop was awarded the Iron Cross, First Class, and in September the Ritterkreuz or Knight's Cross, effectively a double Iron Cross. He was still flying but the logs that might record what he did to deserve the accolades were destroyed in the Second World War. Klop may not have cared much about medals after the loss of his brother. He named his only son in his memory.[20]

In July 1918 Klop won yet another Ritterkreuz, this time with the additional recognition of the Order of Friedrich, a nineteenth-century award created for nobility serving in the Württemberg regiments. In October, a couple of weeks before the war ended, he was transferred out of the front line to a War Office job back in Württemberg. When he enlisted he had described himself as a Protestant Evangelist. By the time he signed his discharge papers he had no religion.

He soon moved to Berlin in search of civilian employment. He abandoned the notion of becoming a diplomat. Representing a defeated and vilified country abroad may not have been the best showcase for his talents but his chosen alternative was scarcely better. He had influential friends and quickly found himself appointed to the *Wolff's Telegraphische Büro*, the national news agency of Germany, as a correspondent destined to report from London, probably the most hostile posting imaginable. *Wolff's* had been founded by Bernhard Wolff in 1849, shortly before his former colleague Julius Reuter set up his eponymous agency in London. They had previously worked together in Paris, for the French news agency Havas. The three agencies represented the great powers of international news reporting, often pooling reports or sharing the telegraph cables that made possible rapid worldwide communication. The strategic significance of communications technology had been recognised during the war, with Britain in particular seeking to control the means of transmission in Europe, across the Atlantic and into the Far East. Intercepting enemy diplomatic and military traffic for intelligence and propaganda purposes played an important part in her strategy. Similarly, the Wolff Bureau had been used before and during the war by the German Foreign Office to challenge Britain's colonial supremacy and to get Germany's message across.

So Klop's new profession was not that far removed from diplomacy, in fact it was ideal cover. Klop was about to become a spy.

While he waited for British clearance to travel to London he was sent by the Wolff Bureau to the Netherlands, reporting from there on Dutch and English news. In 1919 the German ambassador in The Hague was Friedrich Rosen, an Orientalist who had grown up in Palestine and been German consul in Jerusalem at the turn of the century. In 1905 he led a German mission to Ethiopia and so would almost certainly have known Baron Platon Ustinov and Moritz Hall's family. Klop reintroduced himself to Rosen and got to know the counsellor at the embassy, Baron Adolf Georg Otto 'Ago' von Maltzan. Rosen would briefly serve as Foreign Minister in the Weimar Republic conducting lively exchanges with his opposite number in the Soviet Union, Georgy Chicherin, with a view to *rapprochement*.[21] But it was Maltzan who was the architect of German revival by clandestinely subverting the peace treaty of Versailles from the moment when victors and vanquished finally put pen to paper in June 1919.

Germany and Russia had been on opposing sides for the first three years of the war, but after the Russian Revolution hostilities had officially ceased. The Russians were therefore excluded from the Versailles treaty negotiations. In addition, some German soldiers had joined forces with the White Russian armies, which already had British and French support, seeking to depose the new Communist rulers. As these rebellions petered out, hundreds of thousands of troops from either side were left stranded in the Baltic States or held as prisoners on either side. There were estimated to be 100,000 German prisoners in Russia and 1.2 million Russians in German hands. During 1919 Maltzan became commissioner responsible for repatriating these displaced soldiers. These were ideal circumstances for infiltrating agents and Maltzan, who had been First Secretary at the German embassy in St Petersburg before the war, took full advantage.

He was convinced that Germany's best prospect for economic and political recovery lay with Russia – Bolsheviks or no Bolsheviks. Russia needed Germany's technical ability; Germany needed Russia's raw materials and vast labour force. The punitive reparations imposed by the Western Allies meant there was no future in that direction. He built his own career around that concept. By 1921 he was ministerial director of the Eastern department of the German Foreign Office and by 1922 State Secretary and closest adviser to the Foreign Minister, Walther Rathenau, who signed the Treaty of Rapallo which ultimately allowed Germany secret military development facilities inside the Soviet Union.

In 1919 and 1920 Germany did not have normal diplomatic representation in Moscow and was anxious to infiltrate any unofficial observer who could report first hand on the chaos that was enveloping the new regime. One of Maltzan's first sources was a Communist sympathiser, Wolfgang Breithaupt, editor of a small but apparently well-regarded journal known as *The Word in Three Languages*, published by the Pacific-World-Union in The Hague, in fact in four languages – English, French, Dutch and German. It attracted contributions from a number of English correspondents, among them the novelist D. H. Lawrence who provided a four-part series on democracy. He had been introduced to the magazine by the pacifist novelist Douglas Goldring, who visited the magazine's offices in 45 Van Imhoff Street and recalled that the paper was run by Germans pretending to be International Socialists. He thought they were secret service agents.[22] It has since emerged that between November 1919 and March 1920 the magazine was used as a front to gather information from inside Russia, paid for by Maltzan who received the fruits of their research direct from Wolfgang Breithaupt. In January 1920 Maltzan paid an Italian journalist, F. P. Giuntini, the relatively modest fee of 8,000 Marks to travel through Russia, ostensibly gathering material for Italian newspaper articles. A month later, a German businessman using the cover name of Knoll was set up with 30,000 Marks to trade in confiscated or export-prohibited medicinal drugs that the authorities in Soviet Russia desperately needed, while making an objective assessment of the latest political events in Soviet Russia. The German consulate at Vyborg, just inside the Finnish border and only 80 miles north-west of St Petersburg, was weighing in with information gleaned from Bolshevik newspapers and informants prepared to make hazardous border crossings at night.[23] Two German doctors, Julius Borchardt and Georg Klemperer, had been summoned to Moscow to treat Lenin's baffling, persistent headaches and reported back to Maltzan. In 1919 a Dutch journalist by the name of Fabius went on a semi-official trip and was arrested on the Russian border but still contrived to return with copies of correspondence between Stalin, Lenin and the head of the Cheka, Felix Dzerzhinsky.[24]

Maltzan was simultaneously holding secret trade talks in Berlin with Viktor Kopp, Russia's Red Cross representative in the city, and hatching military strategies with General Neill Malcolm, head of the British Military Mission, to overthrow the Bolsheviks. Maltzan was also aware that, however much Britain might appear to oppose the Communist takeover in Russia, Prime Minister Lloyd George saw a potential solution to his country's unemployment problems in opening up the Russian market to British exports. Maltzan was determined to get in ahead of him. On the face of it, Britain was trying to bring down the Bolshevik regime, while Germany was trying to establish good relations with them, in spite of their ideological differences. It was not so straightforward.[25]

Klop was a natural candidate for recruitment. He had strong personal reasons to go to Russia: he had lost touch with his parents and his sister. Early in the war they had corresponded through his mother's younger sister Katia, who was in Bulgaria and managed to pass letters through Sweden and Switzerland. But after the revolution in 1917 Klop lost touch and determined to go to Russia to find out what had happened to them. It was not a journey to be taken lightly or without friends or support. Friedrich Rosen and Ago von Maltzan could help him prise open the door but thereafter he would have to live on his wits. The consequences if he was betrayed or captured didn't bear thinking about.

It probably did not cross his mind that he would find a bride of independent mind, great strength of character and aesthetic talent who just at that moment was in need of a knight in shining armour.

CHAPTER 3: NADIA

Alexandre Benois missed the world premiere of Tchaikovsky's ballet *The Sleeping Beauty* at the Mariinsky Theatre in St Petersburg on 15 January 1890. His friend Dima Filosofov dragged him along on the second or third night, having heard that it was not so bad after all. The composer's earlier ballet, *Swan Lake*, had not been well received. For Benois this was a revelation and he attended every performance from then until March. The impact on him and his friends was such that it changed their approach to art, ballet and music for years to come. Without it, he claimed, there would have been no Ballets Russes.[26]

Tchaikovsky's masterpiece had awakened in Alexandre Benois the creative impulse which led to the founding of *Mir iskusstva* (World of Art), the magazine which dominated the aesthetics and art nouveau movements in the great city of St Petersburg at the turn of the twentieth century. Benois and Filosofov, the supreme ballet impresario Sergei Diaghilev and the artist Léon Bakst, were the driving cultural force and the Mariinsky was its focal point. The greatest talents of music and dance were nurtured there. Alexandre's production of *Le Pavillon d'Armide* was premiered at the Mariinsky in 1907 and performed in Paris by Vaslav Nijinsky and Anna Pavlova two years later. His career as a costume and set designer spanned nearly sixty years with his last production of *Petrushka* staged at Covent Garden in 1957, three years before his death.

For Benois and his young contemporaries, Tchaikovsky opened a gateway to the West, to Europe and progress, without relinquishing the splendour of the eighteenth century when Peter the Great made St Petersburg his model capital. For a while they called themselves the Society for Self-Education of Nevsky Pickwickians, setting out, in the style of Charles Dickens's Mr Pickwick, from the main thoroughfare of their capital, the Nevsky Prospekt, in their quest for the delights and curiosities of life. Alexandre adopted the slogan *'Petersburg über alles'* as a rule to live by and Sergei Diaghilev described their new movement as a generation thirsting for beauty.[27]

The prosperous Benois family, among whom Alexandre was simply the most talented of many talents, had lived in Russia for several generations but they traced their roots to Germany, Italy and France. They were at the heart of the cultural life of the tsar's capital.

Nicholas Benois, son of a farm labourer, was born in 1702 and brought up by his widowed mother, a laundress, in the village of Saint-Ouen-en-Brie about 50 kilometres south-east of Paris. She instilled enough of an education for Nicholas to become the village schoolmaster, a profession his son also followed. But his grandson had grander social ambitions, more suited to a man christened Julius Louis Caesar Benois. He became pastry cook to the Duc de Montmorency. Together they fled the revolution of 1789 and made their way to St Petersburg where the cook found himself more in demand than the duc and was very soon appointed food taster to Tsar Paul I. This prestigious appointment had its drawbacks, since the emperor rightly suspected his courtiers of plotting assassination and became convinced that he was being fed ground glass in his meals.

But the Frenchman survived, adopted the name Jules-Césard and married the royal midwife, Concordia Groppe from Germany. They produced between them seventeen children. Among them was yet another Nicholas, who qualified as an architect and married Camilla Cavos. Her grandfather, the composer Catterino

Cavos, had been brought up in a palazzo on the Grand Canal in Venice and was director of the Imperial Theatre in St Petersburg. Her father was an architect.

Thus there came into being a great theatrical and architectural dynasty. Nicholas Benois, the architect, had as his patrons the Empress Maria Feodorovna and Tsar Nicholas I. He worked on the Cathedral of Christ the Saviour in Moscow and collaborated with his father-in-law, Alberto Cavos, on the design of the Mariinsky Theatre. Three of his nine children were closely connected with the arts. Albert, the oldest boy, was a thrice-married philanderer and an artist whose water colours were popular in the royal household. He was eclipsed by his younger brother Alexandre.

Leontij Benois was the least flamboyant of the three, an architect whose best works were civic and business buildings in a Renaissance style. He enjoyed a reputation as a consummate teacher, holding first a professorship and then becoming rector at the St Petersburg Academy of Arts. He had married Maria Sapojhikova, daughter of a wealthy merchant who ran fisheries on the Volga River.

Leontij's most famous artistic moment came in 1909 when he put on show a 'lost' Leonardo da Vinci painting of the Madonna and Child which he had inherited from his grandfather, Alberto Cavos. Family legend maintained that Alberto had acquired it from a band of itinerant actors. It caused a sensation and Tsar Nicholas II eventually offered $1.5 million to acquire it for the Hermitage museum. Comparing exchange rates over time can lead to wildly differing results but even on the basis, using a reputable academic calculator, that it was the equivalent of £310,000 at the time, it represents £26 million at 21st-century prices. But the payment was to be made in instalments and after the Bolshevik Revolution the new regime reneged on the deal while keeping the painting.

At the time of the painting's first appearance, Leontij's youngest daughter Nadia was thirteen years old and growing up in luxurious surroundings on Vasilievsky Island, the most fashionable quarter of St Petersburg. She could have had little expectation of the terrible events which were to shatter her comfortable existence, nor of the strange 'Dutchman' who would eventually come to her rescue.

Vasilievsky Island was laid out on a grid system. Leontij, who had designed some of the buildings, had a house at Number 20 in the Third Line. As Nadia got older and followed the family tradition by enrolling at the Academy of Arts, she became a frequent visitor at the home of her uncle Alexandre at Number 38 in the First Line, overlooking the Bolshoi Theatre. There she would be likely to meet the composers Sergei Prokofiev and Alexander Tcherepnin, playing the grand piano, or her cousin Nicholas, to whom she was briefly engaged to be married. He later became design director of La Scala in Milan. Prokofiev was in his early twenties, closer to Nadia's age than Alexandre's, but the two men collaborated on ballet productions and became good friends. The composer was a regular guest at the Benois's Thursday night 'At Home' parties and had attended a boisterous New Year celebration.[28]

At that time, St Petersburg was growing faster than any other city in Europe as the Industrial Revolution began to take hold in a country still mainly populated by peasants and serfs. Peter the Great's careful town planning was overwhelmed as factories sprung up everywhere: engineering works for railways and heavy artillery; cotton mills and factories. They produced enormous wealth and lavish spending. The tsar subsidised the Mariinsky to the tune of two and half million gold roubles a year. The nightlife rivalled that in Paris, elegant restaurants like Donon's, Palkin, Barel, and the Bear abounded. European fashions were brought hotfoot from the salons of Paris and London, and demand for the creations of the jeweller Peter Carl Fabergé kept 700 craftsmen busy.[29]

Nadia's friend Tamara Abelson, a merchant's daughter growing up in the city during this period, recalls delicious cakes from the French confectioner Ballet; Einem sweets from Berlin; Druce's, the English shop at the top of the Nevsky Prospekt, the equivalent of Harrods; and Eliseev's great emporium where exotic groceries were imported from East and West and caviar was sold from large wooden barrels.[30]

Beyond the heights of excess though, the warning signs were already present. Among the city's population of 2.2 million, three-quarters were peasants and many of them were starving. Revolution was in the air long before the military follies of the Russian generals in the early years of the First World War left the mass of the population still more deprived. Nadia Benois and Tamara Abelson were witness to the terrors of 1917. Yet so oblivious were the privileged to their imminent fate that on the night before the revolution started, in February 1917, with the army starved of munitions and the people starved of bread, a theatre critic emerging from a particularly lavish production could talk of going to a restaurant 'to eat nightingales' tongues and let the hungry bastards howl'.[31]

Faced with a wave of workers' strikes and demonstrations, Tsar Nicholas II signed a telegram on 25 February 1917 instructing his military commanders to restore order but their efforts quickly collapsed in the face of mutiny and, at the beginning of March, Nicholas abdicated. Tamara Abelson recalled how bands of trigger-happy youths burst into wealthy homes ostensibly searching for arms and enemies of the people. No one dared refuse them admission:

> In our house they passed from one room to another, opening cupboards and drawers, removing anything they fancied while commenting loudly and disparagingly on what they saw, glorifying in their power ... Regardless of these and similar outrages, a feeling of hope, of faith in the future, of a rebirth, pervaded the capital.[32]

During the summer months the Provisional Government under Alexander Kerensky struggled to assert some kind of authority. But with much of the army and navy joining the workers in looting indiscriminately in the stores, palaces and town houses, fuelled by alcohol from the best private cellars, life began to fall apart. In October, with troops refusing to obey orders and sailors bringing the cruiser *Aurora* up the Neva River to train its guns on the on the Winter Palace, the Bolsheviks gained the upper hand.

Novelist Aleksey Tolstoy described what happened next:

> The icy wind sent its icy breath into the darkened windows of the houses and blew through the deserted porches, sweeping out the ghosts of past luxury ... It was terrible, incomprehensible, inconceivable. Everything was being abolished. ... God, private property and the very right to live as one pleased.[33]

For many of the well-to-do, the first instinct was to flee the horror they now beheld. In the next four years almost two million departed, usually believing their exile would be brief and the old order would be restored. They were the White Russians, monarchists and social democrats; business leaders, scientists and increasingly those from the world of arts who discovered that the new regime did not welcome freedom of expression. The stark choice was penury at home or penury in exile. They were permitted to withdraw only a few hundred roubles from their bank accounts, and expected to contribute their wealth and belongings to the welfare of the proletariat. Gold and other precious metals and jewels were liable to confiscation, a black market in artworks flourished. Hyper-inflation made the paper rouble worthless and the economy reverted to barter.

Despite their bourgeois lifestyles, with wealth and privilege that marked them out as targets for the revenge of the proletariat, Alexandre and Leontij Benois stayed and survived. As Alexandre later pointed out, they had not a drop of Russian blood in their veins yet they *were* Russian, by citizenship, language and way of life.[34]

Alexandre remained, as curator of Old Masters at the Hermitage, until 1926 when he joined the procession of Russian exiles that gravitated to Paris. Leontij, after a period of turmoil, was able to retain his professorship and continue teaching until his death in

1928. That is not to say that life continued as normal: the capacious apartments on Vasilievsky Island were requisitioned and had to be shared with a host of revolutionaries who were billeted in them. Leontij grieved over the loss of his summer house in Peterhof, communal living with strangers in his once cosy apartment and most of all the parting with three of his children who fled Russia altogether to escape hunger and other dangers.[35]

In December 1919, the writer Maxim Gorky took over what had been the magnificent Eliseev emporium, on the corner of Nevsky Prospekt and the Moika River embankment, and turned it into a haven for writers, artists and musicians. Their gilded life was gone for ever but they could still live it up a little at the House of Arts, as it was officially known. Fine costumes and caviar were not on offer but alcohol was still available, and on Friday nights the ragged aesthetes could forget the hard times as Albert Benois played Strauss waltzes on the piano. The building, when lit up at night, resembled the prow of an ocean liner and soon acquired the nickname 'the Crazy Ship'.[36] Nadia Benois went there from home some days to fetch a pail of thin tasteless soup which was the best that the epicurean Benois family could now find to put on the table. It was a long walk but infinitely preferable to travelling on the overcrowded trams with the attendant risk of contracting typhoid in the epidemic which swept the city. On one such visit fate provided her with an escape route. Fifty years later, she remembered that day clearly. It was 1 June 1920:

It was a beautiful warm morning. I was walking leisurely and feasting my eyes on the grandiose view of the river … I was in a happy hazy mood.

At the House of Arts my tin can was filled with some unsavoury smelling soup and I was given a sack of potatoes. At that time of famine even unsavoury soups were acceptable. At home one added something to them, either an onion or a little butter and they became quite eatable.

I started on my return journey, one hand holding the sack of potatoes slung on to my back and the other the tin can with the soup. Walking was no pleasure now that I was so heavily laden, and the sun was getting hotter too. When I reached the Fourth Line, and I was just passing the house where my school-friend Valeria worked, I thought how nice it would be to sit down in a cool place and have a smoke.[37]

Valeria Poleschauk worked as a secretary for the former naval officer Nikolai Nikolaevitch Schreiber. She had already told Nadia about the strange visitor who was living there, whom she mistakenly thought was a Dutchman. While Nadia sat on a window seat and smoked her cigarette, the Dutchman appeared. He wore high-laced leather boots, knee breeches, a white shirt and navy-blue, polka-dot tie and altogether cut a rather comic figure, she thought. But he was funny, entertaining her with jokes and double entendres. On a whim she invited him to join her at a fairground that evening and in so doing boarded the gaudy carousel of Klop Ustinov's life.[38] It was Nadia who gave him the nickname Klop soon after they first met.

Shortly before she first set eyes on Klop, Nadia and Valeria had been discussing the prospects of finding a man who would help them flee the country to start a new life. Russians needed an exit permit; girls who married foreigners stood more chance of being allowed to leave. Nadia had already had one such offer, from a neighbour she hardly knew, and was well aware of the pitfalls and potential humiliation that lay ahead for girls who gambled their future happiness on a chance encounter with a stranger. Despite their shared Russian heritage Nadia and Klop did not have a lot in common. Klop had been raised in Palestine, matured in Germany and Switzerland but was not in tune with Russian culture and, although he was fluent in several languages, Russian was not one of them. Yet it took only a fortnight for Nadia to convince herself that marrying him was a risk she was willing to take. Many, many years later, after Klop's death, Nadia would confess to a close friend that he represented a passport to escape the rigours of existence after the revolution and that was a factor in her decision.[39]

The romance began inauspiciously. The amusement park they had planned to visit was closed and, as Klop confessed to her later, he had hoped the switchback ride would provide the opportunity for greater intimacy than would normally be permitted on a first date. But he continued to amuse and entertain. It was the time of the festival of White Nights, when the sun hardly sets and couples strolled along the banks of the Neva until the early hours of the morning and fell in love. Klop met Nadia's various uncles and aunts, but not her parents, and visited the Hermitage to view the Benois da Vinci. With typical bravado, he took her to church and introduced her to his previous girlfriend. They went dancing at the Crazy Ship.

He knew it was only a matter of time before the authorities began to suspect that he was a spy, and his proposal, when it came, was pragmatic and prosaic, anything but romantic: 'Listen, we could be married here and when we are abroad I'd give you a divorce.' Nadia good-naturedly fobbed him off: 'This is of course very charming and simple but there are other matters to be taken into consideration.'

Klop, by now quite accustomed to getting his own way with women, devoted some time to describing the delightful life she might lead with him if she fled from her family and homeland. She in turn, seeing an opportunity about to slip from her grasp, found herself falling in love and praying for guidance. She made an ultimatum. Klop must do the honourable thing and marry her in church, in front of her family. Klop, professing that had always been his true intention, produced an engagement ring of thick silver with a black stone, bearing a carving of an Egyptian princess, which had come from his father's collection of Middle Eastern antiquities.

Klop won doubtful acceptance from Nadia's parents, who were naturally suspicious of a visitor from a country with whom they had so recently been at war. The wedding was fixed for 3 p.m. on Saturday 17 July at St Catherine's Lutheran Church on Bolshoi Avenue, Vasilievsky Island, traditionally the place of worship for the German community in St Petersburg.

Nadia wore a dress of opaque white batiste linen made from an old nightdress of her grandmother's, and borrowed white shoes that were too big for her, a veil decorated with orange blossom and a Fabergé gold bracelet which had been her mother's and was one of the few pieces of jewellery to escape the looters, having been buried in the grounds of their summer retreat at Peterhof. Valeria, who had made the first introductions, accompanied Nadia as she made her way on foot to the church. Klop, whose own wardrobe was limited, wore a borrowed pair of white tennis trousers and greeted her with a bouquet of blue hydrangea. They exchanged rings that had been handed down through their respective families. The reception was enlivened with homemade mocha cake and a couple of bottles of wine that had been hidden under the floorboards.

CHAPTER 4: BOLSHEVIKS

Even before the wedding, Klop had been increasingly nervous about the authorities. A well-wisher in the Soviet Foreign Office warned them that the Cheka – the Communist secret police – were investigating Klop's credentials. He had told them, fairly unconvincingly, that he was a greengrocer's assistant from Amsterdam. He could hardly admit to being a journalist and any suggestion that he was gathering secret intelligence for the German government would have been fatal. He had also begun dealing in black market art, hoping to make a small fortune to start married life in the West.

Nadia, who only seems to have learned that his visit was not solely for the purpose of finding his family after they escaped, was surely being disingenuous years later when she wrote: 'Maltzan asked Klop to keep his eyes open should he succeed in getting into Russia. He did not mean spying of course, only wanting him to report on the whole atmosphere and conditions inside Russia.'[40]

In such a time of turmoil and mutual suspicion, espionage was exactly what Ago von Maltzan had in mind and the preparations could have left Klop in no doubt. He had travelled on a boat taking Russian soldiers and prisoners of war home. Friedrich Rosen obtained a passport for him, in the name of Oustinoff rather than the Germanic 'von Ustinow'. It is not clear what nationality Klop assumed or whether this was an early example of the Nansen passport, introduced by the Norwegian explorer,

diplomat and commissioner for refugees Fridjof Nansen for use
as travel authority for the many stateless displaced people milling
around the continent. Klop passed himself off either as a returning
Russian – difficult when his command of the language was less
than perfect – or a Dutch trader. He travelled light, a solitary bag
with few clothes and gifts of tinned meat and chocolate that might
smooth away some of the minor obstructions to his progress. For
negotiating the major obstacles he had gold coins sewn into the
lining of his coat. The ship dropped them at Hungerborg near
Narva, on the Estonian border, where they began a tediously slow
train journey. The full extent of the famine that was gripping the
Russian countryside quickly became apparent as starving peasants
lined the tracks begging the passengers for scraps of food. A
rumour rippled through the train to the effect that able-bodied
men would not be allowed to disembark until they got to Moscow,
where they would immediately be pressed into military service.
As the train slowed outside St Petersburg, Klop leapt down to the
tracks and completed the journey on foot.

Klop arrived on 7 May and set about ingratiating himself with
officials of the Cheka and the Foreign Office in the course of
searching for his family. At the Cheka his contact was an official
named Rougaev who impressed Klop with his bevy of secretaries.
They obeyed his every word and appeared not to object to sitting
on his lap or being slapped on the backside. Klop was amused to
be offered fish and potato soup by his host, who served it by hand,
disguising the smell of fish with a liberal application of Houbigant's
Quelque Fleurs perfume that he kept in his desk; Klop's memory for
fine detail demonstrating a skill valuable to storytellers and spies
alike. That he should strike up such fellow-feeling in an official
of the Cheka was fortunate. He had discovered on arrival in St
Petersburg that his family had been living on the 'Fifth Line' of
Vasilievsky Island, the once fashionable suburb now overrun by
Bolshevik squatters. To his distress, he soon discovered that his
father had died of dysentery a year earlier and his mother and sister

had moved to Pskov, about four to six hours' rail journey south-west of St Petersburg near the border with Estonia. He needed a Cheka 24-hour travel permit to visit them and the family reunion was necessarily brief, though long enough for Klop to promise to make the arrangements to get the two women out of the country. Typically, his abiding memory years later was of the pretty, freckled peasant girls, their hair tied back by a kerchief, whom he saw on the train. The kerchief became a small fetish that he liked to try out on later girlfriends.[41]

Despite the great risks involved, Klop decided to leave Russia briefly and make contact with Maltzan from the Estonian capital of Reval. There is a record in German Foreign Office archives, dated 13 July, simply stating that the Württemberg citizen Ustinoff was returning to Russia and requesting that Gustav Hilger should be informed by radio. It added that he would not be travelling on a German passport. If Klop filed a fuller report at that stage it has not survived in the records. But it is significant that he was already working with Gustav Hilger, Maltzan's other secret emissary to the Soviet Union. Hilger was born in Moscow in 1886 and brought up there. He studied engineering in Germany but returned to Moscow in 1910 to work for his father-in-law's crane company, travelling all over Russia. He was interned during the First World War and on his release worked for the main commission for aid to German prisoners of war in Russia, assisting their evacuation with only limited and reluctant help from the Soviet authorities. He was briefly expelled when relations between Russia and Germany were broken off but returned in June 1920, and was witness to the starvation, misery, and desperation of the population.[42]

On his return to St Petersburg, Klop had found lodgings with Nikolai Nikolaevitch Schreiber. He was an inventor who had lived in the next street when Klop's parents had an apartment in St Petersburg and had been courting Klop's sister, Tabitha. He was a suspiciously fortuitous landlord for a man who was gathering intelligence for Germany. Schreiber had been a rear admiral of the old Imperial Russian Navy, a specialist in torpedoes and mines. During the First World War he had been in charge of planning the minefields in the Baltic and Black Sea intended to keep the German fleet at bay. He had worked in close contact with the British Admiralty, including the development of a British invention, the paravane, a mine clearance device.

Klop's quest for travel permits for his mother and sister took him from the Cheka to the Ministry of Foreign Affairs. Here again he managed to charm his way into their good books. According to his son, Peter, his best contact there was Ivan Maisky, which would be yet another extraordinarily lucky break. Maisky had been in London prior to the First World War, at the same time as Klop. His circle of friends included the radical writers George Bernard Shaw, H. G. Wells and Beatrice Webb. From 1932 to 1943 he was Soviet ambassador in London, a man of enormous influence and importance in the Allied relationship against Germany. There is no doubt the two knew each other at that time, but it is less clear how they could have met in 1920. Maisky was then a local government official in Samara, near the Kazakhstan border. It is not impossible, with his literary interests, that he visited Gorky's House of Arts club in St Petersburg, which was frequented by Klop and Nadia, but less likely that he was in the Ministry of Foreign Affairs. In any event, Klop's mother Magdalena and sister Tabitha were in due course able to escape via the Crimea and Istanbul. They spent some time in Germany but eventually settled back in the Middle East.[43] Klop's difficulties with the authorities were compounded by his new relationship with the Benois family, some of whom were not entirely above suspicion. They had potentially damning British connections at a time when Britain had been supporting the monarchist side in the civil war with arms, money and men. British secret agents were up to their necks in plots to assassinate Lenin and bring down the Bolshevik regime.

Nadia's aunt, Camilla Benois, had married her English tutor Matthew Edwardes, whose younger brother George introduced the glamorous Gaiety Girls chorus line to the London theatre scene. Matthew became a successful businessman in Russia but he died in 1917 and Camilla escaped to England. Her son Julius stayed behind and became involved in the notorious British action to seize control of the enormous oilfields around Baku, then part of southern Russia. As a result he spent three years in a Russian jail. The two families remained close and Camilla's grandson, Julius Caesar Edwardes, became Peter Ustinov's business partner.

Nadia's cousin, also Camilla, had married General Dmitri Horvath, general manager of the Chinese Eastern Railway. After the Bolshevik Revolution, he led White Russian resistance in the East, declaring himself provisional ruler of all Russia from his power base in Vladivostok. He could never muster sufficient support and eventually threw in his lot with the ill-fated rebellion led by Admiral Alexander Kolchak, with British backing. Kolchak was executed by the Bolsheviks; General Horvath survived in exile with Camilla in Peking. Their daughter Doushka married the British First World War flying ace Cecil Lewis, who in 1922 was one of the founders of the BBC, and in later life lived for a while with Nadia and Klop at their home in Gloucestershire.

In St Petersburg, too, there were dangerous associations about which the Benois family needed to be wary. The Mariinsky Opera had a British conductor, Albert Coates, and in the years prior to the revolution one of his protégés was a young Paul Dukes who had run away from home to join the orchestra. By 1918 he was an MI6 officer, using his old contacts for information and safe houses to hide from the authorities.

In August 1918 an attempt to assassinate Lenin unleashed the Cheka's Red Terror in which thousands of suspects were rounded up and hundreds executed. The British diplomat Robert Bruce Lockhart, who was implicated in the plot, was arrested, only to be freed through the intervention of the lover he shared with Maxim Gorky, Moura Benckendorff. Whether Moura knew Klop or Nadia at this stage is not clear but she would feature prominently in their later lives in her adopted guise as the London society hostess Moura Budberg.

In such turbulent times Klop was running huge risks with his frequent visits to the department of Foreign Affairs, and he compounded those risks with an ill-judged attempt to bribe an official to let Nadia leave the country. Klop told more than one version of this event. According to Nadia he had offered Comrade Rougaev a wad of foreign currency he had smuggled into the country and was immediately rebuffed. According to his son Peter the bribe was chocolate and bacon and the recipient was Ivan Maisky, who rejected it.[44]

Once more fortune smiled upon Klop. Gustav Hilger, in his role of representative of the German Red Cross and the Nansen Relief Agency responsible for the welfare of POWs, could offer Klop an escape route. Klop had good reason to be grateful and he did not forget. Twenty-five years later he returned the compliment.

Hilger took the only photo Klop had of himself and Nadia – from the wedding a few days earlier – and used it to create repatriation authorisations as if Klop were a soldier returning from the Siberian prison camps.

Three days later, on 16 August, Klop and Nadia spent the day getting export licences for Klop's treasure trove of art and that night came the news that they should be at the railway station by 7 a.m. next day. There was a frenzy of packing, and in the dark early hours next morning they crept through the deserted streets, pushing their few possessions and a picnic basket on a handcart. Hilger was waiting for them and guided them swiftly to the top bunks of a civilian carriage where they lay still for hours, not daring to move in case they were challenged. It was gone midnight by the time the hissing steam engine slowly headed south-westward to impending freedom. They travelled all the next day, through searches and security checks, Nadia clinging on to a single brooch and a string of pearls. At Narva, on the Estonian border, they camped overnight before boarding a ferry to spend three days sailing almost the full length of the Baltic Sea to the German port of Stettin – now Szczecin in Poland. Another night in a camp was as much as Klop could bear and he managed to telegraph to Berlin to get money sent to the best hotel in town, where he and Nadia gorged on champagne and lobster before ordering complete new sets of clothes. Nadia was already pregnant, although she may not have been aware of it at the time.

They then spent a week to ten days in Berlin where Nadia was introduced to Klop's relatives – Magdalena's brothers and sisters and his Ethiopian grandmother. Klop had meetings with the directors of the Wolff Bureau and, significantly, spent a good deal of time with Ago von Maltzan at the German Foreign Office.[45]

He wrote a fifteen-page report, closely typed and dated 31 August 1920, which was circulated among senior figures within the Foreign Office. It contained a good deal of pontificating – Klop recognised early in his espionage career that he would do his credibility no harm by telling his masters what they wanted to hear. And of course he could not resist the hyperbole which became a trademark of his later reports for MI5 and MI6. But he also provided, separately and not for circulation, a list of sources that included senior officials of the Cheka, and former ministers and church officials from the Kerensky regime and the last days of the tsar. These indicated that he had indeed been extracting intelligence in high places – some startling new information, of varying reliability, and some particularly acute barbs at his British competitors. Here was a man aged twenty-seven, who had gone pretty much straight from university into the trenches, brimming with self-confidence, politically aware, quick on the uptake and capable of insinuating himself among the powerful elite of a strange country regardless of personal risk.

His stay in Petrograd, the renamed St Petersburg, which he regarded as 'the seismograph of Soviet Russia' covered the period from 7 May-17 August which, he pointed out, ranged from the beginning of the Polish offensive through to the menacing of

Warsaw by the Red Army. The newly created Polish state was bitterly resented by the Germans because the Danzig corridor had divided eastern Prussia from the rest of Germany. The Poles had invaded Russia in April 1920, hoping for territorial gains in Ukraine and Byelorussia, but by early August had been driven back to the gates of Warsaw by the Red Army. There were fears across Europe that, if Warsaw fell, the Communists would sweep onwards across Germany. A peace treaty was signed in October but it was a time of high tension for all those in positions of military, economic and political power. Klop had, he said, attempted to set passion aside and obtain a deep insight through contact with all parts of the population and supporters of all parties. A general overview was impossible; all he could do was report the highlights. Earlier assessments may have overstated the strength and stability of the Red regime but to underestimate it would be equally harmful.

He had concluded already that Communism would not work and that its leaders realised this. They survived only through a bureaucratic reign of terror. The overwhelming majority of the Russian people disapproved of the regime but were too weak and apathetic to oppose it. While an English delegation had been treated to 'six star dinners' in the official Palace of the Workers, he had been with the real workers slurping soup. There was great indignation that foreigners ate so well while the Russian workers starved. Visitors were having sand thrown in their eyes. They were being shown Lenin's version of Potemkin villages – a throwback to an earlier age when temporary villages were created, populated with specially imported cheery peasants, to convince Catherine the Great that her empire was thriving. One of the English delegates privately admitted to Klop: 'My only impression is that we don't get the right impression.'

They were shown hospitals with plenty of food, school children marching in the sun and ruined bankers for whom there was no sympathy. But all these were deceptions. Society and the economy were breaking down. There had been fifty murders in a month in

Petrograd. The head of the Cheka in Petrograd, Gleb Bokii, had personally warned Klop not to put his foreign money in the state bank because it would probably be stolen. A railway maintenance manager explained that for every locomotive they repaired they had to break up two for spare parts, for every new piece of track laid they had to rip up two others to use the rails. Despite steely discipline, the army was decimated by deserters who faced the firing squad if caught. Officers referred to the troops as 'radishes – red on the outside and white on the inside'. Demobilisation of the Red Army would pose a great threat to the regime. It knew that only work and reconstruction would prevent wholesale collapse.

Klop likened the regime to icebound ships in winter on the Neva River that flows through St Petersburg. Often they were rotting from within and liable to sink in the first floods of spring. The Russian regime might slowly go to ground if the ice of war that was their mainstay gave way under the warm sun of peace.

A former high official of the Orthodox Church under the tsar had told him that there was not one man in the current government capable of administering his portfolio. The real problem was that there was no alternative, not tsarists, democrats, Bolsheviks, nor especially anarchists, capable of leading the Russian people. The reign of Faust (the scholar who in German folklore makes a pact with the devil) would be the most likely result of a coup.

Feeble-minded British support for the White Russian rebel forces of Admiral Alexander Kolchak in Siberia and General Anton Denikin in southern Russia and the Caucasus had failed. There was now a view that the perfidious Albion had an interest in leaving the Red regime in place and letting the Bolsheviks 'sit in the saddle until they had ridden the Russian horse to death'. The Red regime recognised that the strength of the revolution was not sufficient and they had persuaded themselves to return to the once much-maligned behind-the-scenes diplomacy.

Klop seems to have been well informed about the secret trade negotiations that had been taking place at the beginning of August

in London between the Prime Minister Lloyd George, Leonid
Krassin, People's Commissar for Foreign Trade, and Politburo
member Lev Kamenev. According to Klop these talks were an
illusion for the benefit of the English workers and the Bolsheviks,
intended to give the impression that a trade deal would create
jobs in Britain and provide food and money to alleviate hunger in
Russia. However, he had received news, from well-informed naval
circles in Petrograd and Moscow, that England had stipulated that
Petrograd should become a free port under the League of Nations.
The Russian regime had agreed to this. An informant reported
that in a food map for Russia that he saw in Moscow, Petrograd
was no longer provided for.

All of which led Klop to the conclusion that:

> In the international race for the great prize of Russia, Germany
> is for the Russian people the hot favourite. The great part of the
> Russian people fully realise that Germany and Russia need one
> another to recover and that this would only be prevented by the
> Allies. Overall they hold the view that: only the Germans know us
> and only the Germans can help us.[46]

There would have to be a 'parallelogram of power' based on German
investment to relieve the sorrows of the people and, consequently,
bolstering the Bolshevik regime. For a start, the entire Russian
transport system would need to be overhauled. Russia was waiting
to see which would be the first country to give them what they
needed. Whoever was first through the door would be last to leave.
It would require vigilance to prevent the Russian sickness pervading
the German economy and workforce and to immunise the country
against the Communist International. A former Russian minister
had described the Bolshevik leadership as the orphan child of St
Ignatius of Loyola, founder of the Jesuits. They had not given up
on their final goal of world revolution and they would pursue it
without consideration by all means possible, including illegality.

Adolph Joffe, chairman of the Petrograd Military Revolutionary Committee which overthrew the Russian government in October 1917, had said to Klop:

> When are we having the revolution in Germany? It will come within two years. We need you unconditionally. Germany will tip the balance. Without Germany the world revolution is impossible.[47]

It was against this background that the German Foreign Minister Walther Rathenau had been persuaded to hold secret talks in the Moabit jail in Berlin with Karl Radek, the Bolshevik agitator who had been incarcerated because of his role in the 1919 Spartacist rebellion in Germany. They discussed industrial cooperation. General Hans von Seeckt, in overall command of rebuilding the German Army by subverting the terms of the Versailles peace treaty, also had talks with Radek and sent emissaries to see him in Moscow in 1920 after he was released from prison. Before the end of the year General von Seeckt had formed the highly secret Special Group R as the means of clandestine cooperation, thus laying the foundation for the rebuilding of the German Luftwaffe and Panzer tank divisions behind the Russian border away from the critical surveillance of the Western Allies.[48]

Early in September Klop and Nadia moved on to Amsterdam to await their visas to travel to London. It was another bewildering phase of married life for Nadia, as she gradually became aware of Klop's previous dalliances and capacity for self-centred insensitivity.

On their first evening they dined with Klop's colleague Felix Banse who was obliged, at Klop's insistence, to explain how he had broken the news of Klop's marriage to the girl he had left behind in Amsterdam, a telephonist named Lenie. She had, Banse assured him, taken it very well in the circumstances.

Nadia's new world centred on a musty one-room bedsit with a rickety washstand, in a tall house on the Singel canal. There was no bathroom and meals had to be prepared on a frighteningly volatile spirit lamp. Nadia had no real experience of cooking for herself and the results were often scorched offerings that filled the room with the smell of burning. She was in despair and Klop showed little sympathy. She confessed later:

> Altogether poor Klop must have been in many ways disillusioned. We had been thrown together by exceptional and highly romantic circumstances, owing to which we got married, disregarding the fact that neither of us represented the ideal of the other, for I was as far removed from a black-stockinged Raphael Kirchner [an illustrator of pin-up postcards] as he was from the David of Michelangelo. But, apart from our physical appearances, we both had something in us which kept us together, forced us to forgive one another for not being ideal and made us even very happy at times.[49]

Nadia was indeed no pin-up: tall and powerfully built, her physical presence served only to emphasise Klop's diminutive stature and appearance of a little bedbug. But she was certainly not ugly and her kindly, expressive face and disposition to accept what fate brought her made her an attractive character. Her imperturbable, pragmatic nature was to be sorely tried by her first experience of Great Britain.

CHAPTER 5: LONDON

Klop and Nadia arrived at Harwich, Essex on the overnight ferry on 22 December 1920. It was, by Nadia's account, about as bleak and unwelcoming as could be imagined. Passport control found a discrepancy with Nadia's visa and detained her while Klop, leaving her some money, hurried on to London, thinking he could sort out the problem from there. Nadia was by now heavily pregnant and dressed in the only clothes that would fit – a brown frock, with horizontal embroidery, and her mother's old sealskin coat. She looked, she thought, like a fanatical female revolutionary. After several hours the police decided she did not represent an immediate threat to the security of the nation and put her on a train to London. She arrived at Liverpool Street station in the dark, to find a thick fog and no one to welcome her. After wandering the streets, being accosted by troublesome strangers, she ended up at the only address she knew – lodgings in Heathcote Street, just off Gray's Inn Road, occupied by Miss Rowe, her English childhood governess. She was not home, her landlord and landlady were scarcely welcoming, and it was several more hours before Klop eventually tracked her down. They retreated to the Liverpool Street station hotel where they spent a miserable few days, dining completely alone in the hotel's vast empty restaurant on Christmas Day.

Nadia's first impression of England was of a benighted country of fog, rain, damp and cold; reeking of coal smoke, mutton fat, gas and tobacco; and deeply antagonistic to 'bloody foreigners' in general and enemy aliens in particular. She and Klop took to conversing in French to disguise their true origins.[50] She must have been desperately lonely. All communication with her family in Russia had been cut off by the Marxist regime.[51]

Nadia's early misadventure at least had the virtue of establishing that there was a room to let at Miss Rowe's lodgings. At the beginning of April they moved to a sunnier top-floor flat in Ridgmount Gardens, near Tottenham Court Road, taking Miss Rowe with them as prospective nanny. Nadia went into labour in the early hours of 16 April. While Miss Rowe searched the empty streets for a taxi, Klop was in the small cubby hole where a telephone had been installed, dictating his overnight news copy to Berlin and demanding that Nadia somehow rein in her contractions until he had completed his story. They eventually made it to the nursing home that another exile, Olia Krohn, had booked for them in Belsize Park and later that day their only child, Peter Ustinov, was born.

Nadia's sister, also named Olia, came to help her through the first six weeks of child rearing before Nadia and Peter were packed off to the Schönblick sanatorium in Württemberg, where Klop's mother and two of his aunts were staying. Klop followed a few weeks later for Peter's christening and, with typical insensitivity, nominated one of his former admirers as godmother. He explained to Nadia that since the girl had hoped to marry him it was the least he could do, even though when he had met her in Munich it was her sister he had an affair with.[52]

They soon returned to Ridgmount Gardens where they spent three years, short of money, initially with few friends and beginning to discover the reality of married life. Nadia recognised that Klop could be a spoilt child, autocratic and averse to criticism. He needed sympathetic company, people to laugh at his jokes and appreciate his repartee, to be sociable and have fun. Nadia seems to have accepted these character traits phlegmatically, balancing them against the gaiety and exhilaration of his good moods. She was not without friends and social connections in London, including the ballerina Tamara Karsinova, a leading dancer with the Imperial Ballet who played a prominent part in the development of the British Royal Ballet. She had married the First Secretary at the British embassy in St Petersburg, Henry 'Benji' Bruce, son of a baronet, and introduced him to Nadia's uncle Alexandre. Benji used to attend his Sunday afternoon drawing master class for the city's leading artists. He and Tamara escaped to London shortly before Klop and Nadia and remained friends.

As Klop and Nadia began to entertain at home, many of the guests had Russian or artistic connections. Among them was Mary Chamot, who had studied at the Slade School of Fine Art and earned her living as a lecturer at the National Gallery and Victoria and Albert Museum. She introduced them to William Constable, then at the National Gallery but later first director of the Courtauld Institute, where he revolutionised the study of art history and in 1933 played a part in the transfer to London of the Warburg Institute, fleeing Nazi persecution in Hamburg. Another visitor was gallery owner Earnest Lefevre, who specialised in French Impressionists, and his wife Nina. Klop was keen that Nadia should pursue the painting career for which her studies in St Petersburg had prepared her. Nina Lefevre was persuaded to pose at the flat, dressed in red evening gown, delicately manipulating a long cigarette holder. Mary Chamot came along to paint her portrait at the same time. Klop was in constant attendance, amusing their model with jokes in French and offering drinks and snacks. Nadia did not find Klop's domineering approach conducive to artistic expression and the result was not a happy one. Her first exhibition failed to sell a single painting, although it got a kindly review in *The Times*. Tragically this professional mishap was overshadowed by the loss of a baby through miscarriage, followed by several weeks of illness, a misfortune which the stoical Nadia dismissed in a single sentence in her account of that time. But she wrote later about how much she regretted that they had not had more children. Klop, on the other hand, seemed to be intimidated by the responsibilities of parenthood and told her, in terms that must have jarred just as much then as now:

> To worry about one is quite sufficient. And what a blessing that it was a boy! I dread to think how it could have been! Fancy us having an ugly daughter whom nobody wanted or, even worse – a very beautiful and attractive one! I would have died long ago worrying and trying to keep her out of trouble![53]

Klop's greatest achievement, in terms of raising Nadia's artistic profile and enlarging their social circle, was his recruitment of a cook (and nanny for Peter) in place of the elderly Miss Rowe, who had died. The enigmatic Frieda, from Hamburg, spoke fluent English in an atrocious accent, cooked like a dream, and in quieter moments posed in the nude for Nadia. She attracted the attention of the *Daily Mirror*. In its 'As I See Life' column, under the headline 'Cooks become models' it reported:

> Mme Ustinov, the Russian artist, who paints under the name Nadia Benois, is the fortunate possessor of an excellent cook who is also an excellent artist's model. I have sampled her cookery and seen her posing. A very graceful tribute to her has been paid by Nadia Benois in the dining room of the South Kensington flat where she lives. Above the service lift she has painted the cook's head surrounded with pots and pans and held up by little cupids.[54]

By that time Klop and Nadia's fortunes and social standing were on the up and in 1924 they moved to a more spacious apartment in Carlisle Mansions, Victoria. Klop's mother, acting on behalf of herself and her four surviving children, had sold a plot of land and three-storey house in Jerusalem to the Empress Zäwditu, co-regent of Ethiopia with Haile Selassie, for use as an embassy. The price was £9,500 – equivalent to nearly £500,000 today.[55] Klop showed his appreciation by escorting the Abyssinian delegation to the British Empire exhibition at Wembley and bringing the entire party, including the emperor, back to their new flat for dinner. The young Peter Ustinov was hauled out of bed to perform party pieces for the Lion of Judah while frantic phone calls were made to the German embassy to prevail upon their chef to despatch a meal suitable for a royal visitor round to the flat by taxi.[56] This more spacious flat had room for a grand piano, helpfully provided by Klop's sister Tabitha and her Palestinian husband Anis Jamal. Nadia painted the ceilings blue, adding figures representing the constellations, and turned a dividing screen door into a medieval icon depicting Klop as a scribe and twenty of their friends in appropriate guises. Here Klop could give full rein to his artistic talents: playing, singing and acting extracts from his favourite operas; mimicking chorus girls and prime ministers and telling tall stories. They could cram as many as eighty people into their Friday night buffet supper parties. Their guest list ranged from the chef Rudolph Stulik to Lady Tyrrell.

Stulik was the proprietor of the Hôtel de la Tour Eiffel, in Fitzrovia, just north of Oxford Street, which in its heyday in the 1920s and 1930s had a slightly louche but glamorous reputation. Royal princes were claimed to be occasional visitors; artists Augustus John and Wyndham Lewis, socialite Nancy Cunard, poet and playwright Dylan Thomas and their literary friends were regular patrons of the restaurant, which after normal licensing hours transformed itself into an amusing but discreet nightclub. The hotel was equally discreet. Lady Tyrrell was the wife of the Foreign Office grandee Sir William Tyrrell who had been a powerful influence on Foreign Secretaries from Sir Edward Grey onwards and had founded the political intelligence department.

Klop's position as the Wolff Bureau representative meant that he had access to German celebrities visiting London. The acclaimed concert pianists Wilhelm Backhaus, Artur Schnabel and the

Russian Vitya Vronsky would visit his flat to practise on the baby grand. Schnabel and Nadia enjoyed a mild flirtation which provoked a jealous response in the constantly libidinous Klop. At around this time they also got to know the Chenhalls family, Alfred and his sisters Hope and Joan. Alfred was an accountant but in reality more of a showbiz agent. Among his clients was the actor Leslie Howard, who played Ashley Wilkes in *Gone with the Wind*. The two men died in 1943 when the Luftwaffe shot down a civilian aircraft carrying them from Lisbon to London. There has long been speculation that they were involved in a secret operation for MI6; Alfred bore more than a passing resemblance to Winston Churchill and he had a connection to the Intelligence services. His sister Joan worked for MI5 for twenty-five years, liaising closely with Klop while maintaining a public persona as a lively spinster, Methodist minister's daughter and head of the international wing of the Girl's Brigade, where she introduced lessons in deportment and encouraged the girls to wear lipstick. Hope had been secretary to the British film star Charles Laughton, worked with Harry Yoxall who founded British *Vogue* and would go on to be chief inspector of the *Good Food Guide*. Yoxall was another of Klop's lunch and dinner guests and a great admirer of his cooking.

With professional musicians to provide the entertainment, Klop could indulge in playing the part of a host, supervising the eating and the drinking, steering the conversation and flirting; above all flirting, with any attractive new female who appeared in their midst, seeking to establish a semi-amorous relationship. For the most part Nadia took an indulgent view:

The adventurous, somewhat Casanovian spirit of his youth never died. He was always on the look-out, eager for new conquests. But as he was superstitious, even a God-fearing man, he never intended 'going the whole hog', for he believed that some terrible calamity would befall us all as retribution for his sins. A mildly amorous relationship sufficed him. His imagination did the rest and the certainty that everything was possible completely satisfied him. Klop's flirtations … were light and gay, like a joyous pas de deux on ice, with lots of slips and slides but never a fall.[57]

What did exasperate her were his frequent attempts to make her a conspiratorial partner in his assignations, trying to draw her into a discussion of their respective merits. He pushed his luck too far over the photographer Thea Struve. Nadia recalled later:

> I had to sit there and listen to their endless tête-à-tête of a rather superficial kind, yet heavily laden with hidden allusions, mainly on Klop's side: I felt like an unwanted old duenna. This was Klop's usual stratagem. He always wanted to draw me into the situation for some reason. I often told him: You know, Klop, I'd rather you had a real love affair without my knowledge – for what I don't know does not exist – than to sit through that kind of insipid deal.[58]

In her mostly affectionate portrait of her husband this is the nearest Nadia ever comes to a reproach for his infidelity, but their son Peter, growing up in this heavily charged atmosphere and occasionally inveigled by his father into comment on his latest amour, was outraged and instinctively recognised the wounds his mother preferred to conceal. His father's entertaining style involved 'galloping like a daring scout in the no man's land between wit and lapses of taste,' full of juvenile double entendres and risqué jokes with which his mother sportingly laughed along. Peter regarded his mother's behaviour on such occasions as 'always impeccable.'[59]

Looking back, the paradoxes of his father were apparent to a son whose relationship with him was frequently antagonistic and bitter. The mask of the convivial party host disappeared when the guests were gone. Klop had 'a mercurial temper and, at times, a wicked and hurtful tongue'. In contrast to his own Calvinistic father, Klop was totally irreligious. Family rows were frequent and he was domineering and didactic with regard to Nadia's artistic method. She stood up for herself only within the bounds that would preserve a fragile peace. And in his early teens Peter turned on his father over his dismissive criticism of one of Nadia's paintings, thereafter treating Klop's sarcasm with cold imperviousness. The atmosphere in the flat was, said Peter, 'glowering and intense'.

Yet he conceded that his father had a distaste for the brutal and cruel and a moral courage surprising in a man so devoted to the good life. Even in later life, in the company of his favourite young women, he 'offered consistent amusement, an elegance of spirit, a sense of joyous irresponsibility'.

Peter shared a greater warmth with his mother, whose benign, liberal nature led her to accept all sorts, even Klop's girlfriends who remained friends with her long after Klop's glad eye had alighted on another social butterfly. Peter was convinced though that this merely disguised the humiliation and degradation she must have felt. He regarded her account of Klop, however affectionate, as a subtle stab at his character that was the only cold revenge her pride would permit. When Nadia died, in February 1975, Peter found conflicting evidence in support of his view. Letters that Klop and Nadia exchanged, even during a long period of virtual separation, were warm and confidential but her private diary was 'searing evidence of the moral injury she had suffered'.[60]

★

When Klop and Nadia were waiting impatiently to come to London, the British-owned Reuters news agency in the city had done its best to help. They wrote to Percy Koppel at the Foreign Office asking him to speed clearance from the British passport control officer in The Hague. Passport Control in those days performed a dual role of vetting foreign visitors and working for MI6.[61]

Reuters and the Wolff Bureau were nominally in competition with each other. Although independent of government both had expected to perform patriotic duties during the First World War. The rapid and reliable transmission of news and propaganda had been increasingly recognised as crucial by governments and journalists – submarine cabling was expensive but essential. In the aftermath of war, Lord D'Abernon, the new ambassador in Berlin, was particularly anxious that British influence should play its part in rebuilding the peace in Germany. He was concerned that reports of British policy were being filtered through the French Havas news agency in Paris and being deliberately distorted.

So, when Klop presented himself at the Foreign Office they were keen to court his favour and he did not disappoint. When he explained to them how difficult it was to recruit servants in Britain – cooks and cleaning ladies were too patriotic to work for a German – the diplomats were sympathetic and persuaded the Home Office to give a work permit to Frieda, baby Peter's German nanny.

When Klop intimated that British foreign policy would get better coverage but for the exorbitant cost of telephoning his copy to Berlin, they intervened with the General Post Office to get him cut-price calls. In return, Klop called daily at the Foreign Office and, in the words of one official 'has been assisted to obtain authoritative statements and comments which have been transmitted without distortion'.[62]

But Klop was not what he seemed. He was still a German Foreign Office secret agent, in their pay and required to answer first to the ambassador and to the senior diplomats of the *Wilhelmstrasse* before attending to the needs of the Wolff Bureau and German newspapers. That had been decided as early as April 1920, before he set out on his Russian mission. Dr Carl von Schubert, a close ally of Maltzan and future Foreign Office Secretary of State, decreed that the London embassy did not need its own press officer and would be better off using the Wolff Bureau representative as a front man. Klop was considered particularly suitable because of his knowledge of Britain and British politics. It is not clear on what basis Klop was considered such an expert, other than his brief pre-war sojourn in London. When he eventually arrived in London it was agreed that three-fifths of his £1,200 a year salary would be paid for by the German Foreign Office. The wage was the equivalent of a fairly senior diplomat – at assistant secretary or undersecretary level – and would equate to £100,000 plus in 2013. And, like most journalists, Klop became adept at recovering his incidental expenses. Part of his rent was paid, plus a newspaper and entertainment allowance and telegraph charges for his reports. In 1923 the ambassador was complaining that nearly all his £500-a-year budget for press and propaganda went on Klop. By 1924 the bill was running at £564 for six months. On the other hand Klop's duties were fairly onerous. He was to cultivate the British press in German interests; and provide daily digests of their reports to the ambassador and Berlin, with particular reference to politics, the economy and culture. He had to monitor magazines, political brochures and books and make comments on them; and report false stories in the London Press and suggest ways to refute them. On top of that he had to supply his agency with reports on all the major British news stories of the day. If he had any time left he was permitted to freelance for other papers and he was entitled to four weeks summer holiday. But on no account was he to reveal that he was anything other than an agency reporter or that he had these obligations to the embassy.

Not surprisingly, Klop managed to ingratiate himself to the extent that he could discuss sensitive political issues with the head of the Foreign Office news department, Sir Arthur Willert, and he formed a crucial and lifelong friendship with Willert's assistant, Clifford Norton. From their attitude it seems probable that they understood perfectly Klop's dual role.

Norton, a clergyman's son, educated at Rugby and The Queen's College, Oxford, was a year older than Klop, and had served with the 5th Battalion, Suffolk Regiment at Gallipoli and in Palestine during the First World War. He knew Klop's home town of Jaffa:

he had suffered a gunshot wound in the back during fighting there in 1917 and from 1919 to 1921 he had been a political officer, advising the Palestine High Commissioner, based for part of that time in nearby Haifa. In 1927 he married Noel Hughes, universally known by her nickname 'Peter', a painter and later leading arts patron with an independent and adventurous spirit. They became close to Klop and Nadia, socialising and sometimes babysitting for the young Peter Ustinov.

Klop's pre-eminence as the German embassy's unofficial eyes and ears in the Foreign Office came under threat at this point from a rival journalist, André Rostin. He had been private secretary to the Social Democrat Friedrich Ebert who was president of Germany from 1919 to 1925. Like Klop, Rostin was partly bankrolled by the embassy while officially working for a trade and industry newspaper. Klop's friend Albrecht Bernstorff, the First Secretary, had recruited him partly because of his socialist and Communist contacts and he spent a good deal of his time at the Soviet embassy, extracting information from the ambassador Ivan Maisky and his colleagues. He also made rapid headway in British society, befriending the Duke of York's private secretary, Sir Louis Greig, and a number of senior government officials. He was remarkably prolific. In a two-month period in the summer of 1926 he filed secret reports containing information gleaned in discussions with three Soviet officials, with John Gregory, the Foreign Office assistant secretary, and with his junior minister Godfrey Locker-Lampson. Klop feared Rostin was after his job and began to bad-mouth him to his friends at the British Foreign Office, whispering that Rostin was in fact a Soviet agent and claiming that he was the son of a Russian Jew, Alexander Helphand-Parvus, who had masterminded Lenin's return from Swiss exile at the time of the revolution. Klop's contacts duly reported this to MI5 and it is clear from the copious files on Rostin that its officers were also monitoring Klop's activities during this period. Rostin, who had money and girlfriend problems, transferred soon after to the

United States and MI5 took some pleasure in warning the FBI about his unsavoury activities.

Rostin resurfaced in London in the late 1930s, working as a salesman for a ladies swimming costume company and as a director of the London branch of Horcher's, a Berlin restaurant fashionable with the Nazi hierarchy. Klop was surprised to bump into him in Piccadilly Circus and realised that despite his Jewish background he was still working for the Nazi regime. He alerted his colleagues at MI5 who would have interned him when war broke out if he had not fled to Switzerland, where Klop and Rostin would have one last, fateful meeting.[63]

With Rostin out of the way, Klop ruled the roost once more and in April 1928 he discussed with Norton the problem of Fichte-bund propaganda – a nationalist group in Hamburg whose pamphlets became part of the Nazi propaganda machine. A few days later Hans Dieckhoff, counsellor at the German embassy, visited Norton who raised the issue again. Dieckhoff handed him a file of correspondence between himself and his superiors in Berlin, showing the efforts he had been making to curb the worst excesses. Norton recorded:

> It reveals (what, indeed, we knew) that the relations between the Wolff Bureau and the German Embassy and Foreign Office are very close indeed. It seems that Mr Ustinov reports to the German Embassy and also to his Chief, Herr Mantler, in Berlin, who takes the question up direct with the Wilhelmstrasse [German Foreign Office], which thereupon asks the embassy to report on it, a system of dual control which post-war Germany has not got rid of.[64]

In December 1930 Klop had a long conversation with Sir Arthur Willert about British and German policy. Three months earlier the Nazis had taken nearly 20 per cent of the vote in Reichstag elections. Lord Cecil had been conducting disarmament talks in Geneva on the British behalf but had predicted a fifteen-month delay. Willert suggested to Klop that although the German government, led by the Centre Party's Heinrich Brüning, professed to support disarmament and to be alarmed by the rising support for Hitler, they might welcome the collapse of the talks as an excuse to break the restrictions placed on the German military after the First World War. Klop had agreed to try to put the British view across in his news agency reports but Willert had a different objective in mind. He wrote:

> Mr Ustinov is very intimate with the German Embassy and one can take it for granted that, if not actually sent to ask questions such as these, he does not fail to report the answers to the Embassy.[65]

Klop would in due course find himself on even more intimate terms with his German embassy colleagues as the Wolff Bureau was absorbed in the German propaganda operation. The pretence of impartiality was abandoned and he became an embassy press officer. In January 1932, Klop presented a fifteen-minute talk about Germany on BBC radio as the first of a series called *Through Foreign Eyes*. He maintained, and even increased, his liaison with the British Foreign Office but from 1930 onwards the records of those meetings have, with one exception, been carefully expunged from the official archives.

It may be coincidence, but 1930 was also the year in which Clifford Norton won a long-awaited promotion. He became private secretary to Sir Robert Vansittart, the permanent under-secretary at the Foreign Office. Throughout the 1930s, Vansittart was the most powerful, and often the loneliest, official opponent of appeasement. He did not trust even his own diplomats to reflect accurately Hitler's true intentions. Nor did he rely on the massively underfunded and often ineffectual espionage efforts of MI6. Vansittart ran his own Intelligence service. Norton was his unnoticed lieutenant, Klop one of his many sources.

Klop had also made the acquaintance of the diplomat Robert Bruce Lockhart who had been implicated in the 1918 plot to assassinate Lenin and was the former lover of the Russian aristocrat Moura Budberg. It appears that Lockhart may have met Nadia during his days in St Petersburg at the time of the revolution, or at least known her family, since he recorded in his diary in March 1929:

> Lunched with Ustinov, an ex-German airman, who is married to Benois's daughter. He is the author of the brilliant expression: There will be no peace until men learn that it is a nobler and harder task to live for their country than to die for it.

A couple of months later he had lunch with Klop and Nadia at their flat in order to meet Hans von Raumer, a former German finance minister who was in Britain to improve his English. Among the other guests were Arthur Willert from the Foreign Office and the German diplomat Count Albrecht Bernstorff.

Bernstorff and Klop made it their business to try to influence British thinking against Hitler, and Lockhart records in 1932 that he met them both at the Carlton Grill shortly after Klop had spent some time in Berlin and both men lectured him on being too pro-Hitler in his *Evening Standard* articles. Klop was at that stage still hopeful that Hitler had lost his chance to seize power.[66]

Lockhart clearly came to admire both men and later wrote:

> From 1929 to 1933 German journalism was strongly represented in London by a brilliant team of foreign correspondents. The brightest star was Ustinov, who not only had a remarkable flair, but also a penetrating mind, illuminated with a scintillating wit.[67]

CHAPTER 6: VANSITTART

Robert Gilbert Vansittart, born 25 June 1881, occupied third place on Hitler's blacklist of Britons whose intransigence he blamed for the Second World War, after Winston Churchill and Leslie Hore-Belisha, the Jewish Minister of War who oversaw Britain's belated drift to rearmament from 1937 to 1940. Even in 1942, in his Wolf's Lair headquarters on the Eastern Front, Hitler's dinner table conversation turned to the supposed iniquities of these three opponents of appeasement.[68]

Vansittart's family origins were in south-eastern Holland, near the German border, but the Vansittarts had been settled in Britain since 1670: merchant adventurers, administrators, admirals and generals, a director of the East India Company, and, in Nicholas Vansittart, Baron Bexley, a Chancellor of the Exchequer from 1812 to 1824. Nevertheless Vansittart's hawkish features and slightly slanting eyes gave rise to rumours that he was of Asian or black lineage, which his detractors thought significant.

His father was an army captain who inherited substantial estates at Foots Cray in Kent. The income paid for Robert to be educated at Eton, where he excelled at languages and determined on a career in the diplomatic service. As a young man, he made extended visits to France and Germany that profoundly influenced his outlook. In Paris, at the time of the Dreyfus affair, he was horrified by the violent anti-Semitism routinely practised. In Hamburg, during the Boer War, he suffered bullying and humiliation as a result of anti-British sentiments. Disappointed to be rejected for military service in the First World War, on account of his protected profession, he mourned bitterly the loss of his younger brother Arnold at Ypres in 1915. From 1916 he was secretary of the Prisoner of War department of the Foreign Office, inevitably concerned daily with allegations of German mistreatment of captives.[69]

In the 1920s his career had advanced rapidly: political secretary to Lord Curzon as Foreign Secretary; then private secretary to Conservative and Labour Prime Ministers, Stanley Baldwin and Ramsay MacDonald respectively. In 1930 he returned to the Foreign Office as permanent undersecretary, theoretically at least the most powerful figure in the diplomatic firmament, and from there he waged a personal and often lonely battle against appeasement for most of the next decade.

His first wife, Gladys, had died young and in 1931 he married Sarita, widow of his diplomatic colleague Sir Colville Barclay. The Vansittart family fortune had been dissipated by his father but his new wife was independently extremely wealthy and this enabled the new permanent undersecretary to entertain lavishly at his country mansion, Denham Place in Buckinghamshire, and at 44 Park Street, Mayfair, where the distinguishing feature was a curved first-floor ballroom. The guest list included King Edward VIII and Mrs Simpson, Churchill, and Ivan Maisky, the Soviet ambassador.

Vansittart opposed a return to the pre-1914 diplomatic policy of alliances, incompatible secret treaties, balance of power bargaining and tariff wars. He feared they would undo whatever progress the League of Nations and disarmament policies had achieved. Over the next six years Adolf Hitler would more than fulfil his worst vision.

Vansittart gathered around him a few rising younger men who became known as 'Van's Boys'. They were in broad agreement with his views about Germany and were prepared to go out on a limb for him, maintaining intelligence contacts, briefing anti-appeasement MPs like Churchill and well-disposed journalists. Apart from Clifford Norton, his two ablest props were Rex Leeper and Ralph Wigram.[70]

The Australian-born Leeper already had close connections to MI6. He had been an intelligence officer at the Ministry of Information in 1916 and had taken a similar role at the Foreign Office in 1918. He was involved in setting up MI6's operations in Poland and in negotiating the release of Robert Bruce Lockhart, the British consul in Moscow. From 1935 he was head of news at the Foreign Office, active in developing the use of propaganda; and in wartime he became director of the Political Warfare Executive.[71] Wigram had been on a secret mission in the Caucasus during the First World War, served as a diplomat in Washington and Paris, and overcame a bout of polio to become head of the central department of the Foreign Office, directly responsible for reporting to Vansittart on developments in Germany. With Prime Minister Ramsay MacDonald's permission, Wigram also briefed his close friend Winston Churchill, at that time exiled to the back benches. He was also behind the leaking to the *Daily Telegraph*, in 1935, of details of the expansion of the Luftwaffe, which caused a political outcry.[72]

Vansittart's private intelligence network was an eclectic mix of nationalities and occupations who shared a deep distrust of German militarist tendencies. Foremost among them was Group Captain Malcolm Christie, who had a First in chemistry from Cambridge, had worked for German industry before the First World War and had then been bitten by the flying bug in its very early days. He served in the Royal Flying Corps during the First World War and was air attaché in Washington and Berlin until retirement in 1930. In that time he had built up a significant range of contacts in Germany which he maintained from his home on the Dutch-German border. He was able to hold lengthy personal conversations with Hitler's Air Minister, Hermann Göring, who could be expansively forthcoming about aircraft development and tactics, and tap into a range of well-placed sources in the aviation world. He was one of the first to reveal the rapidly increasing power of the Luftwaffe and predict Hitler's military and political objectives.[73]

Vansittart's return to the Foreign Office had coincided with the New York Stock Exchange collapse and the start of the Great Depression. In Britain, in 1931, that led to the schism of the Labour Party and the creation of a 'national' government in which Ramsay MacDonald was Prime Minister but Conservatives increasingly dominated. In Germany the collapse of a Social Democrat-led coalition was followed by substantial electoral gains for the Nazis and government by decree by Chancellor Heinrich Brüning, the devoutly Catholic leader of the Centre Party, through the aged President Hindenburg. Hitler consolidated his power base among industrialists and the army while his storm troopers gave the German public a foretaste of what was to come, directing their violence against opponents in general and Jews in particular.

Adolf Hitler came to power in Germany on the morning of 30 January 1933. Over the next twelve months the Nazification of Germany cumulatively destroyed Klop's belief in his nationality. The man who had left London in 1914 to volunteer to fight for Germany, a country he barely knew but whose citizenship he cherished, in the First World War, became an outcast with no right to earn a living from his chosen career.

Klop was one of a number of German journalists who put their names to a letter to the *Manchester Guardian* which appeared, possibly by design, on 1 April 1933, declaring that a full-scale revolution was taking place in Germany and that at such time 'incidents' were inevitable. The correspondents warned that false rumours in the British press about alleged atrocities were reaching the level of psychosis and appealed for everyone 'to avoid sensationalism, exaggeration and distortion'.

Later that month the Law for the Restoration of the Professional

Civil Service meant state employees who were not of Aryan descent could be forced to retire. The law was extended progressively to teachers, doctors and other professions. In October the Reich Press Law made Aryan descent a requirement of journalism and obliged editors only to publish material that did not conflict with the interests of the state under its new leadership. In December the Propaganda Minister Joseph Goebbels absorbed the Wolff Bureau into his state-controlled German News Bureau.

This was part of the process of purging Jews from public life and quickly extended to other ethnic groups and classes perceived to be enemies of the regime. Nadia recognised the implications more clearly than Klop:

> So life went on, rich and varied, until 1933 when the hideous shadow of Hitler loomed for the first time on our horizon. I was full of apprehension but Klop, being an optimist, believed that all would be well. He regarded Hitler as a complete nonentity and could not agree with me that his appearance portended disaster. However, slowly but surely our relations with the German embassy began to deteriorate.[74]

Klop had simultaneously become an employee of the state and rejected by it. The recently appointed head of Foreign Office propaganda in Berlin, Gottfried Aschmann, took immediate steps to move him from the sensitive London posting, where the Nazis were having trouble getting their message across, to Paris. The ambassador, Leopold von Hoesch, who was a constant thorn in Hitler's side, successfully blocked it. On 18 May 1933 he wrote to Aschmann acknowledging that at a time of drastic decisions there was little time for personal issues. But the London embassy was already weak in representing German interests in a country of great importance. Ustinov had over many years mastered the control of the flow of news. He had good relationships in English circles and he knew whom to see and whom to trust. Hoesch went on to praise Klop's knowledge in interpreting press coverage. A new man would be helpless in the face of these difficult tasks, particularly with the forthcoming world economic conference, intended to find solutions to the Great Depression, due in London in June.

Clearly Hoesch was already aware that Klop's racial origins were being held against him because he felt the need to point out that, despite his Russian descent, Klop had volunteered to serve in the German Army, winning the Iron Cross, in the Great War. The fact that his wife was Russian was of negligible importance, he added.

Last but not least, Klop had a good relationship with Reuters and, for example, it was thanks to him that Hitler's speech the previous day had been taken up so quickly and extensively in London.[75]

This was Hitler's famous 'Peace Speech' to the Reichstag on 17 May which the historian William Shirer described as:

> One of the greatest of his career, a masterpiece of deceptive propaganda that deeply moved the German people and unified them behind him and which made a profound and favourable impression on the outside world.

Hitler, responding to disarmament proposals by United States President Franklin D. Roosevelt, had spoken of renouncing all offensive weapons and disbanding Germany's entire military establishment if neighbouring countries did the same. The moderation and peaceful language took the world by surprise. It disguised a condemnation of the Versailles Treaty and a warning that without equality of treatment Germany would withdraw from the disarmament conference and the League of Nations. The warning was overlooked as British newspapers, apparently prompted by Klop, blindly welcomed the new Führer's initiative. *The Times* said Hitler's claim for equality was irrefutable; the *Daily Herald*, official organ of the Labour Party, demanded that Hitler be taken at his word; the Tory-supporting *Spectator* called it a gesture of hope for a tormented world. Five months later, when the Allies failed to deliver immediate disarmament, Hitler carried out his threat. At the same time he dissolved the German Parliament, the Reichstag.[76]

So, for a while, Klop allowed himself to be absorbed into the London end of the new propaganda apparatus established by Joseph Goebbels. He quickly received a direct and salutary warning of what the future held.

In August 1933 the Wolff Bureau's managing director, Artur Rawitski, set out from Berlin to visit Reuters in London, travelling on the German steam ship *Reliance*, bound for America. Before she reached Southampton the German police telegraphed the captain, ordering him to detain Rawitski on charges of embezzlement. On 9 August the captain left him in the custody of the British police and sailed on. By 9:30 p.m. Klop had got wind of what was happening and phoned the resident clerk at the Foreign Office, Geoffrey Wallinger, asking him to intervene. Three hours later Sir Roderick Jones, head of Reuters, added his voice to the protest, pointing out that Mr Rawitski was Jewish and might well be at risk of his life. A pantomime of activity ensued. Immigration officers could not be contacted; lawyers pondered and concluded that formal extradition procedures might not be required in such a case; the Home Office was consulted; and by mid-morning the next day pretty much everyone was satisfied that nothing could be done, which was just as well since the unfortunate Mr Rawitski had already been put on a German-bound ship and sailed away.

Sir Robert Vansittart, when he heard what had happened, was apoplectic. Did the Home Office and the immigration service never read the newspapers? Had they no idea what fate was likely to await Mr Rawitski? Was it not the case that an allegation of embezzlement was among the simplest to fabricate? Surely nothing would have been lost by delaying Rawitski's return for a couple of days while the case was investigated. His mood cannot

have been lightened by a report from the British embassy in
Berlin, which could discover no definite news of Mr Rawitski
but explained:

> Probably his Semitic blood and democratic principles constitute
> his crime ... We should imagine that he will disappear into a
> concentration camp without the formality of any 'proceedings'.

Vansittart's assistant secretary, Sir George Mounsey, was still
able to comment disdainfully that 'all's well that ends well' – a
reference not to Mr Rawitski's unknown fate but to the fact that
Parliament was not sitting so no MP could ask awkward questions
about him.[77]

MI5 still regarded Klop with some suspicion. At the beginning
of December 1933 Sir Vernon Kell, the Security Service's director,
wrote a nine-page report for Sir Robert Vansittart at the Foreign
Office on the Nazi propaganda drive in Britain. Kell dwelt mainly
on Albert Rosenberg, editor of the party newspaper, who had just
paid a notably unsuccessful visit to Britain. He laid a wreath bearing
a swastika at the tomb of the unknown warrior in Westminster
Abbey and an outraged British veteran threw it in the Thames.
Kell warned also of the activities of Joachim von Ribbentrop, later
ambassador to Britain, and Otto Bene, London leader of the Nazi
party whose hectoring demands that Germans living in Britain
should support the party were already viewed with alarm.

Towards the end of his report Kell added a couple of paragraphs
about Klop:

> Representative of the Wolff Bureau, who has a salary of £70 a
> month, although not fully in favour with the Nazis because of
> his Jewish wife, is reported now to be doing a certain amount
> of propaganda work on behalf of the present regime. He seems for
> a time to have given a number of champagne dinner parties and
> generally to have spent money beyond his apparent means.

Aside from the inaccuracy about Nadia – who was certainly not Jewish – and an underestimate of Klop's secret salary, Kell summed up Klop's lifestyle and finances well enough. He went on to make other remarks which unfortunately have been removed from the official Foreign Office record by the simple expedient of cutting off the bottom of the page on which they appeared. In any case, Kell's doubt about where Klop's sympathies lay were directly contradicted in a handwritten note by diplomat Victor Perowne who had his own sources of information from a high-ranking German Nazi. This source described Klop as 'a very dangerous man with wrong ideas. Very bad for Germany.'[78]

The source went on to say that Count Albrecht von Bernstorff had been removed from his position as Secretary at the German embassy in London because he was too friendly with Ustinov and too much under his influence. This was a fairly startling assessment – Bernstorff was one of the most scornful critics of the Nazi regime. A blond giant of a man, he was a familiar, stylish figure arriving at London's best restaurants and clubs in his open-topped Armstrong Siddeley. He was an Anglophile, of liberal convictions, who had been a Rhodes Scholar at Oxford University. The retired diplomat and diarist Harold Nicolson recorded a lunch he attended in August 1932 at The Elms, in Rottingdean, East Sussex, the home of the head of Reuters, Sir Roderick Jones and his wife Enid Bagnold, the novelist. Among the other guests was the Labour politician and former Attorney-General, William Jowitt, and Simone de la Chaume, the French amateur golf champion who married tennis player René Lacoste and founded the sports fashion label, as were Bernstorff and Ustinov. After a good luncheon Klop amused them with imitations of Queen Victoria.[79]

Bernstorff was particularly fond of Enid Bagnold and took pleasure in introducing her to his friends, including Klop. The two men of such contrasting size were nicknamed Big Pig and Little Pig. They seem to have made it their business both to entertain and to warn of the impending Nazi menace. Enid Bagnold was an admirer of Hitler, despite her two friends' protestations and on one occasion invited Klop, Nadia and the teenage Peter Ustinov to a dinner in honour of Hermann von Raumer, Ribbentrop's foreign policy adviser. The devoted Nazi, boasting of the new Germany's efficiency, explained: 'I only have to press my bottom (meaning button) and four policemen come running.' The young Peter Ustinov burst into a fit of giggles and had to be escorted from the room on the instructions of a distinctly unamused Sir Roderick Jones.[80]

It was probably through the Bernstorff and Bagnold social circle that Klop and Nadia got to know Lord Strathcona, under-secretary at the War Office and Captain of the King's Bodyguard. Nadia became friends with his wife Diana and taught her to paint during a holiday at the Strathcona family seat on the Hebridean island of Colonsay. When war broke out, Nadia helped Diana run an emergency canteen at Euston station.

Bernstorff's aristocratic lineage and unstuffy attitude opened up a wide social circle to which Klop also had access. Winston Churchill's controversial cousin Clare Sheridan was among them. She was a sculptress who had been commissioned to create busts of leaders of the Russian Revolution and espoused their Communist creed, scandalising her friends, and agents of MI5 who had her under surveillance, with her advocacy of free love. William Jowitt and his wife Lesley were also close friends and patrons of the arts. They commissioned the Russian mosaic artist Boris Anrep to decorate the entrance hall to their Mayfair home with a series entitled *Various Moments in the Life of a Lady of Fashion* in which Lesley Jowitt was shown in bed on the telephone, in her bath and at a nightclub.[81]

Bernstorff's Establishment friends included British diplomats, newspaper editors, bankers and academics and he liked to enjoy himself, too. He and Klop were no strangers to the London nightclub circuit. Bernstorff spent at least one Christmas with the Ustinov family and invited them for holidays on his country estate on the island of Stintenberg in the Schaalsee east of Hamburg.

Harold Nicolson was a frequent dining companion of Bernstorff's. When the count was forced to relinquish his diplomatic position, Nicolson attended a farewell lunch organised by Enid Bagnold and attended by the author H. G. Wells, who was on the brink of becoming engaged to Klop's friend, Moura Budberg. Nicolson's diaries record a 1936 dinner at the Savoy Grill with Bernstorff, Winston Churchill and Duff Cooper where they discussed how Hitler might be stopped. Bernstorff recommended 'overwhelming encirclement' and Nicolson wrote: 'He is extremely courageous and outspoken in his hatred of the Nazis, and I fear he is not long for this world.'[82]

It was Bernstorff who suggested to an English friend that instead of sending Chamberlain, Eden or Lloyd George to treat with Hitler they should send a sergeant of the Brigade of Guards who would say to him: 'Corporal, stand up when you speak to me,' and Hitler would do as he was ordered.[83]

A year later Nicolson was pondering how he might get Bernstorff an invitation to shoot at Sandringham so that he could get his message across to King George VI. Bernstorff maintained his very public opposition to Hitler, defiantly returning to Germany to join the board of a German-Jewish bank and sheltering Jewish refugees. He was arrested in 1943 for plotting against the regime, suffered terrible torture in Ravensbrück concentration camp and was eventually executed a couple of weeks before the end of the war, apparently on Ribbentrop's orders. This was particularly painful for Klop and Nadia, after their years of friendship, because of a misplaced attempt by Klop to protect him. Shortly after the outbreak of the Second World War, Klop was in Switzerland and bumped into his old adversary André Rostin who, despite his Jewish background, was still working for the Germans. Rostin began to ask questions about Bernstorff and, hoping to deflect an interrogation that he feared could only bring his friend harm, Klop assured the questioner that Bernstorff was in reality a good Nazi. Not long after, he received a mortified letter from Bernstorff reproaching Klop for so blatantly misrepresenting Bernstorff's beliefs. It was the last they heard from him.[84]

At the beginning of April 1933, MI5 had taken the opportunity to take a close look at the new Nazi regime. Captain Guy Liddell, a former police Special Branch officer and deputy director of counter-intelligence, was sent to Berlin, ostensibly to examine a vast cache of subversive Communist literature found in a raid on their massive headquarters, Karl Liebknecht House, a former factory building on the Bülowplatz. Liddell had led the British raid on the Arcos building, headquarters of the Russian trade delegation, at 49 Moorgate in the City of London in 1927. It had produced embarrassingly little evidence of a Communist conspiracy, had been justified in Parliament by revealing information from secret sources and caused the rupture of diplomatic relations between Britain and Russia. Liddell approached his new assignment with a healthy dose of scepticism and the clear expectation that it would reveal more about his Nazi hosts than their Communist enemies.

Liddell was greeted by MI6's man in Berlin, Major Frank Foley. His report went to Clifford Norton in the Foreign Office, Sir Hugh 'Quex' Sinclair, head of MI6, and to Sir Russell Scott, permanent undersecretary at the Home Office.

Liddell got straight to the point, describing their first contact with Dr Ernst 'Putzi' Hanfstaengl, Hitler's personal friend, gifted pianist, financial backer and foreign press liaison officer:

He has travelled a good deal, but his appreciation of foreign affairs and of the psychology of foreign peoples has become somewhat warped by his enthusiasm for the present regime. He is quite unbalanced both on the question of Communism and the Jews and genuinely believes the stories put about concerning the imminence of a Communist rising before Hitler's accession to power, the burning of the Reichstag and the 'International Jewish Conspiracy' ... He is under the erroneous impression that Communism is a movement controlled by the Jews ... I did my best to explain that conditions in England were very different and that violent and indiscriminate action against any section of the community in Germany was bound to be misunderstood in England, and produce unfavourable comment.[85]

This wry, forensic dissection of his host was surely also intended to twist the noses of a number of people in positions of influence at the Foreign Office and beyond, who were at that time full of admiration for Herr Hitler's energetic National Socialism and inclined to think that Sir Oswald Mosley might achieve something similar in Britain. It was typical of the man who was in many ways the embodiment of John le Carré's fictional spy chief George Smiley: a holder of the Military Cross from his service with the Royal Field Artillery in the First World War, he gave up a promising career as a cellist; endured a painful break-up of his marriage to Calypso Baring; successfully countered Communist and Nazi subversion in equal measure but eventually resigned his position as deputy director of MI5 because of an unwise friendship with the defector Guy Burgess. Long before that, he had overseen the embryonic career of Klop Ustinov.

Despite his misgivings, he got on well with Hanfstaengl, who perhaps understood foreigners better than Liddell imagined. When he fell out of favour with Hitler a couple of years later it was to Britain that he turned for asylum, moving next to Canada and then to Washington where he became an adviser to the US government in the Second World War.

Liddell's report continued almost with a sense of disbelief as he explained that public reports that the Communists had been on the verge of armed insurrection, planning to use a network of tunnels spreading out from Karl Liebknecht House, were complete fiction. He reported on Nazi Intelligence services; the assassination of political enemies; and 'amply confirmed' rumours that the Nazis were behind the Reichstag fire as an excuse for the wholesale repression of Jews and Communists. Liddell had drawn up a list of police contacts, who he hoped might prove useful in the future, and had a meeting with Ribbentrop, whose star was rising and whom Liddell found more amenable to reasoned discussion than most of the party faithful.

In 1935 the personal crisis finally engulfed Klop. According to Nadia, the Nazi regime had been treating him with growing suspicion and animosity, while he was boiling with rage and contempt. He was finally required to submit documentary evidence of his Aryan forebears – manifestly impossible given his part-Ethiopian mother and Slavic Russian father, let alone the grandfather who was a Polish Jew converted to Protestantism. He responded to the challenge with breathtaking audacity and an almost cavalier disregard not only for his own safety but that of his wife and family: 'If Herr Dr Goebbels would like first to prove his ancestry, then I will do the same.'[86]

This was more than an act of gross insubordination. Klop would have been well aware that the propaganda chief, although of working-class Germanic parentage, was far from the image of the physically perfect Aryan athlete. He was short, dark and walked with a limp as a result of a childhood illness. His wife Magda, the epitome of a statuesque blonde, had a Jewish stepfather.

Sympathetic staff in the embassy and in Berlin tried to cover up Klop's 'faux pas' but it was never likely to be ignored. He was ordered to return to Berlin for 'consultations', which he wisely refused to do. Then he was threatened with dismissal. He knew he would have to leave but the greatest danger was for Nadia, who was at the time in Berlin visiting her sister Olia and having a minor operation. Klop phoned and told her to come home immediately. Within days of her return Klop was sacked.

He was leaving an embassy more in sympathy with him than with their political masters in Berlin. As his Nazi-inclined successor Fritz Hesse recalled, the ambassador Leopold von Hoesch was no admirer of Hitler and treated the new press attaché with suspicion. Klop had been on intimate terms with the Foreign Office and popular in the highest English social circles. His departure had cut off a very important thread for the embassy.[87]

Hoesch died suddenly, of a heart attack, in 1936. He left behind in the embassy others of a like mind: the military attaché Leo Geyr von Schweppenburg and the Second Secretary in charge of consular affairs, Wolfgang zu Putlitz, who became Klop's most prolific source of information.

CHAPTER 7: EXILES

Although Klop had clung on tenaciously to his position in the German embassy he had surreptitiously made plans for his departure and had already applied for British citizenship. With the help of Vansittart, the official notice of his intention appeared in a Welsh language newspaper where it would not attract the attention of the German authorities. Some people, among them Sir Roderick Jones at Reuters, declined to sponsor his citizenship, fearing to give offence to the Hitler regime.[88] It was finally issued on 21 November 1935, signed by the permanent undersecretary at the Home Office, Sir Russell Scott. Four days later Klop went to Markham House in Kings Road, Chelsea and before solicitor G. F. Wilkins swore 'by Almighty God that I will be faithful and bear true allegiance to His Majesty, King George the Fifth, His Heirs and Successors, according to law'.[89]

He had been a German for one week short of forty-three years and served his country valiantly. For the next twenty-seven years he was avowedly British. His determination to adopt the mores of his new nationality made him reticent about aspects of his own past. Peter Ustinov came home from school in October 1935 to find his father in tears over Mussolini's invasion of Ethiopia. What surprised him more than the tears was the open admission by Klop of his own ancestry. Previously he had suppressed this knowledge for fear that 'a touch of the tar-brush' might make him socially unacceptable.[90] He was similarly disinclined to refer to his Jewish antecedents.

At first his new country scarcely laid out the red carpet. He had no job, no prospects and no way to make ends meet. He and Nadia spent several weeks on holiday in the South of France mulling over their future while Clifford and Peter Norton looked after the fourteen-year-old Peter Ustinov. Their change in circumstances meant that he could no longer board at Westminster School, although he continued as a day boy, doing his best to antagonise his fellow pupil Rudolf von Ribbentrop. To afford the fees, the Ustinovs had to give up their flat in Lexham Gardens, Kensington and move to a three-room apartment at 34 Redcliffe Gardens in Chelsea. Even then, Peter always suspected that the school had overlooked a number of unpaid bills. He felt that Klop simply refused to recognise that he was now poor and behaved instead like a rich man without any money, searching his pockets for non-existent assets and then going shopping anyway and inviting people to dinner.[91]

Klop tried his hand at anything that might make money. He became bookkeeper to the theatre impresario André Charlot. In his heyday, Charlot's West End revues had helped launch the careers of Beatrice Lillie, Jack Buchanan, Gertrude Lawrence and Jessie Matthews, but by the time Klop joined him he was struggling to escape from bankruptcy and reduced to staging round-the-clock semi-nude shows in Soho. The appointment did not last long.[92] He tried his hand at writing short stories, but could not get them published, and served briefly as the art critic of the *News Chronicle* where his views on modern art were too acerbic and he was sacked.

Peter Ustinov, still at daggers drawn with his father, admits to a pang of sympathy for the humiliation Klop clearly felt at his inability to earn a living. Unfortunately this resentment manifested itself in outbursts of anger interspersed with periods of sullen withdrawal and denunciations of his teenage son for laziness when his school reports revealed a lack of academic prowess. In due course Nadia would come to Peter's rescue by recognising that her son's talents lay elsewhere and encouraging him, much against Klop's wishes, to move at the age of sixteen to the London Theatre Studio drama school in Islington run by Michael Saint-Denis, for whom she had worked on set design.[93] Saint-Denis's other protégés included Laurence Olivier, John Gielgud, Alec Guinness and Michael Redgrave. Nadia financed Peter's theatre apprenticeship from the sale of paintings or from savings scrimped from housekeeping money. Encouragement for Peter's dramatic inclinations came not from Klop but from his great uncle Alexander Benois who wrote to him:

> For two centuries our family has been sniffing around the theatre. We have designed for it, we have composed for it, we have conducted in it, and we have applauded and we have slept. At last one of us has had the incredible audacity to clamber upon the boards himself![94]

Nadia was increasingly in demand. In the autumn of 1933 she had been commissioned by the poet Walter Turner to design scenery and costumes for his play *Jupiter Translated* at the open-air Mercury Theatre in Notting Hill, West London. The play was not a success but it led to a new opportunity for Nadia. The Mercury Theatre was run by Ashley Dukes, older brother of Paul Dukes, the MI6 officer active in St Petersburg at the time of the revolution. Ashley's wife was Marie Rambert, who had danced with Nijinsky in the Ballet Russes and was already becoming one of the commanding figures of modern British ballet. She commissioned Nadia to work on scenery and costume design and thus began a long collaboration, which in turn led to further work for the Royal Ballet and Dame Ninette de Valois.

Her paintings were finding an audience, too. Family holidays were spent in the south of France, where she could work on her landscapes. They befriended the American artist Thalia Malcolm who had a studio at Vence, in the Alpes-Maritime region, a few miles from Nice. It was during a solo visit there one summer that Klop had a narrow escape while being driven at high speed by the

Tory MP Arthur Duckworth in his Bentley. They ended up in a ditch, with scarcely a scratch, having narrowly missed tumbling over a precipice on the outside of a bend.[95]

Nadia's work was praised for its 'unabatingly conscientious thoroughness' but she did not lack a sense of humour. Among her commissions was a series called *Three Little Pigs*, seen playing tennis, rowing and cycling in an exhibition of art for children.[96] She was working all hours in her studio on commissions which varied from landscapes to nudes of their German cook Frieda. Klop was always keen for her to paint nudes of his girlfriends. Nadia, unsurprisingly, did not share his enthusiasm although she obliged on some occasions – among them a portrait of Klop's MI5 colleague Joan Chenhalls. Nadia was a member of the New English Art Club, as was James Bolivar Manson, director of the Tate Gallery, who acquired one of her paintings through the Contemporary Art Society. Augustus John was another admirer of her work. Klop seems to have enjoyed mixing in this milieu and regained his earlier penchant for art dealing. He was helped by Manson who introduced him to an elderly collector in Fulham with a dilapidated house full of treasures with which he was willing to part at modest prices. Klop also got to know Daan Cevat, the son of a Dutch art dealer, who was just starting out and became a leading expert on Rembrandt. He brought drawings from Holland for Klop to sell, among them works by Rubens, Delacroix, Ingres and Tintoretto.

Klop's new profession dovetailed neatly with the cover needed for a secret agent. A number of art dealers found their way into MI5 and MI6 before and during the Second World War. In 1935 Klop's old friend Clifford Norton had introduced him to what Nadia described as 'a prominent person from one of the ministries'. Most likely, it was Guy Liddell of MI5 who took him on as a part-time agent. They were anxious to know about potential German infiltrators among the expatriate community in London and Klop was ideally placed. Apart from his journalistic contacts, Klop was in demand as an after-dinner speaker in the German colony in London.[97]

Klop and Nadia's flight from Russia in 1920 had been part of a mass emigration. Around two million left the country, the majority prosperous, educated and part of the cultural elite. Soldiers, peasants and the poor had neither the means nor the incentive to escape but for the bourgeois 'former people', whose homes were being requisitioned, who received the lowest level of rations and who found themselves reduced to hawking their remaining possessions on the streets, it was their best hope of survival. Many had never before had to face the exigencies even of cooking a meal, or earning a living. That's what the servants and the serfs did. And for those who had taken up arms against the Bolsheviks in the White Russian armies, as some of Nadia's relatives had, to return to face the Red Terror of the Cheka meant almost certain death.

The largest number, possibly 400,000, settled in France, where labour shortages after the First World War meant work could be found; 150,000 went to Germany, where inflation meant family treasures realised higher prices; and more to the countries bordering the new Soviet Union on the Baltic, in Eastern Europe and to the Balkans. They did not want to stray too far; they expected to return quite soon when the chaos of the revolution led inevitably to collapse.

By comparison, only about three or four thousand came to Britain. Despite its business ties – and the close relationship between the two royal families – Britain had fewer cultural and social connections to the old regime. Nevertheless the new community followed a similar pattern to that elsewhere, not wanting to fully assimilate or lose their old national identity. They had a very distinct social order to observe.

The Russian colony in London strove to replicate the structure of the old, pre-Revolutionary Russia, including the court, headed by Tsar Nicholas II's sister, the Grand Duchess Xenia Alexandrovna. She had arrived in Britain with her mother, the Dowager Empress Maria Feodorovna, aboard HMS *Marlborough*. The ship had been sent to rescue them from the Crimea at the request of King George V, whose mother, Queen Alexandra, was the empress's sister, after the tsar and most of his family had been executed at Ekaterinburg. Xenia was virtually penniless, sold most of her royal jewellery and lived out her life in grace and favour homes in Windsor Great Park and at Hampton Court Palace.

If she was the figurehead, the Golitsyn – or Galitzine – family were the focal point of the colony's social life. Prince Vladimir Golitsyn and his wife Ekaterina chose to settle in England so that their sons, Nicholas, George and Emmanuel, could attend public schools. To pay the fees Prince Vladimir opened a shop in Berkeley Square, in Mayfair, selling Russian *objets d'art*. During the 1930s Klop would find himself in the same line of business. The Golitsyns were patrons of the Russian Red Cross Society and one branch of the Orthodox Church. The princess was a descendant of the British King George III and so had an entrée at court and became an arbiter of social acceptability. At government level, Eugen Sabline, who had been chargé d'affaires at the Russian embassy at the time of the tsar, was allowed to retain a kind of diplomatic status and he and his wife Nadezhda Ivanovna turned their home in Brechin Place, South Kensington, into an unofficial embassy and museum filled with portraits, maps and ephemera of the imperial regime. Red Cross, Orthodox Church and official business could be conducted there. With his Europe-wide contacts with the Russian émigré community, and personal access to the Duchess Xenia, Sabline was to prove a useful informant when Klop joined MI5. After her husband's death in 1949, Mrs Sabline applied for British citizenship. One of her sponsors was Sir Edward Reid, a former financial adviser to MI5, whose wife was also of Russian descent.

Although their network of friends spread much wider, and Klop's was inevitably more bound up with the German colony, he and Nadia took some part in Russian social life. Peter Ustinov, who displayed an almost total lack of sporting prowess at Westminster School, recalls winning tennis championships at the

Anglo-Russian sports club 'where septuagenarian Czarist officers would lob each other to a standstill in immaculate whites'. The club, at The Lindens in Hartington Road, Chiswick, was co-founded by the former Russian champion and tennis pro Count Mikhail Sumarokov-Elston. He was a cousin of Prince Yusopov, one of the assassins of Rasputin. Both had escaped from the Crimea in 1919 aboard HMS *Marlborough* with the dowager empress.

Among Klop's contacts, who would serve him in good stead, was Captain Henry 'Bob' Kerby, later Conservative MP for Arundel and Shoreham. Kerby, a huge, bald-headed man with a lively sense of humour and pronounced right-wing views, was born in St Petersburg in 1914. His father, also Henry, was a forestry adviser to the tsar and one of MI6's first officers. After the revolution he had helped the dowager empress escape. Kerby and Klop kept in close touch with White Russian circles. The bewildering layers of intrigue that surrounded them, and the perpetual danger of infiltration by the Russian secret police, made them a treasure house of gossip from across the Continent covering a wide political spectrum.

Many of the Whites gravitated towards right-wing politics and Fascism as the best antidote to Communism. As a result, MI5 was constantly on the watch for signs of links between the White Russian community in Britain and Hitler's emissaries, who saw political advantage in cultivating them. Klop helped keep an eye on the main claimant to the Russian throne, the Grand Duke Prince Vladimir Kirillovitch, great-grandson of Tsar Alexander II. His parents had fled to Germany and then France after the revolution but in the 1930s Vladimir came to Britain hoping to study at Cambridge. He was unable to raise sponsorship and instead was assisted by Buckingham Palace to find a job on the production line at the Lister diesel engine factory in Stamford, Lincolnshire. He occupied a workman's house and used the name Vladimir Mikhailov. It was not a success and soon after the outbreak of the Second World War he returned to the family estate at St-Briac-sur-Mer in Brittany. After the German occupation of

France alarm bells began to ring in London. There were rumours that Hitler might offer Vladimir a return to Russia as tsar of a puppet Nazi regime. These fears were in part provoked by a batch of letters that Buckingham Palace handed over to MI5. One of them indicated that Vladimir was actively seeking foreign backers in support of his aspiration to restore White Russian rule. Klop was asked to find out Vladimir's real intentions and, with the help of Sabline and the Grand Duchess Xenia, reported that, despite some resentment that Britain had not done more to support his cause, he was sitting tight in St Briac and not collaborating. In the event he refused Hitler's offer of the regency of the Ukraine or to endorse the Nazi philosophy, and as a result was held in a concentration camp before being placed under house arrest at the home of his brother-in-law, Prince Louis Ferdinand, grandson of the German Kaiser Wilhelm II and one of the focal points of German resistance to the Hitler regime.

Inevitably Sabline knew Admiral Nikolai Wolkoff, who had been naval attaché at the Russian embassy under the tsar. In more straitened circumstances, the admiral became proprietor of the Russian tea rooms in Harrington Road, South Kensington. Like many of his compatriots, the admiral embraced right-wing politics in the quest for means to unseat the Communists. His daughter Anna, a dressmaker whose clients included Wallis Simpson, the future Duchess of Windsor, became an active member of the Right Club, a semi-clandestine pro-Nazi organisation run by Captain Maule Ramsey MP. One of MI5's first successes of the Second World War was a classic infiltration exercise at the Right Club which led to the arrest of Anna and Tyler Kent, a cipher clerk at the US embassy. Between them they had been leaking British government secrets to the Italians, and thereby to Hitler. After a closed trial, Anna was sentenced to ten years in jail. One of the witnesses to her arrest was a very young Len Deighton, the future spy writer, whose mother was working at the tea room.

It was one of Kerby and Klop's contacts, Anatole Baykolov, who alerted MI5 in 1936 to the possibility that Wallis Simpson was supplying intelligence obtained from her lover, King Edward VIII, to the Germans through their ambassador Joachim von Ribbentrop. Baykolov, once a member of the Socialist Revolutionary Party, ran an anti-Soviet newsletter in London during the 1930s and became a valued source for Klop and Guy Liddell. He had been in London since the end of the First World War, working as a journalist, under frequent surveillance through to the 1950s, with the Intelligence services never quite able to make up their minds whether he was a trustworthy source or an undercover *agent provocateur* for the Soviets.

MI5 accumulated thirteen folders of information about him, including occasional contributions from Klop, usually based on commentary provided by Eugen Sabline. Baykolov fed anti-Communist stories to the right-wing *Morning Post* newspaper and became a trusted confidant of the Duchess of Atholl who was one of the first to highlight the repression and exploitation of the people of the Soviet Union. Through her, he was introduced to Winston Churchill and Sir Robert Vansittart. An indication of the ambivalent attitude of the Intelligence services is evident in correspondence in 1934 between Valentine Vivian, the head of the anti-Comintern Section V of MI6, and Jane Sissmore, MI5's Comintern expert. Vivian made the point that all Baykolov's information, in common with other White Russian sources, had to be treated with suspicion, no matter how accurate it appeared, because of the likelihood of penetration by the Russian secret police. It was known that in the early 1930s in Germany he had been in regular contact with them. Nevertheless, MI5 had been in the habit of briefing Clifford Norton, Sir Robert Vansittart's private secretary, on the contents of Baykolov's correspondence and even supplying copies of it. Vivian proposed a conference with Norton to decide how to handle the material in future.[98]

Baykolov had contacts with the main exile groups in Paris, the White Russian Armed Services Union led by Prince Anton Turkul, the NTS or National Labour Group and the Mladorossy or Young

Russians. All these groups had constantly shifting loyalties, were used for intelligence gathering by MI6 and were known to have been heavily infiltrated by Soviet intelligence. Klop continued to keep an eye on Baykolov throughout the war and in December 1941, after the Soviets had been brought into the war on the Allied side, he reported that Baykolov was one of the chief antagonists of Anglo-Russian cooperation. Later still, Baykolov was reported to be a supporter of the Russian Liberation Movement which formed a pro-Nazi fighting force under General Andrei Vlasov in Germany to oppose the Soviet forces. Turkul and Baykolov would feature again in Klop's Cold War investigations.[99]

The Russian influx of the 1920s was overtaken by larger numbers of Germans fleeing the Hitler regime in the 1930s. Klop was among the earliest and, despite the impediments to earning a living, was made a good deal more welcome than many of his compatriots. Long gone was the nineteenth-century open-door policy which prompted the Conservative Lord Malmesbury to proclaim in 1852:

> I can well conceive the pleasure and happiness of a refugee, hunted from his native land, on approaching the shores of England, and the joy with which he first catches sight of them; but they are not greater than the pleasure and happiness every Englishman feels in knowing that his country affords the refugees a home and safety.[100]

In the last twenty years of that century approximately one hundred thousand Jewish refugees arrived, mostly fleeing persecution in Russia, and the foreign population more than doubled. Many were poverty-stricken and their presence was emphasised by their congregation in areas like the East End of London. The Aliens Act of 1905 gave immigration officers the right to refuse entry to 'undesirables'.

The First World War, and the years immediately before it, fostered anti-German and anti-immigrant feeling, sometimes to the point of hysteria, and led to the internment of 40,000

Germans, four-fifths of the total resident in Britain. Additional legislation in 1914, 1919 and 1920 required immigrants to be able to demonstrate that they had the means to support themselves and to obtain a Ministry of Labour permit before they were allowed to take up employment.

The idea that immigrants were a threat to the livelihoods of the native population were all the more prevalent during the Depression years of the early 1930s and initially the British government tried to limit admission to those who would bring economic advantages: manufacturers and industrialists, who were directed to the high unemployment areas in the north east and north west, and eminent scientists whose skills were of identifiable value. Nevertheless, in 1933, when Hitler came to power, between three and four hundred refugees a month arrived in Britain. By the time war broke out, in September 1939, 55,000 refugees had been admitted. Despite the concerns about unemployment there was a counterbalance in the Foreign Office's desire to maintain Britain's reputation abroad as a haven for the downtrodden. Other countries, including the Colonies, progressively closed their doors.

There was another fear, in which MI5 became embroiled. The influx, about 90 per cent of which was Jewish, was used as an excuse for Oswald Mosley and his British Union of Fascists to carry their violent anti-Semitic propaganda campaign into the East End of London and other districts with a large Jewish population. Nazi propaganda attempted to whip up this virulent hatred. The Home Secretary, Sir Samuel Hoare, told the Cabinet in March 1938 that MI5 believed it was deliberate German policy to export anti-Semitism by inundating Britain and other countries with poverty-stricken Jewish refugees to create the social problems that accompanied such an exodus.[101] Among the exiles were a relatively small number of political activists, representative mostly of the banned German Communist Party, the KPD, the Social Democrats and a smattering of senior Conservative politicians who had held office and attempted to thwart Hitler's ambitions. Among the latter group were Heinrich Brüning, Hermann Rauschning, Carl Spiecker and Gottfried Treviranus.

Brüning had been leader of the Centre Party and Reichs Chancellor from 1930 to 1932. He fled to Britain in 1934, later moving to the United States. Rauschning was a former Nazi leader who turned against Hitler and went into exile, arriving in Britain in 1939. Spiecker was another member of the Centre Party under Brüning and a special commissioner for combating National Socialism. He had originally gone into exile in Paris but became a contact of MI6's assistant chief Claude Dansey and, as will be seen, was the instigator of one of their worst wartime blunders. Treviranus, a member of the Conservative People's Party, had been a minister in Brüning's administration.

As they maintained their opposition to the Nazi regime in speeches and publications, German government policy was to deprive them of their citizenship, rendering them stateless and dependent on their new host countries, then to try to bully those countries into silencing the dissidents in the interests of good diplomatic relations. In Britain this policy was largely ineffectual, on account of the attitudes of those charged with implementing it. The German embassy counsellor Count Albrecht Bernstorff, who was frequently to be found with Klop decrying the Nazi regime, reported disingenuously to Berlin in 1933 that no anti-German activity by the émigrés had been brought to the embassy's notice and they appeared to be acting with restraint.

Two years later Wolfgang zu Putlitz, Klop's close friend at the embassy, made a half-hearted protest to the Foreign Office about refugees – especially the playwright Ernst Toller – making speeches against the German government. The Gestapo and the Nazi party soon recognised that their diplomats were reluctant informers and began to post their own people abroad.[102]

It was in this context that Putlitz warned Klop and MI5 in 1936 against the activities of Otto Bene, the Nazi leader in London whom the new ambassador, Joachim von Ribbentrop, hoped to appoint as Consul General.

Klop was also one of a number of people keeping an eye on Gottfried Treviranus. They had something in common: both had been part of Sir Robert Vansittart's private intelligence network while still German citizens. Treviranus had been introduced to Foreign Secretary Anthony Eden by Vansittart. The German politician had a much narrower escape than Klop. He was in his back garden when SS men arrived to arrest him and fled by jumping over a wall to his waiting car after his young daughter cried out a warning. The SS men opened fire and only narrowly missed – he later claimed he had kept his hat with bullet holes in it. His escape was engineered by another of Vansittart's men, the former Labour MP Major Archibald Church who provided him with a false British passport and escorted him through Holland back to Britain.

In 1936 Klop reported to MI5 that he did not think Treviranus posed a threat to British security or was engaging in 'unpleasant activities'. He revealed that, apart from working for Vansittart, Treviranus was also briefing Winston Churchill on the situation in Germany.

Treviranus set himself up as an arms dealer and was allowed to open a gun-manufacturing plant in Lancashire. Among his clients was David Hall who was buying arms on behalf of the Ethiopian government of Haile Selassie, whose country had been invaded by Mussolini's Fascist Italian regime. David Hall was Klop's uncle, his mother's brother who had maintained the family's Ethiopian heritage by becoming an adviser to the emperor. After war broke out Sir Louis Greig, who had been an equerry to King George VI and was working for the Air Ministry, helped find Treviranus a job with an aeronautical engineering firm who employed him as their representative in Canada – thereby neatly removing him from contentious political manoeuvring in Britain.[103]

Apart from a favoured few, like Klop, German journalists were regarded with suspicion by the Foreign Office and MI5. Klop used his journalistic background to keep tabs on them, including Karl Abshagen, correspondent of the Prussian newspaper *Schlesische Zeitung*. Doubtless he did not find it too much of an imposition to accompany his colleague to his favourite watering hole, the Paradise Club in Regent Street, where they could enjoy late night drinking, a cabaret with jugglers, stand-up comedians, 'exotic' dancers and music provided by the resident pianist Arthur Rosebery and his band. Abshagen was held in much the same esteem in the 1930s by senior figures at the Foreign Office, including Clifford Norton, as Klop had been during the 1920s. His reports were considered objective and well informed – too well informed sometimes and there was at least one investigation into a suspected Cabinet leak. It was assumed that he had an unofficial intelligence role and, after a foreign correspondents' visit to the battleship HMS *Nelson*, the director of naval intelligence somehow got the idea that Abshagen's wife had a miniature camera concealed in her umbrella. A Foreign Office note about Abshagen noted that he was in a mood of exasperation and despair at Britain's failure to heed his warning that a strong and forthright condemnation of Hitler's diplomatic bully-boy tactics was what was required. Hitler was scoring points at home and intelligent opposition to him in Germany was becoming stultified. At the highest level of the Foreign Office there was general agreement. Sir Robert Vansittart commented that he was talking admirable sense and even the pro-appeasement Alec Cadogan, the rising star at the Foreign Office who would eventually supplant Vansittart, described him as 'a fairly acute observer'. They were aware of reports from Klop identifying Abshagen as one of at least half a dozen German journalists using their official role as camouflage for intelligence gathering. Klop knew, probably from his own experience, that they wrote special reports, with a circulation of only about 200 to the most senior officials in the German government.[104]

These documents went first to General Hans Oster, deputy to Admiral Wilhelm Canaris, head of the Abwehr, German military intelligence. Abshagen's reports were often in complete contradiction to the wilder flights of fancy of the German ambassador Joachim von Ribbentrop. The Third Reich's propaganda minister Joseph Goebbels warned his editor:

> Abshagen must continue to report quite frankly, whether or not his reports agree with those of the embassy in London. But tell him to take care that his phrasing gives no offence, for they will be read by our Führer in the original.[105]

Klop had already reported to MI5 on what could happen when the Führer took exception to a news man's interpretation of events. Count Carl Heinrich Pückler of the *Deutsche Allgemeine Zeitung* had commented favourably on the strength of Britain's anti-aircraft defences and had received such a fearsome dressing down from Hitler that he was a broken man and later lost his job. Under such circumstances his colleagues were most reluctant to file any news stories that might incur their leader's wrath.[106]

CHAPTER 8: SECRET AGENT

Klop's introduction to MI5 put him in the position of answering to two masters. Vansittart at the Foreign Office still wanted to know what was going on in Germany; Liddell was concerned with counter-espionage on the home front. But there were no hard and fast demarcation lines. When Liddell recruited Dick White to MI5 in 1936 his first act was to send his future deputy on a tour of Germany to improve his language skills and familiarise himself with the Nazi regime.

On his return he became Klop's case officer and, as he later told his biographer:

> Here without question we had picked a natural winner who would not let us down … the best and most ingenious operator I had the honour to work with.

Klop and White also shared a certain disdain for some of the old-fashioned MI6 officers whom they encountered and who appeared to be 'ivory from the neck up'.[107]

White had been assigned to fill the void of MI5's ignorance about German intelligence activities in Britain and was coached by Klop and Putlitz, who also introduced him to Vansittart's private intelligence system. Thereafter White often served as a staging post at which high-ranking anti-Nazi visitors from Germany could stop off to deliver their warning messages for Vansittart.

Although Klop was by now an employee, albeit a part-time one working at arm's length, he was rarely referred to by name but by his soubriquet U35. The U might almost stand for ubiquitous – it appears in the MI5 wartime records and those of the Foreign Office in a way that no other agent does. But it is a curious choice. Taken at face value it could be short for Ustinov 1935, the year he was recruited. That seems too transparent to be true, and he had in any case been unofficially recruited some time earlier. It is also out of keeping with normal practice. MI5 rarely gave its officers a cover name consisting of initial and numbers. They were more likely to use a pseudonym. MI6 did use initials and numbers in the 1920s but had largely abandoned the practice by the 1930s, preferring a five-digit code in which the first two digits signified the country of operation.

There is, however, a curious anecdote about U35 which, if connected, would indicate an unsuspected sense of humour among the heads of the Intelligence services. It concerns Admiral Wilhelm Canaris, who became head of the Abwehr, German military intelligence, on his forty-seventh birthday, 1 January 1934.

He was small, shrewd and secretive, fluent in English, French and Russian, educated, well travelled and an officer of the old school. He despised Hitler and it is now generally accepted that, while he performed his duties effectively enough to remain in office until 1943, he was throughout working in what he believed were Germany's best interests, not the Führer's. At times that meant lending active assistance to the Western Allies. He stood back from the conspiracies to depose Hitler, while doing nothing to discourage his deputy Hans Oster from playing a leading role, and both men were executed after the assassination attempt on Hitler in July 1944. The Nazis condemned him as a traitor.

During the First World War he was an intelligence officer in neutral Spain where his reports enabled U-boats to wreak havoc on Allied shipping in the Mediterranean. Such was his notoriety that a young British intelligence officer, Captain Stewart Menzies, was sent to kill or capture him. More than twenty years later Menzies would become head of MI6, once more in direct opposition to Canaris. But it was the German who won that first encounter. Knowing that the British were on his trail, and despite two French submarines patrolling the coast, he took refuge in a small boat among the Spanish fishing fleet in Salitrona Bay near Cartagena, southern Spain. Germany's most successful U-boat commander Lothar von Arnauld de la Perière slipped in unnoticed to rescue him. His vessel was U-35.[108]

★

On 7 March 1936 Hitler reoccupied the Rhineland. Vansittart's assistant Ralph Wigram was given the task of escorting the French Foreign Minister Pierre Flandin to London where he tried without success to persuade the Prime Minister, Stanley Baldwin, to take a robust stance against the aggression. A sympathetic Wigram arranged meetings with every influential person he could find, including Churchill, but as it became clear Britain was neither inclined nor prepared for a confrontation, the despondent official told his wife:

> War is now inevitable, and it will be the most terrible war there has ever been. All my work these many years has been no use ... I have failed to make people here realise what is at stake.[109]

Before the year was out he died of cancer. On 31 December 1936, Vansittart wrote a memorandum entitled 'The World Situation and British Rearmament', in which he observed: 'Time is vital and we have started late. Time is the material commodity the Foreign Office has to buy. Our aim must be to stabilise the situation till 1939.'[110]

This was the strategy which in part influenced Chamberlain's ultimately fruitless endeavour to find solutions to Germany's grievances. Even officials who no longer believed that such a policy could appease Hitler found it difficult, given Britain's lamentable strategic position, to recommend alternative courses.

Around this time Klop also had the opportunity to enter a rather different, risqué artistic clique. It came about through his intimate relationship with the photographer Thea Struve which had threatened to drive a wedge between him and Nadia. When Nadia and Klop lived at 72 Lexham Gardens, Kensington in the early 1930s, Thea had been a near neighbour at No. 64, a house occupied by a coterie of respectable individuals, among them Etheldred Browning, founder of a housing association for single women, the religious writer Arthur Howell Smith and Nadia's fellow artist Vere Lucy Temple. Thea was, like Klop, a German exile. She had taken pictures at Marie Rambert's Notting Hill theatre where Nadia designed the sets.

Nadia recognised that Thea was attractive in a rather special way. Her elongated figure reminded Nadia of a Modigliani or El Greco painting. She was broad-minded and unpredictable which made her intriguing to Klop and infuriating to Nadia, who admitted to powerful feelings of jealousy as she was obliged to witness their exchanges of sexual banter. As ever, she later tried to make light of it, recalling a wild Bohemian party in Bloomsbury when the lights went out. Klop had taken the opportunity to surreptitiously fondle his latest amour in the darkness, only to discover when the lighting was restored that he had missed his target and was greeted by the loving glance of a bearded Hampstead poet.[111]

It was in this Hampstead world, populated by a number of German cultural exiles, that Thea's ambitions lay. She began photographing the sculptor Jacob Epstein and the surrealist painter Sir Roland Penrose at work in their studios. Penrose, friend and biographer of Pablo Picasso, and a Communist sympathiser, lived at 21 Downshire Hill and was a notorious party-giver. Many of the guests would have been of interest to Klop as would his neighbours in the Isokon building, better known now as the Lawn Road flats where some of the KGB's best agents made their homes.

Thea moved in with Penrose and is believed to have been the model for one of his nudes, but it was to be a short-lived affair. He was already involved with the American photographer Lee Miller, who would become famous later as a *Vogue* war photographer and come under Klop's scrutiny because of her Communist activities. She was married to an Egyptian diplomat and when she returned briefly to him Penrose wrote to her that Thea was now occupying his bed but added:

> I almost feel ashamed to make love with her. She is very sweet and is perhaps the only person who could console me of this bitterness. She puts up with my gloom with great patience though I talk of you whenever I can and tell her of the lump that I can't move at the bottom of my heart.[112]

Thea left Penrose in December 1938 to start a new career at the Buchholz Gallery in New York, an occupation which would be of interest to Klop during his wartime duties in Lisbon.

In April 1937 Klop and Wolfgang zu Putlitz were involved in the expulsion of the German spy Otto Ludwig who was caught during a customs search at Harwich carrying blueprints for a new type of armour-piercing bullet. As head of the consular department at the German embassy, Putlitz was responsible for looking after Ludwig's interests while he was in custody. Simultaneously he briefed Klop on every legal move and contact that Ludwig made.

Klop was able to report that Ludwig's first instinct was to ask Ambassador Joachim von Ribbentrop to intervene. Instead, Putlitz sent his assistant to interview Ludwig, who was anxious to warn his contacts in Britain to lie low. One of these was the German journalist Franz Wrede, who had been asked to establish contacts with Oswald Mosley, leader of the British Union of Fascists, and evaluate the group's attitude to Hitler. Wrede's colleague, Werner von Crome, was supposed to find out what were the prospects of Edward VIII being able to return to the throne. Edward had abdicated the previous year, over his determination to marry the divorcee Wallis Simpson, and was considered to be sympathetic to the Nazi regime. Later that year he paid a controversial visit to Germany and met Hitler. Karl Friedrich Basedow had posed as a British tourist and managed to get on board a British warship in Majorca to question the crew. He tried a similar stunt at the naval dockyard in Gibraltar.

Klop, playing the sympathetic fellow journalist, was able to chat to Ludwig's colleagues about their plight and to feed back to MI5 the consternation that his arrest had caused in the German embassy and in Berlin. Klop went through Ludwig's papers and diaries and concluded that he was an agent of the Gestapo who intended to set up a secret political intelligence unit to operate in peace and wartime. His notebooks revealed that among the tasks Ludwig had been set was to find out what Klop had been up to since he left the German embassy. Unfortunately, the spy charge would not stick because it turned out that the blueprint was the property of a foreign inventor who had already offered it to the British government and been rejected. Sir Robert Vansittart reported Klop's findings to the Prime Minister who authorised the Home Office to expel Ludwig along with seven German journalists. Ludwig was convinced he had been betrayed – how else did customs know to search him? – and was also incensed that Putlitz had treated him in such heavy-handed fashion. Putlitz was summoned back to Berlin to explain himself, particularly his very public remarks that Ludwig had behaved like 'a complete fool'. Luckily for him, his outspokenness diverted attention from the possibility that he was the mole who had given away Ludwig's mission in the first place.[113]

Wolfgang Gans Edler Herr zu Putlitz was a member of a Junker family – Prussian landed gentry – born in 1899 at Laaske in the Brandenburg province. His ancestors had been rulers in the Middle Ages until they were supplanted by the Hohenzollerns who eventually ruled the German empire until 1918. The Gans in the middle of his name means goose – the family estate was famous for them. After service in a Prussian cavalry regiment on the Eastern Front and Finland in the First World War, he had forsaken the family estates at Putlitz, midway between Berlin and Hamburg, for a university education and a career in the diplomatic service. Even in those days he had a reputation for left-wing sympathies and had supported the Communist-inspired revolution of 1918–19 which led to the replacement of the imperial government with the Weimar republic. He was nicknamed *das rote puttchen* – the little red chicken – in a derisive reference to the traditional family association with geese. He had a letter of introduction to Klop and got to know him and Albrecht Bernstorff in London in the 1920s, while broadening his education with a spell at Oxford University. At Oxford he was befriended by Claud Cockburn and their paths later crossed in Washington, Berlin and back in London where Cockburn's scurrilous newsletter *The Week* acquired an influence way beyond its meagre circulation and despite its editor's unwavering commitment to Communism.[114]

In the late 1920s, when Cockburn worked for *The Times* in Berlin, Putlitz had been his best source in the German Foreign Office and they met again a couple of years later when both were posted to Washington. Cockburn recalled him as a big man, with gleaming grey eyes and a face like a hooded eagle. He occasionally thought wistfully that he might have been Germany's ruler had his ancestors anticipated, as the Hohenzollerns had, how useful gunpowder could be in wartime. He was prone to moods of profound Prussian doom and occasionally envisaged himself leading his country away from the abyss towards which Hitler was leading them. In anticipation, he practised carrying large amounts of gold around in a body belt and concealed elsewhere about his person. It did not take Cockburn long to realise that Putlitz had no interest in women and preferred the company of young men whom he met in bars or in servants' quarters. He scandalised the American diplomatic circuit by having an affair with the French ambassador's valet.[115]

Putlitz was well connected. He was already friends with Franz von Papen, son of the former German Chancellor, and when he returned to work in London in 1934 he was greeted by the ambassador, Konstantin von Neurath, an old family friend who became Hitler's Foreign Minister until 1938. He was in touch with 'Putzi' Hanfstaengl, who at that time was the Führer's confidant.[116] Claud Cockburn did him no favours though by reporting in *The Week* an incident in which Putlitz had posed as an American journalist for an interview with Joseph Goebbels. It had backfired, convincing no one and making Hitler's Propaganda Minister look rather foolish.[117]

Klop initiated him into the mysteries of Fleet Street and introduced him to Sir Robert Vansittart. When Putlitz came under pressure to join the Nazi party, Klop persuaded him to comply so that he could fight the regime from the inside. He was promised a safe haven in Britain if he was caught. He was remarkably productive; it was Putlitz who urged MI5 not to accept the appointment of Otto Bene as Consul General because of his thuggish Nazi attitudes. He briefed them on social connections between the German ambassador Leopold von Hoesch and King Edward VIII's mistress Wallis Simpson. When Hoesch died, to be replaced by Joachim von Ribbentrop, Putlitz explained that he had ordered the German press to avoid mentioning the King's affair because he thought he would retain the throne and be sympathetic to Germany. The abdication came as a shock to the inexperienced diplomat – nicknamed Herr Brickendrop by the British press – and took some explaining to Hitler. At that time some German military leaders were trying to persuade Hitler to attack Russia, rather than Western Europe, confident that Britain would not come to the Soviets' aid. As Ribbentrop's attitude changed to one of hatred for the British, Putlitz kept Vansittart fully briefed. He tipped off immigration authorities about intensifying attempts by German agents to infiltrate Britain; throughout the first half of 1938 he warned of the increasing bellicosity of Hitler; and he predicted the invasion of Czechoslovakia. His message, repeatedly passed on by Vansittart, was that Britain was letting all its trump cards fall from its hand.[118]

Putlitz cannot have been an easy agent to run. He was actively homosexual and found his way into an Establishment network that brought him into dangerous company, in particular Guy Burgess, whom he claimed to have first met at Cambridge in 1932.

Jackie Hewit, who was successively the lover of Burgess then Anthony Blunt, two of the Cambridge spy ring, has described how he first met them. He was a nineteen-year-old working-class boy from the north east, who had run away to London and was appearing in the chorus line of the revue *No, No Nanette* at the London Hippodrome. He was picked up by a Hungarian in the Bunch of Grapes pub in Westminster and found himself at a party in a flat inside the War Office, the home of the resident clerk, Tom Wylie. The guests were about twenty gay men, all with upper-class accents, behaving as if they were appearing in a scene from a Noël Coward play. Burgess and Blunt were among them and it was Burgess who took the young man home to his flat in Chester Square, Belgravia, that night.[119] This was the milieu in which Putlitz mixed and he was a frequent visitor to the Chester Square apartment. Hewitt was persuaded by Burgess to sleep with Putlitz, describing it as 'comfort for the troops', and was under the impression that he was acting as a kind of Mata Hari, seducing the German diplomat for the benefit of Theodor Maly, Burgess and Blunt's Russian intelligence handler.[120] This was not necessarily so. As MI5 would discover many years later, Putlitz was probably working for the Russians even before he signed up for Vansittart's private intelligence network.

Nevertheless, Peter Wright, the assistant director of MI5 who investigated the Cambridge spy ring in the 1960s and 1970s, regarded the information Klop extracted from Putlitz as priceless – 'possibly the most important human-source intelligence Britain received in the pre-war period'.[121]

General Leo Geyr von Schweppenburg left his position as military attaché in mid-October 1937 to take over command of the 3rd Panzer Division in Berlin. During his four-year tenure in London he trod a difficult line between loyalty to his country and anxiety to avert the war that he knew was coming. His relations with some of the British military establishment were good, among them the director of military operations and intelligence Major General Sir John Dill, Colonel Bernard Paget, head of the Western European section at the War Office, and Sir Basil Liddell Hart, the anti-appeaser and military strategist. Geyr had formed a firm friendship with Klop, whom he regarded as an exceptional journalist and 'a clever and most amusing person who had many good friends among the English'.[122] The general's father had been Master of the Horse to King Karl of Württemberg whose wife Olga granted Klop's father German citizenship.

One evening in 1938, shortly before Prime Minister Neville Chamberlain flew to Munich to try to reach a deal with Hitler over his demands to redraw the Czech border, Peter Ustinov returned to the Redcliffe Gardens flat from drama school to find Klop in a state of mysterious agitation. There were glasses on the table, a bottle of champagne on ice, an open box of cigars. Guests were clearly expected imminently. Peter was ordered to make himself scarce and given ninepence for a cheap seat at the local cinema. He met the guests on the way out:

> We lived on the fourth floor. As I went down the stairs there was a
> group of old men climbing the stairs laboriously. They were like a
> lot of elephants looking for somewhere to die. I stood flush against
> the wall as they passed.

The meeting had been arranged by Geyr von Schweppenburg who brought with him other members of the German high command who had flown to London incognito. He had apparently phoned from a call box to arrange the meeting and told Klop:

We simply must get the British to stand firm at Munich. It is the
last chance we have to stop Hitler. [123]

It was to no avail. The British suspected a trap to goad them into a
war they were still in no position to fight.

That, at least, was the explanation Klop gave to his son Peter
some years later and the substance is confirmed by unpublished
MI5 files.[124] The exact date of the secret rendezvous is not clear but
it appears to have been in the second half of August. It was not the
only indication that the British government had during August
that some senior figures in the German Army would contemplate
overthrowing Hitler to prevent the forthcoming conflict. Apart
from Klop's rendezvous with the generals in his flat, there were at
least two other secret military visits to Britain.

Geyr von Schweppenburg handed over a 'strictly secret' four-
page directive circulated by Ribbentrop saying that the problem
of Czechoslovakia must be solved by early autumn, by war if
necessary. Hitler was confident Britain and France would not
intervene. Detailed instructions for mobilisation were given and a
date for action was stated as before 20 September.

However, Hitler's army chief of staff, General Franz Halder,
and his commander-in-chief, General Walther von Brauchitsch,
believed that the projected invasion of Czechoslovakia would
provoke a response from Britain, France and Russia that
would lead to a world war that Germany could not win. They began
drawing up plans for the army to arrest the Führer if he tried to
declare war on France and Britain. In August 1938, Ewald von
Kleist visited London as an emissary of the dissident army faction
to urge Britain to stand firm against Hitler. He saw Vansittart
and told him Hitler was determined on war and that although
the generals were opposed to it they could not prevent it without
outside help. He wanted a guarantee that France and Britain
would intervene if Hitler ordered an attack on Czechoslovakia:
that would be sufficient for the generals to act. Vansittart informed

the Prime Minister and the Foreign Secretary. Chamberlain's vacillating reaction was to say: 'I don't feel sure that we ought not to do something.' Kleist then saw Churchill, who was more positive, saying that he felt certain France and Britain would respond to an armed attack by Germany on her neighbour but that once committed there would be terrible warfare that might take years to resolve. Within a fortnight the generals tried again. Colonel Hans Böhm-Tettelbach, acting on behalf of Halder and General Hans Oster, deputy head of the Abwehr, visited his old friend Julian Piggott who had been British Commissioner in Cologne after the First World War.[125] Piggott was an occasional lunch guest of the director of MI5, Sir Vernon Kell, who sent a major from the Intelligence service, probably Dick White, to hear what Böhm-Tettelbach had to say and passed it on to Vansittart.[126] But the Prime Minister still doubted the resolve of the German officers to stage what would effectively be a military coup. Chamberlain also had to be careful not to be trapped into conspiring to overthrow the legitimate government of a country with which Britain still officially had good diplomatic relations. And, if the putsch failed, he would face leading a woefully unprepared country into war against an enemy whose military might and ambition was becoming ever more apparent.

The result was the opposite of what the German generals had hoped. On 15 September 1938, Neville Chamberlain boarded an aeroplane for the first time in his life and flew to Munich to try to reach some kind of compromise with Hitler over his demands for Czechoslovakia to cede the Sudetenland. On that very day, Geyr von Schweppenburg contacted Klop again and warned him that Hitler intended to bring about the dissolution of the Czech state by all or any means and that by 25 September mobilisation would have reached a stage whereby Hitler only needed to give the word and the invasion would start.[127] In Munich, on 29 September, Britain, France and Germany agreed, without consulting the Czechs, that the Sudetenland should be ceded to Germany.

That postponed Hitler's invasion plan, since he got what he initially demanded without the need for it. The consequence, as explained later by those dissident generals who survived the war, was to deprive them of their excuse for overthrowing him. There would be other occasions, before war was finally provoked a year later, when a putsch would have been justified but the moment had passed and the impetus was dissipated.

On 7 November 1938, MI5's senior staff handed to the director, Sir Vernon Kell, a dossier running to around forty pages setting out the array of warnings they had received from four highly placed German moles about Hitler's intentions. The bulk of it was Klop's work, particularly from his contacts with Putlitz and Geyr von Schweppenburg. Kell took it to Vansittart and to his replacement as permanent undersecretary at the Foreign Office, Sir Alec Cadogan. He in turn showed it to the Foreign Secretary, Lord Halifax, upon whom it is said to have made a considerable impression and he showed it to the Prime Minister. In diplomatic language it made clear that MI5 did not understand the government's emollient attitude to Hitler when so much of the evidence pointed to his aggressive attentions. Nothing that had happened in Czechoslovakia should have come as a surprise, they said. It was beyond doubt that there were forces in the German government, represented by Ribbentrop and Goebbels, that had not hesitated to risk war with Britain over Czechoslovakia. Hitler may have taken notice of the more cautious advice of his chiefs of staff on this occasion but, the report went on:

> these aggressive elements are, and will continue to be, a very dangerous factor in the general situation. There is however reason to suppose that since the crisis Hitler, convinced of the weakness of England, is likely to adopt a different attitude in future.

They highlighted reports coming out of Germany that the government intended to put up to half a million people in concentration camps and authorise mass executions of political prisoners at Dachau.

Without naming him, the authors described Putlitz, making clear that he was working in what he believed was the best interests of his own country and accepted no payment for his information, which they described as scrupulously accurate. They made special mention of the dismay and exasperation Putlitz felt at the hopeless failure of the British government to recognise Hitler's Machiavellian tendencies. He had told Klop that 'the English think they are wise and strong. They are mistaken. They are stupid and weak.'

The report revealed that Geyr von Schweppenburg had also warned the government during the Munich crisis that if war had been declared the Luftwaffe's first act would have been to concentrate all its resources on a bombing raid on London. The authors concluded:

> It need hardly be emphasised that in giving us this information Herr von S has been risking his life. On the 28 December so strong was his desire to do everything possible to bring about the defeat of the Nazi regime – in the event of war – that he was attempting, in spite of the immense difficulties in the way of rapid and safe communication, to send through information which he hoped would have given the British Air Force a few hours more warning than they would have otherwise received.[128]

Putlitz left London in May 1938 to take up the position of First Secretary in the German embassy at The Hague. MI5 still had excellent sources within the German embassy, presumably still using Klop as an intermediary. They were better informed about what was going on inside the German embassy at 9 Carlton House Terrace than they were about 10 Downing Street, with the result that they found themselves spying on their own Prime Minister.

On 23 November 1938 they trailed the embassy press officer Fritz Hesse, knowing that he had arranged a clandestine meeting, supposedly with someone from No. 10. They observed a two-hour discussion with a man the watchers did not immediately recognise but who was soon identified as George Steward, the Prime Minister's press secretary.

Within days MI5 was able to lay a copy of Hesse's account of the meeting on the desk of Alec Cadogan. They even updated it with a revised version which had been sent to Ribbentrop after amendments by the ambassador Herbert von Dirksen. It showed that Steward had proposed an extraordinary agreement to limit the horrors of war, including a ban on poison gas and limitations on bombing civilians or a nation's cultural treasures. Steward said it would paint Hitler in a more sympathetic light with the British public. Hesse reported:

> This surprising suggestion is another sign of how great the wish for an understanding with us is here in England and is also evidence for the point of view that Great Britain is ready, during the next year, to accept practically everything from us and to fulfil our every wish.

The meeting took place only weeks after Chamberlain had returned from meeting Hitler in Munich, waving aloft the piece of paper representing 'peace for our time'. But the deal, which followed Hitler's occupation of part of Czechoslovakia, was already falling apart. Early in November, the Kristallnacht, during which Nazis ransacked synagogues and Jewish homes across Germany, had outraged British opinion.

Cadogan, generally perceived as far more appeasement-minded than Vansittart, agonised over what he should do. His private thoughts, only released in the National Archives in 2011, were that if he revealed to his own Foreign Secretary, Lord Halifax, that Chamberlain had gone behind his back to do secret deals with Hitler, Halifax might resign. If Halifax confronted Chamberlain, the PM would probably think his policy of appeasement had been torpedoed by the wicked anti-German Foreign Office ... he would probably take steps to clip the wings of the FO as much as possible and at the same time carry on with his clandestine negotiations. He would either have to have a General Election or carry on with some dummy in the FO. He might well take over the entire Secret Intelligence Service and put it under his personal control.[129]

Britain would look weak and divided. Hitler might be tempted to stage an immediate military showdown before Britain had a chance to rearm and prepare to fight. On the other hand, Cadogan did not want to be accused later of suppressing vital intelligence. He described the appeasement faction as 'Tiger-riders' who were playing an appallingly dangerous game. He decided he must tell Halifax, who in turn confronted Chamberlain. The Prime Minister professed he was 'aghast' at the revelation and promised to put a stop to it, although the idea that Steward might have acted without Chamberlain's authority seems preposterous. In reality, all that happened was that Steward was warned about 'indiscreet talk'.

Dick White had befriended Hesse when he spent several months of 1936 in Germany, but Hesse was a loyal servant of Ribbentrop and continued to work for him throughout the Second World War. In 1946 he was flown to Britain to be interrogated by his predecessor, Klop, who revealed that MI5 had kept a record of his conversation with Steward. Hesse told him that he had been in secret contact with Steward from 1937 onwards and with Chamberlain's special adviser Horace Wilson after Munich. He explained:

My relations with the Foreign Office were quite normal and they helped me in any way I asked them. The secret talks I had here were at the instigation of No. 10 and I was their instrument ... My defence is that I was used from the other side. I was a journalist, half and half in disfavour with the Germans. Then there comes the secretary to the Prime Minister and asks me to help.[130]

The incident did not dissuade Chamberlain from pursuing his appeasement policy. Neither did the warning, three weeks later, from Sir Hugh Sinclair, director of MI6, that Hitler was bent on world domination and that:

> Among his characteristics are fanaticism, mysticism, ruthlessness, cunning, vanity, moods of exaltation and depression, fits of bitter and self-righteous resentment; and what can only be termed a streak of madness; but with it all there is a great tenacity of purpose, which has often been combined with extraordinary clarity of vision.[131]

From that point onwards warnings came thick and fast about Hitler's aggressive intentions, not only in the East towards Czechoslovakia and Poland but in the West where war with Britain and France was also countenanced. Between December 1938 and April 1939 there were twenty secret reports, among them the dire threat that Hitler's first aggressive act would be to bomb London, possibly as early as March 1939. Not all the reports were accurate and some may well have been planted by Admiral Canaris of the Abwehr, either to provoke Britain into a robust response or to test Chamberlain's resolve. MI6 predicted that Hitler would find a quarrel to justify an invasion of Holland, initially wrong but ultimately true, and accurately forecast the annexation of the remainder of Czechoslovakia.[132] And while the Prime Minister clung to the hope of peace he was not blind to the fact that Britain was unprepared for conflict if it came. Production of aircraft, particularly fighters, was stepped up, and a Military Training Act requiring all men aged twenty and twenty-one to spend six months under arms was passed in April 1939. An agreement was entered into with the French to defend Holland if Hitler attacked and talks began in Moscow to persuade Stalin to side with the Western Allies, effectively encircling Germany. Stalin, fearing that the Allies hoped to turn Hitler eastwards for an attack on Russia, chose instead to sign a peace treaty with the German dictator.

From the perspective of the German Army officers still trying to avert a war with Britain and France, none of these measures was likely to convince Hitler to back off. As late as July 1939 they despatched Lt Col. Gerhardt Count von Schwerin, the head of the British section of the German war ministry intelligence department, to warn of Hitler's determination to attack Poland. Schwerin was a guest of the director of naval intelligence, Admiral John Godfrey, at a dinner party given by retired Admiral Sir Aubrey Smith at his home in Gloucester Place, Marylebone. Also present were James Stuart MP, parliamentary whip, representing the Prime Minister, and General Sir James Marshall-Cornwall, a former MI6 man who was now director general of air and coastal defence. He recalled that 'a good deal of good champagne was consumed'.

Schwerin recommended that Churchill should replace Chamberlain as PM, a battle squadron should sail to the Baltic to make a show near Danzig and RAF bombers should be stationed in France. His hosts severely deflated these ambitions. James Stuart explained that replacing the PM would bring down the government; Godfrey said the Admiralty would never allow its capital ships to be at risk in the Baltic where they could be mined or torpedoed; and Marshall-Cornwall pointed out that French airfields had already been prepared to meet RAF bombers if needed. Schwerin's proposals were duly passed to the Prime Minister who balked at anything so provocative.[133] One Foreign Office official dismissed Schwerin's arguments as 'gross treasonable disloyalty', while another pointed out that the German Army seemed to expect Britain to save them from the Nazi regime.[134]

CHAPTER 9: WAR

With war looking ever more likely, Klop made frequent visits to Holland to hear how Wolfgang zu Putlitz gauged the situation. He had used his journalistic credentials to obtain a freelance position as European correspondent of an Indian newspaper and established an office in The Hague for the purpose. Although Klop was still technically working for MI5, his duties in Holland brought him under the aegis of MI6.

Putlitz told Klop that Holland was now the frontline for Abwehr intelligence operations against Britain. MI5 submitted a report to the Foreign Secretary, Lord Halifax, who in turn relayed the information to the Prime Minister. It included a character assessment of Hitler, based on information from Putlitz and others who were in touch with his closest entourage, saying that he was now pursuing in high politics tactics which he had previously confined to smaller matters:

> He caused his opponents to be confused with a feint here and a serious blow there, and simultaneous offers of peace, and when having given them no rest, he had got them where he wanted them, he made an energetic attack, falling on them like lightning.

The report added a comment from Hitler's Propaganda Minister, Joseph Goebbels, to the effect that the only person who made an impression on Hitler was one who could firmly say 'no' or answer threats with counter threats. Any sign of weakness only egged him on and it was a mystery that other countries did not see this. MI5 concluded that

> it must be anticipated that Hitler would make increasingly drastic demands. This was extremely probable if, as seemed beyond doubt, he was convinced that Great Britain was decadent and lacked the will and power to defend the British Empire.[135]

No action was taken on the Security Service's request for additional manpower to match the German effort. The lack of preparedness would cost them dear when war was finally declared on 3 September 1939. Klop was again at the heart of events, in what came to be regarded as MI6's worst humiliation of the war.

Klop's intelligence from Putlitz in the last days of peace was confusing and, with hindsight, wishful thinking. In the first week of August 1939 Klop reported that the German military were on standby but not yet on full alert. On 30 August he declared that 'the Germans have got the jitters' and Putlitz was under the impression that: 'We have got Hitler on the run and that nothing should be done to provide him with a golden bridge to make his getaway.'

He reiterated this message the following day and Guy Liddell noted that he seemed very confident that disintegration had set in and even suggested that it was doubtful whether the German Army would march if the order were given. Liddell found it difficult to judge whether his two agents' views were based on hard evidence or gossip in diplomatic circles. He feared it may be another bluff but did not rule out the possibility of serious internal dissension between the German Army and its political masters. The information was passed to Vansittart, who said it confirmed what he was hearing from other sources and that he still hoped there might be no war; or that if there were it would not last very long.[136]

Klop was not the only agent feeding back intelligence that elements within the German Army were anxious to avoid a conflict.

This coincided exactly with what Chamberlain continued to hope and strive for, and appears to have persuaded those involved, Klop included, to ignore a dire warning sign.

Putlitz was doing his very best to pass on every item of useful information. He compiled a list for Klop of Dutch businessmen who were collaborating with the Germans to transport vital imports of oil, coal and raw materials from their ports before a British naval blockade could come into effect. He was horrified when, three days later, he was summoned into his ambassador's office and confronted with the list, which had apparently come into the hands of the Gestapo direct from the office of MI6's main officer in The Hague, Captain Richard Stevens. He was asked to conduct an investigation into how such a leak had occurred. Putlitz knew immediately that the game was up. It could only be a matter of time before the ambassador realised he was the mole. He had to get out … fast.

Putlitz had a live-in lover – his manservant Willi Schneider, a former waiter who had fallen foul of the Gestapo and spent some time in a concentration camp. If Putlitz was going to escape, Willi had to come too. He had often acted as a go-between with Klop and it now fell to Willi to arrange the getaway. Within twenty-four hours he and Klop had lined up the Dutch air ace Dirk Parmentier, who could circumvent wartime emergency flight restrictions. The two fugitives carried only one small suitcase each. German propaganda later claimed that Putlitz had filled his with stolen Nazi gold. He denied it.[137]

On 15 September, at Shoreham airport near Brighton, they were met by Dick White who took them to his brother's flat, close to the British Museum in Bloomsbury, central London, where they were to live. Within days Putlitz found himself under arrest by the British police. He had gone, quite innocently, to a local cinema where he was recognised by a Belgian diplomat who happened to be in the audience and denounced him as a probable Nazi spy. This kind of hysteria was, understandably, rampant on both sides in the phoney war period and may partially account for the way warning signs were disregarded.

Reaction in Germany was equally bizarre. The news of Putlitz's defection was deliberately concealed from Adolf Hitler. There were various vested interests at work. The German ambassador at The Hague, Count Julius von Zech-Burkersroda, no Nazi sympathiser, had to account for the missing money that Putlitz had taken with him, and his failure to spot a mole at the heart of his embassy. The Gestapo could equally be found to be at fault for the security blunder. Joseph Goebbels seized the opportunity to put round a story that Putlitz and Willi Schneider had been murdered and thrown into a canal by 'Jewish robbers' who made off with the money. But there were plenty of people who knew this to be a fiction and word penetrated through to Putlitz's old school friend Count Michael Soltikow, who was working for Admiral Canaris in the Abwehr. He was told that the missing pair were 'living in clover' in London. Canaris, calculating that this was an opportunity for one-upmanship over the Gestapo, despatched Soltikow to the Netherlands to investigate.

He quickly established that on the day they were supposed to have been murdered the pair had sold a private car and a motorcycle and that payment had been transferred to London. Putlitz had signed a receipt for the money. Dutch police had investigated the disappearance and were mightily put out by the slurs broadcast by Goebbels. They had obtained from Scotland Yard a photograph of Putlitz in a London street, which was date stamped and showed in the background young women in military uniform, demonstrating that it could only have been taken after war was declared. They also had a copy of a letter, signed and dated, that Putlitz had written to various former diplomatic colleagues in London explaining his reasons for defection and revealing correspondence between Hitler and Ribbentrop exposing Hitler's double-dealing over the naval treaty he signed with Britain in 1935. The police were able to tell Soltikow that the spy and his lover were disguised in women's clothing when they fled the country.

It was weeks after the disappearance that Soltikow found himself summoned one evening, with Canaris, to face the Führer at the Reich Chancellery in Berlin to explain his findings. On the way Canaris warned him not to mention the document revealing the double-dealing over the naval treaty. It might be interpreted as painting Hitler as 'War Criminal Number One'.

Hitler demanded to know every detail. How long had the treachery gone on and what were Putlitz's motives? Soltikow showed him the photographs and traced Putlitz's history back to his days at Oxford University. He told Hitler that Putlitz had been the victim of British blackmail over his homosexual relationship with Willi. He had been given the choice of betraying his country's secrets or being arrested and deported back to Germany where he would certainly find himself in a concentration camp, brutally treated and probably hounded to death. When he worked in the London embassy he had access to the safe where secret documents were kept and would copy them with a miniature camera.

Hitler seems to have been impressed and wanted to promote Soltikow to be a lieutenant in the SS. Canaris persuaded him that his agent could be put to better use in the Abwehr.[138]

Wolfgang zu Putlitz, meanwhile, found himself rather surplus to requirements. He no longer enjoyed access to German diplomatic secrets and his potential value to the British war effort was either as an analyst or a propagandist. Vansittart's principal agent, Group Captain Malcolm Christie, recommended him for a role on an Anglo-German committee pursuing long-term propaganda aims, not just to refute 'Nazi lies' but to prepare the way for eventual peace. Putlitz, according to Christie, was eminently suitable because of his friendships with exiled anti-Nazi German politicians and for his flexible mind and constructive, creative mentality. Vansittart reported this to the Foreign Office, having first consulted MI5, and proposed taking Putlitz and Christie to talk it over with the

Ministry of Information.[139] It came to nothing and Putlitz was reduced to working as a production assistant to the film director Alexander Korda at Denham Studios.

After the Nazi invasion of France, anti-German feeling became so intense that he and Willi Schneider decided to move to the United States. They were initially refused a visa and spent an unhappy time under effective house arrest at a Canadian Army camp on the Caribbean island of Jamaica. When he was finally granted a US visa he teamed up with a number of dissident Germans, among them his old friend Dr Carl Spiecker, who, as will shortly become clear, had not endeared himself to the British. The group wrote copious briefing notes for the Americans on German resistance to Hitler, nominating their exiled friends as a replacement government if the Führer could be deposed. Putlitz, in particular, does seem to have been instrumental in briefing Allen Dulles, who would play a key role as head of US intelligence in Switzerland. Not all of their intelligence was of the highest calibre, as the following excerpt from Putlitz demonstrates:

> Dr Wolfgang Klaiber is in his early forties, a rather good looking blond fellow, trying to be immaculately well-dressed without always succeeding (he likes spats and similar gadgets) to look really smart. By natural inclination he cannot be much of a Nazi.[140]

Their hosts soon tired of this flummery and Putlitz eventually returned to Britain, without Willi Schneider, in 1944, to a new role as a propagandist, and a controversial future in peacetime Germany.

It must have been obvious from the circumstances in which Putlitz's role as a British agent was jeopardised that there was a serious leak in the British Intelligence services' Dutch network. The culprit was not identified until after the war when a German intelligence officer under interrogation, Traugott Protze, named the mole as a Dutchman, Folkert Arie van Koutrik, whom the British had believed was working for them. He had fled to

London shortly after the outbreak of war and continued to work for MI6.[141]

It might be expected that the reaction to the exposure of Putlitz would be caution. Yet the first thing MI5 did was to send an officer using the cover name Susan Barton to join Klop in The Hague, where she had worked previously. Mrs Barton, real name Gisela Ashley, was German by birth and had a brother who was a U-boat captain. She had married a British man and although they had divorced by the time war began she retained British citizenship and loyalty. She later became one of the leading members of the hugely successful Double-Cross operation, running agents supplying the Germans with bogus intelligence.[142] It was hoped that she might entice the German naval attaché, Käpitan Kurt Besthorn, into believing that she could provide him with intelligence from the British military censorship department, where she purported to work, and then use him to obtain naval intelligence from Germany. She shared a flat with Besthorn's secretary Lili, who was an old friend from Germany. This, Guy Liddell thought, would partially compensate for the loss of Putlitz.[143]

But the greatest risks were taken by Richard Stevens and Sigismund Payne Best of MI6. In theory, the two should not even have been working together. For the previous twenty years, MI6's rather sparse and underfunded network of agents had been based on the British embassy passport control officers whose official role was to scrutinise applications for visas. It was a convenient cover, in peacetime, for defensive intelligence to keep a check on foreign agents intent on coming to spy on Britain but less effective in gathering intelligence about foreign governments. And, inevitably, the cover story was fairly transparent. The head of MI6, Admiral Sir Hugh 'Quex' Sinclair, commonly known as 'C', had given his deputy Claude Dansey the job of setting up a parallel, undercover team, known as the Z organisation. Dansey was something of a maverick but he had a background in business and set about recruiting fellow businessmen.

Major Richard Stevens was the passport control officer in The Hague. He had only been appointed in 1939, having previously served as an army intelligence officer in India. He was multilingual (languages included German) but inexperienced. He was also, according to one contemporary, 'a man of almost overbearing confidence'.[144] As part of his induction he was introduced to Klop and briefed on the relationship with Putlitz. It is clear that MI5 feared that Stevens's cover had been blown almost as soon as he was appointed and that even in London he would be under German surveillance. John Curry, the MI5 official who took him to Klop's London flat, recalled that as they drove off a man jumped into a taxi on the rank immediately behind them and followed. Curry instructed their driver to make a series of quick turns in the side streets and lost their pursuer.[145]

By contrast, Sigismund Payne Best was an intelligence veteran. He had worked for the first director of MI6, Mansfield Cumming, during the First World War, directing military espionage from Holland. He had married the daughter of a Dutch general and lived in Holland for twenty years, setting up an import-export consultancy for British businessmen wanting to trade with Holland and Germany. He spoke both languages fluently and had extensive contacts, among them the German-born Prince Henry of Mecklenburg-Schwerin, consort of Queen Wilhelmina of the Netherlands. Best and his Dutch business partner, Major Pieter van der Willik, were recruited by Claude Dansey for the Z network. Best was not exactly inconspicuous, every inch the English gent with a private income, affecting both a monocle and spats, but he kept himself apart from the British embassy. With the outbreak of war, a reluctant Best was persuaded to subordinate himself to Stevens on the grounds that they would need to coordinate their efforts and use the embassy's secure means of communication, either through wireless or diplomatic bags which were immune from inspection by customs or other authorities.

The chain of command at the top of MI6 was altered, too. Dansey was to operate from Paris or Switzerland so Best would be reporting direct to 'C' – except Admiral Sinclair was seriously ill with cancer, and died on 4 November 1939, so his deputy, Stewart Menzies, handled the day-to-day business and was effectively in charge.

The Prime Minister was clinging to the hope that war might still be averted by a change in the Nazi regime. Two days before war was declared he told the House of Commons:

> We have no quarrel with the German people, except that they allow themselves to be governed by a Nazi Government. As long as that Government exists and pursues the methods it has so persistently followed during the last two years, there will be no peace in Europe.[146]

He reiterated that position in the Commons on 12 October, saying that the German government was the sole obstacle to peace, which he was sure the German people desired, and playing on what he believed was serious dissent within the German high command. He had good grounds for believing it to exist.

In 1951, Sigismund Payne Best published a book giving his account of what happened next but it was heavily circumscribed by the Official Secrets Act. He wrote a much more explicit private version in 1947 to an old friend, Lt Col. Reginald Drake, who had joined MI5 in 1912 and was helping Best to claim a proper pension and compensation for what became known as the Venlo Incident.[147]

Best says that he was contacted from London on 30 August 1939 by Dansey's right-hand man, Lt Cdr Kenneth Cohen, and instructed to make urgent contact with one of Dansey's agents, Franz Fischer. Best maintains that he knew of Fischer and did not trust him. Nevertheless, knowing that it risked blowing his cover, he invited him to his office and Fischer explained that he was working with a former press secretary from the German Chancellor's office, Dr Carl Spiecker, who was in contact with the anti-Nazi faction of the army and had organised anti-Nazi radio broadcasts from a pirate radio ship in the North Sea. Dansey vouched for Spiecker's reliability but Best reported to London that he did not believe Fischer's story.

A senior official came over from London to impress on Best and Stevens the importance and urgency of the contact and they pressed ahead, meeting yet another intermediary, Johannes Traviglio, a Luftwaffe major from the Abwehr, in the Wilhelmina Hotel at Venlo on the Dutch-German border. Best was led to believe that at least three generals were involved in the anti-Nazi faction: Werner von Fritsch who had been driven out of his position as commander-in-chief by Heinrich Himmler on trumped up charges of homosexuality; Gerd von Rundstedt, who had supported Fritsch against Himmler; and Gustav von Wietersheim, the Panzer Division commander who had had a face-to-face clash with Hitler over his plans for the invasion of Czechoslovakia. Fischer indicated that one of the three was prepared to meet Best and Stevens personally.

It seems doubtful whether there was ever any truth in Fischer and Traviglio's claim to speak on behalf of those involved. Both men were double agents working for the German SD – the *Sicherheitsdienst* or SS security service. Certainly there were factions within the army that contemplated the removal of Hitler, and there were fears among the generals, shared by Himmler and others in the Nazi leadership, that a war in the West simply left Germany open to invasion by Russia in the east, despite Hitler's non-aggression pact with Stalin. The Venlo operation seems therefore to have been an attempt either to find out to what extent Britain was conspiring with dissident factions in Germany, or to see if there was still a last chance of a peace settlement even though war had been declared.

The latter view is supported by events elsewhere. Prince Max von Hohenlohe had the ear of many in the Nazi regime and plentiful contacts with the Allies. He had sent a note to Goering and Hitler, arguing that only Bolshevism would benefit from war between

Britain and Germany. Although Hitler dismissed his 'defeatist scribblings', Goering and the Gestapo showed some interest. Accordingly, he took his proposals to the Royal Hotel in Lausanne in Switzerland in October 1939 and put them to Sir Robert Vansittart's agent, Group Captain Malcolm Christie.[148] Christie, using a highly placed source in the German Air Ministry, had been able to warn Vansittart on 15 September of German military plans to invade Holland and sweep down through Belgium into France.

Separately, Theodor Kordt, who had been German chargé d'affaires in London prior to the declaration of war, was visited in Berne in October 1939 by Dr Philip Conwell-Evans, acting as Vansittart's intermediary. He reiterated Chamberlain's assertion that their quarrel was with the regime, not the German people, and that a just peace might still be negotiated. This was supposed to be the incentive the army dissidents would require to carry out their coup. And in Rome Dr Joseph Müller, a Munich lawyer sent by the deputy head of the Abwehr, Major General Hans Oster, was making similar overtures via the Pope to the British ambassador to the Vatican. Oster had already leaked to the Allies Hitler's projected date for an invasion of Holland and Belgium, on 12 November, adding urgency to the quest for a solution.[149]

What occurred at Venlo has to be viewed in this context. It was an intelligence operation but it was sanctioned by the Prime Minister and the Cabinet in pursuit of a compromise peace.

In any event, Fischer kept the talks going and demanded that, as evidence of British sincerity, a coded message should be broadcast by the BBC which the conspirators in Germany could recognise as a sign of encouragement. Klop was called upon to make the arrangements, planting a story in a Swiss newspaper which could then be taken up by the BBC. On 11 October Guy Liddell noted in his diary that Klop had just got back from Holland:

It seems that SIS [MI6] are in touch with certain disaffected elements in the Reichswehr [German armed forces], who are proposing to organise a coup d'état within the next few days. Their programme is to arrest all the principal leaders of the Party on the grounds that they have sold their country, and laid up large balances for themselves abroad. Hitler is to be the only exception and will be allowed to remain as a puppet head. The army could not attack him on account of their oath of allegiance, but they would see to it that he was rendered entirely innocuous.

Two envoys are said to have come to Holland on this mission and were anxious to see a British Cabinet Minister to get some assurance that if they took over and proposed the restoration of Poland and Czechoslovakia, Germany would be given an honourable settlement. They were told that it was impossible for a British Cabinet Minister to be involved in a matter of this sort but that if a notice which they had prepared found its way into the Basler Nachrichten before Thursday they could go ahead. The message in the paper is that it is reported that there is a movement by certain elements in the German Army to arrest all Party leaders on the grounds that they have betrayed the State etc.

U35 in order to get this message through to the BN approached a contact of his in the Swiss legation. This was necessary in order to get the use of the Press telephone line. The Swiss legation must have had some idea of what is intended but they put U35 in touch with the representative here of the BN, which is generally speaking anti-Nazi in tone. This representative thought the story was a good one and worth publication, and a message was telephoned through last night. When it appears it will be broadcast two or three times as a news item by the BBC and this is supposed to give the signal for a general revolt.[150]

Liddell was not convinced by the German story, any more than Best was, although the form of the proposed coup described fairly accurately what the real dissidents had in mind. The stumbling block of the officers' oath of allegiance did prey on their minds. Stevens, however, does seem to have been taken in. He and Klop had obviously been working on it together for some time. Klop had also spent some time in Switzerland on an unspecified mission. On a brief visit to London in the middle of the operation, Klop invited Putlitz round to his flat and Stevens regaled him with stories of how they had celebrated Putlitz's escape from the Gestapo with champagne and oysters at the Restaurant Royale in The Hague. He then revealed that he was in radio contact with army dissidents in Germany and predicted confidently that Hitler was 'nearly finished'. The war would be over before it began. Putlitz cautioned him against Gestapo double-dealing but Stevens assured him everything was under control. His confidence was misplaced.[151]

According to Best, the BBC message appeared to have the desired effect and he was told by Fischer that General von Wietersheim was prepared to meet him to discuss terms. At this point Stevens and Best decided they had better tell the Dutch secret service what was afoot and, to help things run smoothly at the border, they were assigned a Dutch escort officer. He was Lieutenant Dirk Klop, an extraordinary coincidence given Klop Ustinov's involvement. On 20 October, two junior German officers using the names Seydlitz and Grosch crossed the border into Holland and were taken by Fischer to meet Stevens, Best and Lt Klop in a café at Dinxperlo. There were Dutch soldiers in the café and Best decided it would be more discreet to continue the conversation at the home of his cousin in Arnhem. The soldiers in the café had been suspicious and called the police, who raided the house in Arnhem. With some difficulty Lt Klop persuaded them that all was above board.

After some delays a further meeting took place in The Hague on 30 October. By now Fischer had faded from the scene and von Wietersheim did not show up. In his place, with Grosch, came Major Schaemmel and Colonel Martini. These two were, in reality, Walther Schellenberg, head of counter-intelligence in the Gestapo, and his friend, Professor Max de Crinis, a psychologist. The bogus Major Schaemmel impressed the British delegates and in lengthy discussions they drew up proposals that would involve German withdrawal from Czechoslovakia and Poland, plebiscites in Sudetenland and Austria and restoration of Jewish rights. Best was sufficiently encouraged to entertain the German party to dinner at his home and allow them to sleep over. Next morning Stevens presented them with a two-way wireless set to make communication possible without hazardous border crossings.

These developments were reported back to Stewart Menzies, acting head of MI6, who in turn briefed the Foreign Secretary and the Prime Minister. Chamberlain authorised MI6 to pursue the talks 'with energy' and notified the War Cabinet on 1 November. They approved his action although Churchill, in particular, was unenthusiastic.

After radio contact Best and Stevens met 'Major Schaemmel' again on the 7th and 8th of November at the Café Backus, just on the Dutch side of the German border near Venlo. Von Wietersheim still did not materialise, the excuse being that he could not get away because he was obliged to be on hand to attend meetings with Hitler at short notice. On the morning of 8 November, the Queen of the Netherlands and the King of the Belgians, fearing an imminent invasion, had issued a joint appeal for peace. It was promised that von Wietersheim would show up on 9 November.

On that fateful, overcast day Best, Stevens, Lt Klop and their chauffeur Jan Lemmens intended to set out early. They were delayed by a long coded message coming in over the wireless that they had given to Schaemmel, although when deciphered it contained little of consequence. By the time they set off they were aware that an attempt had been made on Hitler's life the night before when a bomb went off in the Bürgerbräukeller in Munich, the traditional gathering place of the Nazi party. As they travelled the 120 miles to the border in Best's distinctive two-door American Lincoln-Zephyr car, they considered the significance of that event, although they knew only the bare details. On the face of it, it lent credence to the idea that there were forces at work in Germany ready to remove Hitler from power by whatever means necessary.

It was getting dark as they drove through the pine woods to the red-brick café with its first-floor veranda and children's playground with swings and see-saws. It was almost opposite the Dutch border post and only 200 yards from the black-and-white painted barrier that marked the German frontier. Best was driving, despite the presence of the chauffeur, and recalled a feeling of impending danger although outwardly there was nothing to fear. A German customs officer was lounging at the roadside; a little girl was playing ball with a black dog. As the Lincoln cruised slowly into the car park Major Schaemmel appeared on the veranda and raised his hat to signal the all clear.[152]

But as Best reversed into a passageway to park, his way out was blocked by a German Adler car. A snatch squad of ten SS men led by Major Alfred Naujocks came running towards them, firing their weapons to scare off any Dutch customs officers who might otherwise consider intervening. Naujocks was already a veteran of Nazi intimidation techniques: he had murdered a Czech dissident famous for broadcasting anti-German propaganda and he had faked an attack on a German radio station which was then blamed on the Poles and used as justification for Germany to invade Poland. In due course Hitler would use the Venlo Incident to justify the invasion of Holland.[153]

The gallant Lt Dirk Klop was the only one of the British party to put up a fight. He leapt from the front passenger seat and opened fire, and was gunned down for his trouble. He died later the same day in hospital in Düsseldorf. The other three members of the party were captured and driven at high speed into Germany where Best and Stevens were interrogated and made scapegoats for the Bürgerbräu Keller bomb, of which they knew nothing. The chauffeur Jan Lemmens was later released but the two MI6 officers spent the war in prison and concentration camps.

Walther Schellenberg would claim after the war that he had embarked on this exercise with the intention of discovering whether Britain might be prepared to reach a peace settlement without denying Germany the territorial gains she had already made. He had the authority of his boss Heinrich Himmler and, initially, the acquiescence of Hitler, who had believed that Britain would not go to war over Poland. But Hitler was quickly losing patience as his projected date approached for invasion via Holland and Belgium into France. By 9 November it was only three days away, although he was later persuaded to postpone it repeatedly until May 1940. And he was understandably enraged by the Munich beer hall bomb on 8 November which he escaped only because he left early. It remains the most likely explanation that this outrage had been engineered by his own people as a propaganda weapon against the West just as they had faked provocative incidents to justify military actions in the East. Schellenberg maintained that he was only told on the morning of 9 November that he was to act as the bait for the SS hit squad.

On the face of it, Klop Ustinov's role in this fiasco was peripheral. But there remain many unanswered questions and there were other figures lurking in the shadows. It is known that Klop was working with Stevens in London in October – hence the meeting with Putlitz – and that he was at some point in Switzerland. And it is apparent from Group Captain Christie's personal papers that his talks with Prince Max von Hohenlohe were not just taking place in parallel but were inextricably interlinked. Moreover, Prince Max at one point had talks with a second Englishman, who may have been Klop. Christie seems to have been in no doubt that Prince Max was genuine, that he acted on behalf of Göring and that he also briefed Hitler from time to time. Christie adopted a fairly transparent disguise for his communications with Max, and his reports back to Vansittart in London, presenting them in terms of competing groups of shareholders and directors of a Mexican oil company. Sir Nevile Bland, ambassador in The Hague, was being kept in the loop.

So on 12 November 1938, three days after the Venlo Incident, Christie told Prince Max that his shareholders were deeply dissatisfied with the way the merger was being handled and added:

The fact is that the Mexican chairman and his supporters have exhibited so often the worst side of their treacherous characters, amounting to sharp practice and misrepresentation of the company's affairs that my company's directors and shareholders will have nothing more to do with them. ... If you want my company's cooperation in price adjustment, an entirely new operating company must be formed to deal with your Mexican interests.[154]

These comments make apparent the disillusion and dismay that must have been felt in London at the loss of two valuable agents and the diplomatic loss of face at falling for a Gestapo sting. They also imply that a peace manoeuvre was still considered viable. A series of scribbled jottings on rough notepaper with frequent crossings out and overwriting capture something of the confusion and panic that gripped both sides. It is not always clear whether Christie was making notes of conversations with Vansittart or Prince Max. But it emerges that the Prince had been in Holland at around the time of the Venlo Incident and that he was trying to set up a face-to-face meeting with Christie or better still Vansittart. A royal personage was lurking in the shadows, ready to take on the role of peacemaker if Göring could be persuaded there was a real prospect that he could emerge with a favourable peace. Several names were mentioned in this context – the British Duke of Kent, the King of Sweden, or the King and Queen of Belgium and the Netherlands respectively. The latter pair had made a public appeal to Hitler to talk. On the German side, Prince Louis Ferdinand, grandson of the kaiser and a sympathiser with the anti-Hitler social democrat factions, was mooted as a potential monarch in a reformed state if Hitler could be deposed.

After the Venlo Incident, Prince Max, using the codename Smiler, called to make excuses and Christie reported back to London, in his Mexican oil company code:

The Rowdy meeting down South was not at the Chairman's incentive or that of his supporters. On the contrary, the entourage of the Vice-Chairman was perhaps not entirely blameless in this hooliganism.

The implication appears to be that Göring played a part in the sabotage of discussions controlled by his rival Himmler while simultaneously conducting his own negotiations via Prince Max and Christie.

Post-war even this episode took on an element of conspiratorial farce as SS officer Klaus Huegel revealed that they were so cock-a-hoop over their success at Venlo that they planned to kidnap Vansittart by luring him to a meeting in Switzerland.[155]

Astonishingly, the Venlo operation did not end with the capture of Best and Stevens. MI6 maintained radio traffic with the wireless set they had given to 'Major Schaemmel' because they were not certain that he did not genuinely represent the dissident generals. It seemed possible that Schaemmel had been as surprised as Best and Stevens by the arrival of the SS hit squad. Since MI6 knew that Hitler had planned to invade Holland on 12 November, and that did not happen, they suspected that the army dissidents had prevented it.

Schellenberg kept the game running by sending a message on the two-way radio on 13 November asking what had happened to the British representatives at Venlo. On 16 November, the acting head of MI6, Stewart Menzies drafted a message to be returned by radio from The Hague to the German dissident faction. In the absence of Richard Stevens, who was by then under interrogation in Germany, it may have been Klop who took responsibility for the radio traffic. The message repeated an earlier British stipulation that for peace talks to progress there would have to be regime change in Germany. Schellenberg replied, asking which British politician would be nominated to conduct the negotiations. This charade continued, with Chamberlain and his Foreign Secretary Lord Halifax still discussing how to handle the conspirators, until Schellenberg brought it to an end with an abusive message on 22 November.

From reports Klop wrote for MI5 it is clear that he was well versed in the minutiae of the Venlo discussions, and the radio traffic between Stevens and his supposed contact in Cologne. Klop had also visited Brussels soon after war was declared for talks with an SD man who was in touch with Group Captain Christie.

Klop's news story, planted in the Swiss newspaper *Basler Nachrichten*, was a bizarre choice of signal and it had a damaging side effect. While the Gestapo were duping British intelligence in Venlo, genuine peace feelers were being made by Hans Oster of the Abwehr via the Vatican. He had sent a Munich lawyer, Josef Müller, a Catholic who had access to Pope Pius XXII, and messages were relayed via the British ambassador to the Holy See, Sir D'Arcy Osborne, to the Foreign Secretary. But Schellenberg's superior officer Reinhard Heydrich, head of the Reich's security service including the Gestapo, had got wind of the discussions and when he saw the newspaper article his investigations intensified, forcing Oster to back off.

Since Klop was responsible for the newspaper article, and the BBC follow-up, he may also have been behind another unexplained element of the fiasco. There are reports that, on the day that Stevens and Best were captured, a pirate German radio station or *Freiheitsender* broadcasted a call to arms to anti-Nazi Germans to rise up and overthrow Hitler. The BBC ran this as a news story and reported a 'manifesto' of this dissident station. Yet the BBC's own monitoring service maintained that it had not picked up the pirate broadcast. As already mentioned, Dansey's contact Carl Spiecker claimed to be able to make such broadcasts from a ship in the North Sea. And there was another highly secret outfit, the Joint Broadcasting Committee, which had been set up to make just the type of propaganda that this illicit broadcast represented. Among its early recruits were Guy Burgess and Klop's close friend Moura Budberg. It later emerged that this team, run either by MI6 or by Vansittart's personal intelligence agency, claimed to be able to deliver recorded messages for broadcast either inside Germany and its occupied territories or from Switzerland.[156]

One interested observer of this debacle was the young Nicholas Elliott, just starting out on a career as a diplomat and MI6 officer.

He was the son of a headmaster at Eton and his social network included members of the royal family, the Cabinet and the Establishment at large. Through a family connection he had been recruited when he came down from Cambridge as an honorary attaché at The Hague by the newly appointed special envoy, Sir Nevile Bland. Bland was a close friend of the head of MI6, Admiral Sir Hugh Sinclair, who visited the legation during the summer of 1939 and got to know Elliott. The aspiring spy also got to know Klop and acted as a go-between with Wolfgang zu Putlitz, who sagely advised him not to take a holiday in Russia at the end of August 1939 as war would break out before he could get back. Elliott had met Best a couple of times and thought him 'an ostentatious ass blown up with self-importance'. Stevens he liked, but concluded that his intense ambition to take the credit for ending the war before it really got started warped his critical faculties and prevented him seeing through the deception. The consequence was 'as disastrous as it was shameful.'[157]

Elliott's superior, ambassador Nevile Bland, took a different view, telling the Foreign Office in London that Best had been viewed with intense distrust by other members of the Passport Control Office and that they had resented the increasing ascendancy of Best over Stevens in the weeks running up to the Venlo Incident. Bland went on to report gossip that Best had been in the pay of the Germans all along and was expecting a German war decoration for his betrayal. He complained, too, that Stevens's deputy was not up to the job. All these allegations were emphatically rejected by Stewart Menzies.[158]

One of the unexplained elements of the Venlo Incident is the role of the Czech Intelligence Service. They and the Poles had borne the brunt of Hitler's aggression but they had offered more than passive resistance. They had well-developed networks of agents whose information they were willing to share. They had also, inevitably, been the target of penetration attempts by Hitler's secret services, some of which succeeded. Klop and Dick White were responsible for liaison and by the end of the war Klop was regarded as a walking encyclopaedia on their activities.

František Moravec, who had been appointed head of the Czech Intelligence Service in March 1934, had formed a close working relationship with MI6's man in Prague, Harold Gibson. Despite the debacle of Munich, in which Chamberlain effectively sold out the Sudetenland to Hitler behind the backs of the Czechs, Moravec still believed Britain was his best ally. He shifted £1 million in secret funds via neutral countries to London. On the eve of Hitler's occupation of the Czech capital in May 1939, Gibson laid on a private plane to fly Moravec and ten of his most senior staff to London. Moravec transferred his most secret files to the British embassy, who shipped them to London in diplomatic bags that the Germans could not intercept. He liaised closely with the heads of MI5 and MI6 and was able to pass on to them intelligence brought out of Germany by his best agent, codenamed A-54 and later identified as Paul Thümmel, a high-ranking Abwehr officer. Since 1937 he had correctly predicted every step on Hitler's route into Czechoslovakia.

Moravec was delighted when Thümmel re-established contact with him in London and set up a meeting for 15 June 1939 at the Hotel des Indes in The Hague. He revealed the existence of Plan White, for the invasion of Poland and information about the increased number of Panzer divisions. A-54 made another trip to Holland on 3 August. His rendezvous point on this occasion, with two of Moravec's senior staff, was a small shop, known as De Favourit van Jansen, in Noordeinde in The Hague. It was run by an exiled Czech couple, Charles and Antoinette Jelinek, who traded in small *objets d'art*, Czech glass and leatherwork. Thümmel spent the evening sitting at a table in a backroom typing from memory full details of the invasion plan for Poland.

At the end of November, a matter of weeks after the Venlo fiasco, Thümmel was back in The Hague for three days, giving early warning of the rocket development that would lead to the

V1 and V2 weapons. The bric-a-brac shop became Thümmel's cover address for mail drops. Towards the end of March 1940 he revealed, using invisible ink in an otherwise innocuous letter, the plans for Germany's attack on the West. On 1 May he correctly predicted that it would take place on the tenth.[159]

Klop had been in The Hague for most of the final months of 1939, gathering all the intelligence he could from Wolfgang zu Putlitz before he had to flee to Britain and assist Richard Stevens in the Venlo negotiations. Another of Moravec's agents was also in evidence. This one was less trustworthy. William Morz had worked for the German police in Hamburg and belonged to the *Schwarze Kapelle* – the resistance movement against Hitler – before becoming a collaborator with Czech intelligence. Unbeknown to them, he was a double agent working for the Nazis.

In April 1939 Dick White had issued a special clearance for Morz to be allowed into Britain. He had visited Major Josef Bartik, the Czech head of counter-intelligence, at his new home at 53 Lexham Gardens, South Kensington, and been despatched on a secret mission to Holland. He then tried to lure Bartik to a meeting near Venlo but the Czech officer, who had lost men to Gestapo kidnap squads in the past, was suspicious and insisted that the meeting take place well away from the German border, on the Dutch coast. He decided to hand control of Morz over to the British. Whether Klop was the liaison officer in the case at that stage is not clear but in 1940 he was involved in a frantic manhunt for Morz, who had by then been exposed as a German agent. Special Branch spent some time visiting West End nightclubs and Soho cafes after various sightings of the agent. Dick White thought he had spotted Morz working as a waiter in a Chinese restaurant but, like every other sighting, it proved to be mistaken. He noted:

> It is only the great importance of his case that makes me anxious
> to leave no stone unturned to try to find him. He is in fact one of

the cleverest secret agents the Gestapo has, and he is believed to have been responsible for betraying certain members of the British S.S. [Secret Service] in Holland and thus contributing to the kidnapping of Stevens and Best at Venlo in November last year. [160]

Morz was never found but it was discovered that Franz Fischer, the instigator of the whole sorry Venlo episode, had also worked for the Czech Deuxieme Bureau. [161]

Back home Klop felt that it was time his artistic son joined the family business in secret intelligence. He arranged an interview which required Peter to meet a stranger, identifiable by his copy of the *News Chronicle* and an exchange of passwords, outside Sloane Square Underground station. A brief and inconsequential conversation took place, in elementary German and French, before the two parted and Peter later learned that he was considered unsuitable for secret work because he could not easily blend into a crowd. This may well have been true, but his father was hardly inconspicuous either and it represented yet another disappointment for Klop in his son's progress into adulthood. Instead, Peter got a part in a revue. His father was dismissive: 'Not even drama ... vaudeville.' For much of his son's early career Klop maintained an ambivalent attitude, outwardly dismissive, even hostile, yet he would often sneak in unannounced, in the company of friends, to observe his performances and bask in the occasional successes. Peter was called up in 1942, serving briefly as a private in the Royal Sussex Regiment and the Royal Army Ordnance Corps before being transferred to a propaganda film unit under the aegis of the Directorate of Army Psychiatry. In 1940, at the age of nineteen, he had married the actress Isolde Denham. As he later admitted, he was ill-equipped to sustain such a relationship and Klop seems to have had little to offer in the way of parental advice or encouragement. Indeed, he had never felt able to explain the facts of life to his son, despite their lecherous conversations over ice-creams in the park during Peter's childhood.

Klop worked throughout the war and beyond in close collaboration with Czech intelligence but it was a complex relationship. His contact, Vaclav Slama – Agent Sloane – was a lawyer and head of counter-intelligence. He had sources all over Europe, one of the most important being a mole inside the Swedish embassy in London. The Swedish minister to London, Bjorn Prytz, had been involved in one of the most controversial peace feelers of the war. On 17 June 1940, only a fortnight after the evacuation of Dunkirk, he had met his old friend Rab Butler, deputy to the Foreign Secretary Lord Halifax, strolling back from lunch across St James's Park. Prytz reported this casual encounter with one of the arch apostles of appeasement back to his government, including seriously injudicious remarks by Butler that appeared to have Halifax's tacit encouragement. He said that no opportunity would be missed of compromise [with Germany] if reasonable conditions could be agreed and no diehards would be allowed to stand in the way. Halifax was reputed to have said that common sense and not bravado would dictate British policy.

The Swedes passed on these comments, with their implied criticism of Churchill, to Hitler. News of it leaked to a British journalist in Stockholm whose report back to London was quickly quashed by the censors but Churchill soon got to hear of it, from his ambassador and, most likely from surveillance by MI5. He issued a strong rebuke about Butler's 'odd language' and impression of defeatism.[162] This directly contradicted Churchill's famous 'fight them on the beaches' speech on 4 June and another, made the day after Butler's meeting with Prytz, in which he warned of the likelihood of imminent invasion and declared that if Britain and the Empire could stand up to Hitler men would forever say: 'This was their finest hour.'

It is clear from MI5's file on Prytz, only released in March 2014, that he was considered a continuing risk of indiscretion and unauthorised attempts to broker peace deals in contravention of Churchill's policy of unconditional surrender. Sloane and Klop were able to report the content of discussions among Swedish diplomats and their contacts throughout 1941–42 on the Russian campaign, morale among German troops and civilians, and the influence of Japan on the war. Telephone taps recorded Prytz's unofficial conversations with British sympathisers.[163]

The Czechs had good sources and were crafty operators but they had been the targets of determined penetration efforts by the Germans in the years of harassment and intimidation prior to 1939, while simultaneously providing a haven for persecuted German Communists. MI5 had been warning from early in the war that refugees had to be regarded as potentially subversive in the German and Russian cause. There was enormous pressure on the Czech government in exile, prompted both by their British hosts and Stalin once Russia entered the war on the Allied side, to mount a showpiece act of resistance. The opportunity came with the appointment of the sadistic security chief Reinhard Heydrich as Deputy Reich-Protector of Bohemia and Moravia. With the help of the British Special Operations Executive, two Czech agents, Jan Kubiš and Jozef Gabčík, were parachuted in to assassinate him. On 27 May 1942 they succeeded in fatally wounding him by throwing an anti-tank mine at his car as it slowed to take a hairpin bend. Terrible reprisals followed after the two assassins had been traced to the crypt of the Karl Borromäeus Church where they committed suicide rather than be captured. Many of their supporters were killed, and in the villages of Lidice and Ležáky every man was executed, as were many of the women, while those left alive were sent to concentration camps. Children were sent to an extermination camp and the villages obliterated. This had a devastating effect on morale and naturally raised questions of why the British and Czechs in London sanctioned it, knowing there must be reprisals. One suggestion is that the Intelligence services feared that Admiral Canaris was losing his grip on the Abwehr. They knew that in October 1941 the Gestapo had captured the Czech's best agent, Paul Thümmel, who officially worked for the Abwehr. Under interrogation he admitted he had also worked for the British and been in touch with Best and Stevens prior to their capture at Venlo. There was a distinct possibility that Heydrich was on the verge of seizing control. This would inevitably have led to a purge of Abwehr agents and their sources, depriving the British of one of their most valuable weapons – the double agents whom Klop and others ran so successfully throughout the war feeding the Germans false information which deceived them over Allied strategy including the landings in Sicily and the Normandy beaches.[164]

CHAPTER 10: VERA

Early on the morning of 30 September 1940, Vera Schalburg waited on the platform of Portgordon railway station on the north-east coast of Scotland. She was cold and frightened and not sure where she was. Beside her, silent and anxious, stood Theodore Drücke.

Stationmaster John Donald cast a suspicious eye over the well-dressed, well-spoken woman and her morose companion. He summoned PC Robert Grieve, who noted that the lady's silk stockings and shoes were soaking wet. The constable guessed, correctly, that she had recently waded ashore after being dropped by a German flying boat. He was about to arrest the first woman spy sent to infiltrate Britain in the Second World War.[165]

Vera's possessions were a handbag full of drugs and make-up, a spare pair of stockings and a pair of kid gloves. The couple had about £300 on them. She and Drücke were taken to Latchmere House at Ham, an interrogation centre on the edge of Richmond Park. There were listening devices in the cells and the radiator system had been blocked off to stop inmates tapping out Morse code messages to each other on the pipes. The interrogations, under the control of Colonel Robin 'Tin Eye' Stephens – so-called because of his thick glass monocle – were harsh but elicited little. Drücke and a fellow spy, Walter Werti, who had arrived on the same seaplane and got as far as Edinburgh before he was caught, were executed.

MI5 was concerned that the trio had been on a special mission and they had good reason to think so. Vera admitted under interrogation that she had been married to Hilmar Dierks who had been a member of the German secret service since 1914, running agents in Holland, Belgium, France and the UK. He was known to MI5 because in September 1925 he had offered to change sides and was rebuffed. He had been interviewed at the time by members of MI6 in Amsterdam. He told them he would not spy against Germany but offered his services in Russia, Scandinavia and Turkey. They concluded it was a bluff and that he was trying to infiltrate them. But they had kept watch on him and knew that in 1938 he had been running a spy ring in Holland, under cover of a legitimate business. Dierks had died in 1940 in a car driven by Drücke, the man who was now in custody with Vera. Vera suspected it was not an accident and that the two men had fallen out over her or her mission.

A new tactic was needed to find out how much Vera knew. Dick White decided on a bold experiment. Vera was to have a holiday in the countryside, in different and pleasant surroundings with a 'sympathetic' couple who spoke her language. Her freedom required the Home Secretary, Sir Alexander Maxwell, who took a personal interest in Vera's progress, to revoke her detention order.

At the beginning of February 1942 she was moved, in the interests of secrecy, from Holloway prison to Aylesbury jail, where nobody knew her, before being released and taken by a Mrs Gladstone for a restorative hair-do and an Oxford Street shopping spree. Mrs Gladstone's main role in MI5 was the use of the Ellen Hunt employment agency in Marylebone as a front for MI5 to place staff in foreign embassies. Two minders were deputed to shadow the women and make sure Vera did not escape. She was handed an emergency ration card, number 520460, in the name of Veronica Edwards, giving her address as Klop's flat: 904 Chelsea Cloisters.

Then she was taken to meet her holiday hosts, Klop and Nadia Ustinov, at their Gloucestershire retreat, Barrow Elm House.[166]

The isolated Victorian farmhouse, north of Fairford, had been loaned to them by Sir Thomas Bazley, a wealthy eccentric who worked for MI5 during the war, occasionally acting as the director general's personal assistant. Sir Thomas shouldered the bulk of the work of investigating the Czech Refugee Trust and its Communist influences, a task that required regular liaison with Klop, Dick White and their Czech Intelligence contact Agent Sloane. In March 1941 Klop and Nadia spent a weekend as guests of Sir Thomas at his principal residence, Hatherop Castle, which was later taken over by the Special Operations Executive as a training school for the Danish Resistance. A few weeks earlier a bomb had badly damaged their flat in Redcliffe Gardens. Klop and Nadia had found temporary refuge with the Chenhalls sisters, Hope and Joan, in Belsize Park, and Nadia painted Hope's portrait out of gratitude, but they needed something more permanent. Nadia savoured the isolation of the rather stark but substantial farmhouse with its overgrown courtyard and ramshackle outbuildings. The rooms were spacious and light. There was no gas or electricity, heating was from coal and oil fires and an old-fashioned boiler. But she made it habitable and welcomed Dick White as one of the first house guests. He became a regular weekend visitor, sometimes accompanied by his secretary, Joan Russell-King.

Klop also came for weekends, always bringing several visitors, mostly girls, and laden with all kinds of provisions and bottles of gin and whisky. He would cook while the visitors piqued their appetites in the country air. He stayed in London during the week, moving into a small ninth-floor flat in Chelsea Cloisters, Sloane Avenue. It had only one room, crammed with his collection of bronzes and *objets d'art*, with a foldaway bed, kitchen alcove and bathroom. Yet he was ever the effervescent host and this was a period when his marriage to Nadia was under considerable strain. They were effectively leading separate lives. He threw parties in his tiny London flat that was so crowded there was hardly room to move or else invited girlfriends round for intimate dinners. She recorded:

I think he was thrilled to have a place of his own and to feel a bachelor again, just as I was enjoying my independence and complete freedom at Barrow Elm. I believed that it was good for us to be separated for a while. Neither of us was really made for matrimony. We could not become 'one' – our personalities could not merge. The separation however, strangely enough, fortified our bond and at a distance we had a much greater sense of belonging together than when we were actually together.[167]

It turned out that Vera had rather more in common with Nadia than she did with Klop. Vera Schalburg was born on 10 December 1912 in Siberia where her Danish father was a farmer. The family was ruined by the 1917 Bolshevik Revolution, fleeing Russia in poverty. They gravitated to Paris during the 1920s. Vera claimed to have danced with the great ballerina Pavlova, star of the Ballet Russes; appeared at the Folies-Bergère; and with the Russian Opera in the Champs-Elysées. This was the great era of Ballet Russes, which had grown out of the World of Art movement led by Nadia's uncle and artistic mentor Alexandre Benois. Under the direction of Sergei Diaghilev, it featured the dancers Vaslav Nijinsky, George Balanchine, Anna Pavlova, Tamara Karsavina and Alicia Markova. They performed to music by Stravinsky, Prokofiev and Tchaikovsky in costumes designed by Coco Chanel and sets designed by Henri Matisse, Pablo Picasso, Leon Bakst and Alexandre Benois himself.

It was a world of high art and low dealings as exiled Russians intrigued for and against the new Communist regime in their homeland. The penniless and naive eighteen-year-old Vera was seduced by a man who was to shape her destiny. Vera believed his name was Count Ignatieff but was unable to identify him fully to her captors. She said that he was a friend of Prince Serge Wolkonsky who had been director of imperial theatres under the tsar and patron of the likes of Diaghilev and Benois. Ignatieff introduced her to cocaine and persuaded her to spy for the Bolsheviks. She acted as his courier, running drugs and secret documents. Vera's interrogation records show that MI5 was intrigued by Ignatieff's identity and tried to get the Soviet defector Walter Krivitsky to help. For unexplained reasons, MI6 was reluctant to pass on their inquiries and Krivitsky, who was supposed to be under guard in the United States, was assassinated two months later.

Vera had tired of Ignatieff's attentions and fled to Antwerp, pursued by one of his hired assassins who stabbed her in the chest but failed to kill her. Terrified for her life, she turned to her pro-Nazi brother, Christian, for help. He introduced her to a member of German Intelligence and not long after Vera married him. Christian von Schalburg went on to join the German SS and was killed in June 1942 when commanding the Danish Freikorps in battle in Russia.

Vera's new husband, *Oberleutnant* Hilmar Dierks, fifty-two, was part of a team run by spymaster Major Nikolaus Ritter. Under Admiral Wilhelm Canaris, head of German military intelligence, Ritter was tasked with setting up spy networks in the US and Great Britain. Believing any agents he sent would be quickly followed by invading German forces, Ritter blitzed the country with poorly trained spies. As far as is known, they were all caught and either executed or turned into double agents, feeding duff information back to Germany. Vera had been groomed by Ritter before the war, and sent early in 1939 to stay in London with the right-wing Countess de Chateau Thierry, whom he was bankrolling to extract military gossip from her rather limited social circle. The countess was to have been Vera's first port of call in 1940. Then she was under instructions to take a room in the Dorchester Hotel in Park Lane and wait to be contacted.[168]

It emerged that Vera had an uncle, Ernst, who had been in business in Britain for many years and was serving with the RAF. He was questioned and confirmed Vera's family history but could tell the authorities little about her more recent past.

After her fortnight's holiday, Vera, having satisfied Klop that she had told him all she knew, had to return to custody. She wrote him a polite little note:

Dear Klop!

I have been very happy staying with you both and I hope the time
will come when we shall meet again under more normal circumstances.

Vera

The note was sent to a graphologist who concluded that Vera was
a cold, calculating person, selfish, hard, lost and lonely. A month
later, Klop returned to see Vera in prison once more and reported
in rather florid terms on their encounter:

> I stressed that Vera had now 'made her peace with us' and noticed
> unfeigned happiness descending over Vera's anxious features. I also
> emphasised that she now had a chance to live up to the trust put
> in her by showing that she wants to collaborate loyally with the
> people who have shown her consideration. This really moved Vera
> and she was quite sincere (I believe) when she said: 'Life is not
> worth living for me if it starts again with distrust. The Russians did
> not trust me, the Germans distrusted me the whole time and if you
> now start with distrusting me, then it would be much better for me
> to make an end of it.'[169]

Vera's newfound loyalty led to her being sent as an informant to
the Isle of Man where Germans suspected of pro-Nazi sympathies
were interned. Klop advised her 'to act as though she was the only
agent we had on the island'.

In December 1943 she wrote from there in Russian, which
Nadia translated. It was a rather plaintive Christmas greeting
which began:

> I have been always waiting for a letter from you but you seem to
> have forgotten me and that hurts because I have grown very fond
> of you and [Nadia] ... Write me a few words, how is everything;
> are you still polishing your bronzes and can you still faire la cuisine
> as well as before?

I think I had been a good girl as I had promised you to be. I am now very lonely. The females here are awful, they gossip and they knit and sometimes, presumably out of boredom, they fight. It is fun and it is sin all in one (a Russian expression).[170]

Klop and Nadia both replied, although their letters had to pass through MI5 censorship controls, and the correspondence was first shown to the director general, Sir David Petrie, who had asked to be kept informed of Vera's progress.

Much of the information about Vera's activity later in the war is still classified as secret and has been withheld from her files. Her case was dealt with by Joan Chenhalls, a friend of Klop and Nadia.

After the war, in October 1945, Vera was apparently deported to a British Army of the Rhine camp while remaining on MI5's 'A list' of surveillance subjects. When her Uncle Ernst asked after her in 1948 he was told she had disappeared. Miss Chenhalls claimed to have no record even of which camp she had been sent to.[171] Was Vera abandoned to her fate by a callous British intelligence, or did she begin another espionage career behind the Iron Curtain? It is hard to believe that a woman whose trade had been espionage all her adult life was allowed to slip away into the shadows. Certainly Major Nikolaus Ritter, the Abwehr officer responsible for sending her to England in the first place, did not believe it. In memoirs published in 1975 in Germany he claimed that she had been turned to work for Britain and married a British officer.[172]

The success of Vera's holiday in the countryside prompted MI5 to repeat the exercise with another, more troublesome woman agent. Mathilde Lucie Carre, alias Victoire, La Chatte, had been second in command of the Interallie organisation with around 100 agents. It was run by a Polish major, Roman Czerniaski, codenamed Walenty, from a Paris café. Victoire had become one of his lovers, taught him to speak French, and helped organise the network. Trouble began when Walenty imported his long-term mistress, codename Violette, and a jealous feud began. MI5 never entirely got to the bottom of who betrayed whom but in a very short time the whole organisation had been rolled up by the Nazis. Victoire admitted that under interrogation by the Germans she had implicated a number of her former Resistance colleagues, to save her own neck, and then become the lover of one of her captors. He organised her escape on the understanding that she was to be his double agent. She managed to link up with a new Resistance group, run by Agent Lucas, who brought her to London in February 1942. There she confessed her misdeeds and offered to turn the tables once more and work for the Allies. Lucas, who had become her latest lover, was keen to maintain the liaison.

MI5 was not about to trust her out of their sight – Lucas returned to France alone. But she did have her uses. She could broadcast radio messages to one of the Walenty sets in German hands, feeding them disinformation about the Lucas group's plans. Susan Barton was given the job of minding her, first at a flat in Rugby Mansions, Kensington, and then at Stratford Court, Oxford Street, where there were more distractions for Victoire's restless ambitions. It quickly became apparent where those ambitions lay. Through a Harley Street doctor who was treating her, Victoire got an introduction to Lord Selborne, the Minister for Economic Warfare and political head of the Special Operations Executive, the sabotage organisation for which Victoire worked. On 2 May 1942 Mrs Barton reported:

It seems that Victoire's party last night with Lord Selborne at Claridge's was a great success. She was so excited that she woke me up when she got in about 11.30 to tell me about it. I gather that apart from exceedingly intelligent conversation Victoire put forward some ideas on propaganda which impressed Lord Selborne very much and he said nobody had ever thought of them before. In order to have a long talk about everything Lord S suggested that he take her out to dinner alone next Tuesday. This is a definite appointment unless he has urgent business of state. He also told her that a man who wanted to get on always needed the advice of a clever woman and that there were several women around Churchill. He further said that he was going to talk to Churchill about her and that he wanted a woman painter to paint her portrait. As far as I can gather Victoria seems to be dreaming of becoming Lord S's mistress. According to her he has all the attributes she admires in a man except that he cannot dance, but that for the moment has become a minor matter. Lord S may be merely playing up to her but even if only half of what she has told me is true it seems that he is behaving exceedingly foolishly and is not doing himself any good, nor for that matter us as she will get more and more above herself.[173]

Mrs Barton was no prude but she took a very dim view of Victoire, concluding:

She has a thin veneer of charm, kindness and consideration but underneath it all she is an utterly egotistical woman who cares for nothing and nobody but herself and her own pleasures. She is clever, but not half as clever as she thinks she is. She can be very amusing but goes in a lot for dirty stories and her sense of humour is almost infantile. Added to all this there is, of course, her interest in men. She feels she is irresistible to men anyhow and to sleep with a man seems to be a necessity for her. Once she gets hold of a man it is up to her to drop him or be unfaithful to him. God help the man, or for that matter the Service he is in, if he dares to drop her ... She is a very dangerous woman.[174]

Christopher Harmer, the MI5 officer responsible for Victoire, added tersely:

From the point of view of running the case I don't much mind whether she goes on seeing Selborne or not, but whether we owe a duty to him to prevent him making a fool of himself is a matter I must leave for someone else to decide.

MI5's lawyer, Gonne St Clair Pilcher, reviewing the case, commented:

In addition to being unscrupulous and fickle, she has extremely expensive tastes. Her goodwill can only be retained by the satisfaction of her appetite for luxury and lovers, the former of which is constant and the latter constantly changing![175]

More man trouble swiftly followed. Her doctor friend now introduced her to Richard Llewellyn Lloyd, a wealthy army officer and author of the bestseller *How Green Was My Valley*. Within days she had installed herself in his Mayfair apartment. At first MI5 suspected that Captain Lloyd was simply providing a love nest for Victoire and Lord Selborne but it transpired that he had fallen for her himself and after a brief affair had offered her the use of the flat while he was away on military duty. At this point Victoire was persuaded that what she needed was a weekend in the country with Klop. He took against her in a big way:

To put it bluntly: I did not believe and do not believe a single word Victoire says. I tried in further contacts with Victoire to find confirmation for my doubts – a hopeless task with a person so tricky and so alive to the dangers of contradiction ... If anything, her confidence in her immunity from being unmasked grew in proportion to the comfort which surrounded her.[176]

Seeking confirmation of his opinion, he interviewed two other agents from the Walenty organisation who had managed to escape the Gestapo. Both condemned her. Klop believed that her whole story was a carefully thought-out and well-rehearsed German fabrication. She told him that she found Walenty dirty and repulsive as a lover and reckless and indiscreet as an agent. This, Klop thought, was part of a smokescreen to obscure her own role in the cascade of arrests that obliterated the organisation. She made anti-Semitic remarks about Violette, whom she considered ugly, and accused her of implicating Victoire to the Gestapo when she was captured. Klop suspected the reverse, and put it down to jealousy. It took Victoire only two days after her arrest to become the mistress of a Gestapo officer named Bleicher. This would not wash with Klop:

> I cannot believe that the confidence of the German Intelligence Service can be won by giving yourself to one member of this service … With all due respect, too, to Victoire's seductive powers, I firmly believe that every German officer in Paris had the opportunity to 'write on better paper' (as they so delicately say in German) and was not dependent for his amorous exploits on the rather faisandé [corrupt] charm of Victoire. This is all nonsense. In my opinion German confidence in Victoire started earlier than one day after her arrest. It was based on a more solid foundation than a bed. The Germans needed Victoire. They needed her for rounding up the rest of the Walenty organisation; they needed her for maintaining wireless transmitter traffic with England, and they needed her as a bait for future fry, small and big … Nothing will ever make me believe that the Germans, however stupidly they may sometimes behave, would take such risks without good reason.[177]

He concluded that it would not have been enough for Victoire to betray her friends to save her own neck after her arrest. For German Intelligence to have 100 per cent confidence in her, and to release her on a mission to England, she must have been a German agent in the first place, infiltrated into the Walenty organisation to destroy it from within. He paid tribute to her intelligence, courage and sangfroid, all qualities of a perfect double agent, but regarded her motivation as purely venal, unmitigated by patriotism, idealism or decency.

Surprisingly, given this opinion, he introduced her not only to Nadia, the chatelaine at Barrow Elm, but to his son Peter and their friend 'Dan' with whom Victoire began a flirtatious correspondence. Dan was almost certainly Daan Cevat, the Dutch art dealer and Rembrandt expert who had teamed up with Klop pre-war buying up paintings at country house sales for export. By 1942 he was working with the Dutch government in exile in London. The correspondence, monitored by Klop without Victoire's knowledge, was presumably intended to extract some unwitting confirmation of Klop's opinion of her but petered out inconsequentially.[178]

Nevertheless, Dick White and his colleagues at MI5 were in full agreement with Klop's scathing assessment and Victoire very soon found herself interned on the Isle of Man for the duration of the war. In 1945 she was handed back to the French who sentenced her to death for collaboration with the Nazis, although the penalty was later commuted and she was released after serving a prison term.

★

On Tuesday 10 November 1942, at the Lord Mayor's Luncheon in the Mansion House, a jubilant Prime Minister told his audience:

Now this is not the end. It is not even the beginning of the end. But it is, perhaps, the end of the beginning. Henceforth Hitler's Nazis will meet equally well-armed and perhaps better armed troops. Henceforth they will have to face in many theatres of war that superiority in the air which they have so often used without mercy against others, of which they boasted all round the world, and which they intended to use as an instrument for convincing all other peoples that all resistance to them was hopeless...[179]

Churchill was celebrating the triumph of General Montgomery

over Field Marshal Rommel at El Alamein at the end of October, the Allies' first victory. He went on to point out that their fortunes continued to prosper in North Africa now that America had entered the war. Two days before his speech they had launched Operation Torch, the invasion of Morocco, Algeria and Tunisia previously controlled by the Vichy French. For Major Richard Wurmann, chairman of the German Armistice Commission liaising with their puppet regime in Algiers, Operation Torch was the beginning of the end. Dressed in French Army uniform, he headed for Tunisia hoping to escape the advancing American and British Forces. He successfully bluffed his way through several roadblocks until he was unmasked by French soldiers who had switched to the Allied side. The British quickly discovered that they had an important prize in their hands. His real job was as head of the Abwehr station in Algiers. He had extensive knowledge of Germany's military intelligence set-up throughout Europe and America. MI5 gave him the cover name Harlequin and even now expunge his real name from their files when they are released to the National Archives. What he told them, coupled with the Enigma decrypts, enabled British Intelligence to penetrate the Abwehr so deeply that no important activity remained unknown to them for long.[180] One commentator concluded that it was probably not an exaggeration to maintain that, as a result, Allied intelligence understood the Abwehr better than its own high officials did.[181]

To get him to talk, Guy Liddell, director of counter-espionage at MI5, made a promise he knew he could not honour: to protect Richard Wurmann by offering him a new identity and British citizenship. In perpetrating this deception he inveigled Sir Alexander Maxwell, permanent secretary at the Home Office, into writing a letter seeming to confirm the deal. Wurmann naturally assumed that such matters could be fixed quite easily. Yet, even in the midst of war, neither Guy Liddell nor Alexander Maxwell had the power to put this into practice. The law said that he could only obtain British citizenship after five years' residence. And the law brooked no exceptions.

So Maxwell's letter simply stated that it was intended to grant Wurmann citizenship in five years, starting from the date of his capture. In addition, it explained that it was not the custom of the British government to deport aliens if by so doing they would be liable to persecution by their own authorities. The letter was addressed not to Wurmann but to the Director of Military Intelligence, who got cold feet and refused to endorse it. Nevertheless, Wurmann was eventually given a copy and taken along to the Midland Bank in Sloane Street, Knightsbridge to put it in a safe deposit box. Sir Edward Reid – in peacetime a director of Barings Bank, in wartime a financial fixer for MI5 – helped Wurmann to open an account in his new false identity: Count Heinrich Stenbock, an aristocrat from the Baltic states. He was to receive £400 a month plus his rent, of forty-nine guineas a week, for his flat at 184 Chelsea Cloisters, in the same block as Klop. In Wurmann's absence, Sir Edward Reid had a quiet word with the bank manager, the delightfully named Mr Skull, and explained to him, as one banker to another, that under no circumstances should Count Stenbock be allowed to remove the letter from the safe deposit box. If he attempted to do so Mr Skull was to notify the appropriate authorities immediately.[182]

Wurmann was already acquainted with his new neighbour, Klop Ustinov. He had spent a fortnight at Klop's country retreat at the end of January 1943. He passed the time sketching out charts on A3 size sheets of paper showing the entire structure of the Abwehr, starting with Admiral Canaris at the top and details of each country headquarters and sub offices, with names of the operatives where he knew them.

Wurmann had satisfied his own conscience by making it a condition of his cooperation that he should one day play a part in initiating a peace deal with Germany. He accepted that they would not win the war and implied that his boss, Admiral Canaris, recognised this too and would negotiate. MI5 played along and Klop proposed that interrogations should take the form of casual conversations at his flat rather than formal questioning where Wurmann might feel he was betraying his country.

Klop shared the task with Major Victor Caroe and between them they covered a range of topics. Guy Liddell regarded Wurmann as 'a useful reference book on all Abwehr matters'. Klop, at the end of a long report, some of which is still classified secret, felt that 'Wurmann is not the type of person I ever want to see again once the orange has been squeezed dry.'[183]

His personal assessment of Wurmann was scathing: a member of the Prussian officer class distinguished by physical courage and moral cowardice. He had embraced Nazi-ism as the antidote to the Treaty of Versailles, Bolshevism and Judaism and was now ready to disown it since it had failed to deliver the anticipated results. He went on:

True to type, Wurmann lacked the courage to face a prisoner's future. He saw only mud not stars. He burnt his boats as thoroughly as anyone can. I firmly believe that having taken the plunge and having soothed his conscience with patriotic and humane formulae, he is playing fair with us and will continue to do so, not because fair play is part and parcel of his moral make-up, but because he is much too intelligent and much too disinclined to face discomfort of any description.

Wurmann characterised Admiral Canaris as having an ice-cold brain but a friendly disposition, on first-name terms with his subordinates. His aim was to 'secure big stuff through big people' and to that end he cultivated agents like Prince Max von Hohenlohe, an aristocrat with estates in Czechoslovakia, Spain and Mexico. Among Hohenlohe's contacts were Sir Samuel Hoare, British ambassador in Madrid, and Allen Dulles, Swiss station chief for the American secret service. Wurmann's previous posting had been in Biarritz, where Hohenlohe had a villa. The prince had confided in him that as early as February 1941 he had put peace feelers out to Sir Samuel Hoare but they came to nothing.

Wurmann had also been in contact with Charles Bedaux, the notoriously right-wing American millionaire. He had befriended the Duke and Duchess of Windsor after the abdication and engineered their visit to Germany and meeting with Adolf Hitler in 1937. Bedaux had used his Nazi connections to put pressure on the Vichy government in North Africa to sign commercial deals with him and boasted to Wurmann that he held an honorary rank of major in the German Army. He knew Admiral Canaris, and Wurmann thought he might be one of the admiral's special agents. Bedaux had also been captured during Operation Torch and committed suicide in the United States while awaiting a grand jury investigation for alleged treason.

MI5 was reassured by Wurmann's admission that the Abwehr had poor agent coverage in England but dismayed to learn that their radio intercepts had given them a full picture of the distribution of army divisions and numbers. Similar results came in from Allied radio traffic in Egypt. Guy Liddell had been warning for some time of lax signals security. The Prime Minister was given a special report on Wurmann's information and noted that it was 'deeply interesting'.

Eventually Wurmann's usefulness came to an abrupt halt as a series of Abwehr failures made it apparent that Admiral Canaris was increasingly out of favour and liable to be dismissed. Wurmann realised that his dream of playing a prominent role in making peace and salvaging Germany's pride would never be realised and refused all further cooperation. Klop took him out for a final dinner before leaving it to Major Caroe to hand him over to an escort party to send him to America as a prisoner of war. As a PoW, Wurmann was entitled to wear his German officer's uniform. Fearing that this might cause some consternation around Chelsea Cloisters, Caroe took him to a nearby office to change and then to Waterloo station, only to find the escort was waiting for them at Paddington. They dashed across London and made it to their train with minutes to spare. Major Caroe was careful to take possession of the Home Office letter offering Wurmann British citizenship.[184]

A top secret report issued by the British to the United States on the intelligence value of Klop's interrogations concluded:

Only after the Allied landings in North Africa in November 1942, and the capture there of responsible Abwehr officers, was it possible to balance our theoretical knowledge against the evidence of knowledgeable men with practical experience. From that moment our penetration of the Abwehr became increasingly deep so that by the time of its dissolution and the fall of its head in the Spring of 1944 there was no important activity which it directed unknown to us.[185]

CHAPTER 11: LISBON

Towards the end of 1943 Klop became a KGB agent carrying out an important mission of special interest to Joseph Stalin. Klop was oblivious to this, of course. He was acting under orders from Kim Philby, the Russian Intelligence service's main man inside MI6. Philby's duties for Britain left him in charge of counter-espionage against the Nazis in the Iberian Peninsula. Among other things, that meant assessing the frequent peace feelers put out by secret contacts with German politicians and agents. Lisbon and Madrid, along with Berne and Stockholm, were the favoured neutral locations for this traffic and during 1943 it began to reach a crescendo.

The presence of Sir Samuel Hoare as ambassador in Madrid had made the British embassy a magnet for German dissidents and secret service mischief makers. Hoare was a former Foreign Secretary who had been strongly pro-appeasement. He had been sent to Spain as a sympathetic ear to the Fascist dictator Francisco Franco, who needed oil and provisions to fend off starvation in a country ravaged by three years of civil war. The supplies could only reach him by running the gauntlet of a British naval blockade. Hoare, supported by a vast array of agents from MI5 and MI6, played a canny hand, bribing and cajoling Franco's government with cash and goods to keep them from entering the war on the Nazi side. The Germans were playing the same game to less effect. Hoare was seen as a potential intermediary by those Germans who thought a peace deal was still possible, or even that Churchill, once he took over as Prime Minister in May 1940, might still be undermined and supplanted by a leader more sympathetic to the German cause. Albrecht Haushofer, representing the Führer's deputy Rudolf Hess, turned up in Madrid, as did Prince Max von Hohenlohe, Walther Schellenberg's agent, who previously had dealings with Sir Robert Vansittart's secret agent Group Captain Malcolm Christie. Hoare, against instructions, saw Hohenlohe in March 1941, and was told firmly from London that the discussions should be broken off. Churchill had made it abundantly clear in the aftermath of Dunkirk that his government would not participate in peace negotiations and that such approaches should not even be dignified with an answer. Silence should prevail.

This was reinforced by the US President Franklin D. Roosevelt at a conference with Churchill and de Gaulle in Casablanca in January 1943. Roosevelt proclaimed that the war would be fought relentlessly by the Allies to the point of unconditional surrender by Germany and Japan. There was debate later about whether this had the effect of prolonging the war by giving the Germans no option but to fight to the bitter end. The intention was to demoralise them and, equally, to reassure Stalin that the Allies were committed to the fight and would not leave the Soviet Union to bear the brunt of the losses nor make a separate peace and turn against the Communist regime.

Silence did not prevail. Stalin was not convinced. MI6 had an interest in hearing what the Germans had to say. It was a means of gaining intelligence, of finding out who might be joining the ranks of the disaffected, of feeding back disinformation and of sizing up likely defectors.

Philby's task, for Soviet intelligence, was to keep Stalin informed of any indications that the Allies were wavering from the stance of unconditional surrender. During 1943 the head of the Abwehr, Admiral Canaris himself, had made several trips to Spain and Portugal and sent a message inviting his opposite number,

Stewart Menzies at MI6, to meet him face to face. Menzies wanted to go but the Foreign Secretary, Anthony Eden, absolutely forbade it. Almost simultaneously, a German agent with Abwehr connections, Otto John, leaked to MI6 in Lisbon a report that revealed the existence of the weapons research establishment at Peenemunde, on the German Baltic coast, where the V1 and V2 rockets were being developed. In August 1943 the RAF were able to mount a major bombing raid on the facility.[186]

Otto John was one of the key figures in the German resistance to Hitler. He was a frequent visitor to Madrid and Lisbon in his capacity as a lawyer for the Lufthansa airline and from May 1942 onwards was in touch with MI6. He was a friend of Prince Louis Ferdinand Hohenzollern, grandson of Kaiser Wilhelm II and a rallying point for monarchist elements among the anti-Nazi factions. Acting on the directions of Colonel Claus von Stauffenberg, who would eventually lead the ill-fated assassination attempt on Hitler's life in July 1944, Otto John made contact with the American chargé d'affaires in Madrid, William L. Beulac, and his military attaché Colonel William Hohenthal. He also had a meeting with an MI6 officer from Lisbon, whom Otto John referred to as 'Tony'. Some accounts identify him by the name Graham Maingott, others say it was Guy Burgess. It might equally have been Kim Philby's deputy, Major Tim Milne, who occasionally used the name Tony. Whoever it was, Otto John gave him information, nearly a year in advance, that there was a plan to assassinate Hitler. He asked for support. It was not forthcoming.

There were doubts about Otto John's Resistance credentials and fears that he might be an agent provocateur for the Gestapo, but Allen Dulles, senior representative of the OSS (American secret service) in Switzerland, was convinced of his bona fides and angered by his colleagues' apparent lack of enthusiasm. In January 1944 he sent a coded message to Washington saying he had heard about Otto John's mission from a Resistance contact who told him that it had not been well received in Portugal. Dulles asked his boss,

Whitney H. Shepardson, to find out discreetly what had happened at this 'exceedingly secret' meeting because the Resistance, whom he codenamed the Breakers, needed encouragement and support. He added:

> I would appreciate hearing of any indication with which you could supply me regarding what you would be interested in achieving via the Breakers, and could be pursued effectively at this time. I do not understand what our policy is and what offers, if any, we could give to any resistance movement.[187]

The message was passed on up the chain of command to the US State Department but only in order to tell the Russians of the approach and assure them there was no intention to broker a separate peace.

Two of MI6's most formidable analysts, the historian Hugh Trevor-Roper and philosopher Stuart Hampshire, had drawn up a report on the dissident faction within the German Army. Philby refused to circulate it, describing it as mere speculation, and likewise suppressed Otto John's supplications for encouragement. Trevor-Roper later wrote that they were baffled by Philby's intransigence and, looking back, wondered whether the reason was that it was not in Russia's interest for the Western Allies to support Hitler's conservative enemies within while the Red Army was still too far away to intervene.[188]

Philby decided he needed a man on the spot to keep him up to date with what he described as 'dickering with the Germans'. Klop was that man. His mission, initially for three months, was agreed by the Intelligence services towards the end of November 1943. He was to 'make contact with his former German connections in the Embassies and ultimately worm his way into Abwehr circles'.[189]

It was around this time that Baron Axel von dem Bussche, a relative of Klop's godmother, offered to give up his own life to assassinate Hitler. Due to model a new army greatcoat before the

Führer, he intended to hide two grenades beneath the coat and, when he got close enough, pull the pins, annihilating them both. The fashion show was cancelled, because of an Allied air raid, and another opportunity passed.[190]

MI6 had been under pressure on financial grounds to reduce its presence in Lisbon, where it employed more than fifty people. Philby had to refer Klop's mission to Peter Loxley, MI6's liaison officer at the Foreign Office, and in December 1943 he cleared it with the Foreign Secretary. Anthony Eden made clear that Klop was to refrain from discussing peace proposals and engage only in intelligence work, which was exactly what Philby's Soviet paymasters wanted. Klop was to report direct to MI6's head of counter-intelligence in Lisbon, Count Charles de Salis, who in turn was to inform the British minister on the spot, Henry Hopkinson.[191]

Years later Philby, basking in the reflected glow of a visit to Moscow by Peter Ustinov to meet President Gorbachev, claimed he got to know Klop well after sending him to Lisbon to meet Germans 'who were thinking mainly of saving their own skins'.[192]

While Eden was making up his mind to approve Klop's mission, new evidence of German peace feelers emerged. Walther Schellenberg, MI6's nemesis at Venlo, sent the French fashion designer Coco Chanel and her English friend Vera Lombardi to Spain in an abortive attempt to make direct peace overtures to Winston Churchill via Sir Samuel Hoare. Chanel had been conducting an affair with a German officer but had made at least one earlier visit to Madrid to pass on intelligence to MI6. This time she was unsuccessful although it is clear that Churchill was informed of her mission because he later intervened to help Vera Lombardi, who had been left stranded and penniless in Madrid.

Klop departed for Lisbon in mid-February 1944. An American intelligence report from that time described Portugal as a happy hunting ground for racketeers, double agents and double-crossers. The dictator Antonio Salazar was well disposed towards Britain but many of his middle-ranking officials were pro-German Fascist sympathisers and his secret police were German-trained. The poverty-stricken peasant classes were socialist or Communist inclined and both groups were open to corruption and bribery. It wasn't even safe to go for a haircut. One of the Abwehr's best sources was the Portuguese barber who trimmed the locks of many an American and British diplomat and agent. The report added:

> Lisbon is as extraordinary a meeting place of all the homeless, the unfortunates, the arrivistes, the scoundrels as can be found in the world today. Most of the refugees from Hitler's New Order arrive finally in Lisbon en route for the new world. ... The temptations to shady activities by some of the refugees, who have lost everything, including their families and their countries, must be overwhelming. There are always agents of the Germans or their stool pigeons [in the secret police] to act as *agents provocateurs*. The traffic in passports and visas, in reply paid cables, the white slave trade, the smuggling of diamonds, gold, platinum – all these flourish.
>
> More perhaps than any other place in Europe, Caldas da Rainha [the main refugee camp] is a place where the fundamental human urges of love, hate, hope and the will to live have been exploited by a clever and ruthless enemy.[193]

Among those who arrived in Lisbon in late 1943 was one of Hitler's favoured art dealers, Karl Buchholz. He had been permitted by the Führer to buy up and resell confiscated 'degenerate' art. In 1937 Hitler and Goering had displayed 16,000 examples of modern art that they had removed from Germany's museums and galleries. After ridiculing and condemning it they burned more than 1,000 items, provoking a stampede of art lovers around the world prepared to pay good money to rescue the remainder. Buchholz was one of four people authorised to dispose of it. Another was Hildebrand Gurlitt, whose son Cornelius was discovered still to be hoarding 1,500 of the treasures in his Munich flat in the year 2013 when police raided it. Buchholz had a ready outlet for his share of the works in America because he owned a gallery in New York. As it became known that he was an authorised outlet, many Jewish owners, desperate to dispose of their art collections at any price, also turned to him. Once the US entered the war the dealers had to find a neutral point of sale. Some chose Switzerland; Buchholz opened an antiquarian book shop and dealership in the Portuguese capital.

It would be surprising if Klop did not know of this, given his own interests in art dealing. Certainly British intelligence was aware of Buchholz's activities and investigated them in some detail. Klop's close friend Clifford Norton was coordinating reports in Switzerland and at the end of the war these investigations formed the basis of the records of looted art which continue to be sought to this day for return to their rightful owners. Klop, of course, had a potential source within the smuggling operation in the shape of his former mistress, Thea Struve, who had moved to New York in 1938 to work for Curt Valentin, manager and later owner of the Buchholz Gallery there. Valentin handled many prestigious exports from Berlin, including works by Picasso, and his close relationship to the New York Museum of Modern Art later came under scrutiny.

★

Klop was met on arrival in Lisbon by Desmond Bristow, a Cambridge graduate in his mid-twenties who was born and brought up in the Sotiel Coronada area of southern Spain where his father was a mining engineer. He had been recruited to the Iberian section of MI6 by Kim Philby in September 1941 and had spent the previous two years in Gibraltar and Algiers. He was there to watch Klop's back as he made contact with an old friend from Germany who was part of an anti-Nazi group plotting to get rid of Hitler. Bristow never met this agent and gives no clue to his identity in his memoirs but the timing coincides very closely with

Otto John's visit to Lisbon, at which he revealed the existence of the plot to assassinate Hitler. Bristow's value was as an unfamiliar face, not immediately recognisable to the Abwehr agents in Lisbon or to the ever vigilant and frequently pro-German Portuguese secret police, the *Polícia Internacional e de Defensa do Estado*.

Bristow made a big show of being a wide-eyed tourist new to the pleasures of Portugal, sightseeing, taking a river cruise and visiting the casino at Estoril before meeting Klop for dinner at the Hotel Avenida Palace in Restauradores Square. It was one of Lisbon's finest and most glamorous, and at the heart of political intrigue in the city. Klop was not stinting on the expense, immediately ordering lobster and Vinho Verde as they made their introductions.

Tradecraft – the skill of conducting undercover operations – seems to have been rudimentary. Even in such a cosmopolitan city the diminutive Klop must surely have been conspicuous, dressed in a long Russian astrakhan coat and wide-brimmed black hat, smoking gold-tipped Sobranie black Russian cigarettes, as he and Bristow strolled by the River Tagus. They were stopped by two secret police officers and required to prove their identities – which revealed the fact that Bristow's room at the Europa hotel had been booked by the British embassy. They borrowed a black Citroen saloon, identical to those used by the police, from Count Charles de Salis and moved into an apartment in Estoril where they began to play cat-and-mouse with the secret police officers who constantly shadowed them. While Klop hung around in Estoril – gambling heavily, Bristow suspected – Bristow attempted to lead the unwanted shadows a dance around Lisbon, testing their ability to keep him in sight.

It was several days before Klop could make his rendezvous. Klop and Bristow spent the morning sitting on the coast, gazing out over the Atlantic Ocean, while two teams of watchers gazed at them. Bristow was first to make a move, sauntering along to the Tamaris restaurant in Estoril, casually carrying out an inspection of the toilets out the back and establishing that there was a small door leading to a garden gate which opened almost directly on to a side entrance of the railway station. After an early lunch, Klop rose at 1:10 p.m. and went, ostensibly, to relieve himself. Five minutes later he had followed his pre-planned escape route and was sitting aboard the 1:15 p.m. train to Lisbon as it pulled out from platform three. Four detectives sat under a tree in the square at the front of the restaurant quite oblivious to their quarry's departure.

Klop did not return until the early hours, and next day offered only the noncommittal opinion that the meeting had gone well. Two more rendezvous followed before Klop returned briefly to London to report back. Bristow stayed on for another month, working on providing stories from North Africa that could be fed to the Germans through British double agents, and then returned to Algiers. He regarded his time with Klop as two of the most thrilling weeks of his MI6 career, remarkable considering he later became MI6 head of station in Madrid and Lisbon, retiring in 1954 to work for the De Beers diamond company investigating the illicit gems trade. He had been instrumental, with Kim Philby, in recruiting the most successful of the double agents, Juan Pujol Garcia, Agent Garbo, who went on to deceive the Germans about the location of the D-Day landings and employed a safebreaker to steal Spanish ciphers from their consulate in Algiers.

Bristow maintains that he never knew the identity of the agent whom Klop was meeting but clearly he regarded it as of the highest importance and later wrote:

> It was our hope and the hope of MI5 that this rendezvous might bring the war to an earlier end than could possibly happen without inside help from this German anti-Nazi group.[194]

In his recently published memoirs, Philby's deputy, Major Tim Milne, confirms that he and his colleague Noel Sharp, who were monitoring and evaluating the peace feelers, had become increasingly interested and optimistic about the plotters and willing to encourage them. Their concern was that they must have been infiltrated by the Gestapo.[195]

Milne's and Bristow's views are at odds with the stated aims of the British government and the brief that Klop had supposedly been given before his departure from London. It is likely that Klop was not fully informed of higher government policy but it is also the case that MI6 tried hard to deter Bristow and Milne from publishing their rather too frank memoirs. By implication, Klop's contact must have been of great significance and the most likely explanation is that it was Otto John, who is known to have been in Lisbon at around that time. He had held a rendezvous with the MI6 officer Rita Winsor. According to John's own account, there was a hurried conversation, sitting in her car, parked in a side street, in which he passed on more specific details of the impending assassination plot but again got no encouragement. However that does not preclude a separate meeting with Klop. Kim Philby later told an interviewer:

> John was a difficult man. We tried to use him as a double agent but he was always changing sides. The trouble with the German peace terms was that they were too demanding to take seriously. They were suggesting terms that might have been appropriate if Germany had still been winning the war instead of losing it. We rightly turned them down, so the good Germans had to go it alone, and unfortunately for them, they failed.[196]

They failed through one of those minute quirks of fate by which even the best laid plans go awry, despite a host of conspirators who had in place not only the means to assassinate the despised Führer but to declare a new government in Germany. On the morning of 20 July 1944 Count Claus von Stauffenberg, colonel and chief of staff to the head of the German Home Army, arrived at the Wolf's Lair, Hitler's military headquarters east of Rastenburg, to report on the training of fresh troops to reinforce the rapidly disintegrating Eastern Front. He walked with a limp and was badly disfigured. His staff car had hit a landmine in Tunisia fifteen months previously and he lost his left eye, his right hand and two fingers of the left, plus he had injuries to his ear and knee. But he had insisted on returning to military service. His briefcase was packed with English explosives obtained through the Abwehr and as he entered the conference room he broke a capsule of chemicals that would activate the device in ten minutes. He stood about 6ft away from Hitler and placed the briefcase underneath the heavy trestle table around which more than twenty senior officers were gathered. The conference room, about 30ft by 15ft, had 18in. thick concrete walls that would contain the blast but all ten windows were open on a sweltering day. At 12:37 p.m., with five minutes to go, he left the room, with the excuse of taking a phone call. He did not return. His fellow officer Colonel Heinz Brandt, finding the briefcase in his way, moved it to the far side of a heavy wooden trestle. That saved Hitler's life. By 12:42 p.m., when the bomb went off, Stauffenberg was a couple of hundred yards away. He heard the roar of the explosion, saw bodies hurtling out of the window and debris everywhere. Convinced his mission had succeeded he headed for Berlin to join his co-conspirators. By the time he got there just over three hours later, word had reached Berlin that the attempt had failed. By that evening Stauffenberg and three of his fellow conspirators had been executed and the round-up of suspects commenced. There were as many as 7,000 arrests.[197]

Hans John was tortured to death. His older brother, Otto John, fled to Spain. There he took refuge with Juan Terraza, one of the principal diplomatic secretaries in the Spanish Foreign Office and a close friend of Prince Louis Ferdinand of Germany. With the help of MI6 officers in Madrid he was smuggled to Lisbon in August and spent a couple of months hiding out at a safe house, the Boa Vista, which was also used by Spanish Communists. In October, Portuguese police raided this house and arrested him along with the housekeeper and seven of the Spanish Communists.

After several days he was released on the orders of the Portuguese general staff and handed over to the British. Count Charles de Salis arranged for him to be transported secretly to Gibraltar and on 3 November he was flown to the UK under guard.[198] The long delay arouses suspicion that Philby deliberately blocked his return to prevent him revealing the extent of opposition to Hitler and the potential for a negotiated ceasefire. Otto John, in his own account, insists that he was anxious to get to Britain to reveal all he knew and to resuscitate the remains of German resistance by broadcasting the true story of the assassination attempt. He was first taken to London Reception Centre for screening alien arrivals at the Royal Victoria Patriotic School in Wandsworth and questioned by a Captain F. Basett, who was deeply suspicious and dismissive. He thought John's muddled replies showed a lack of candour and made plain that the opposition in Germany was unwilling to recognise the inevitability of unconditional surrender. He suspected that John was working for the SS, or being used by them as an unwitting agent. He also knew, from Enigma decrypts, that John had sent radio reports from Madrid to the Abwehr. John consistently denied any link to the Abwehr and Basett was unable to challenge him on that point without compromising the Enigma source. He surmised that John, and some of the other conspirators, may have been unwittingly controlled by the Gestapo as front men for a peace initiative and concluded:

> Quite clearly John's case will have to be gone into very thoroughly and in the meantime he cannot be considered a suitable prospective candidate for use by either SIS or PWE [Secret Intelligence Service or Political Warfare Executive].

Basett was working for department B1D of MI5, reporting to Lt Col. H. J. Baxter who in turn forwarded Basett's report to Major Tim Milne, Kim Philby's deputy in the Iberia section of MI6, on 14 November 1944. Somehow it did not find its way to the

Above: Freed hostages at the siege of Magdala. Klop's grandmother Katarina is at the very centre, clutching the barely discernible infant Magdalena on her lap. Moritz Hall is fourth from the right in the back row.

Above left, and cover: Klop in his German army greatcoat, with the Württemberg 123rd Grenadiers in the Forest of Argonne in 1915. *Above right*: Klop's brother Peter in his flying kit shortly before being killed on a mercy flight for the German air force.

Klop's spymasters:

Ago von Maltzan.

Sir Robert (later Lord) Vansittart.

Guy Liddell.

Sir Dick White.

Klop's contacts: Albrecht Graf von Bernstorff, *right*; Wolfgang zu Putlitz, *below left* and General Hans Spiedel (*below right*, with Adolf Heusinger).

© Getty Images

Above: Triple defector
Otto John.

© Getty Images

SCHELLENBERG

Left: Klop's deadly rival,
Walter Schellenberg of the
German Security Service.

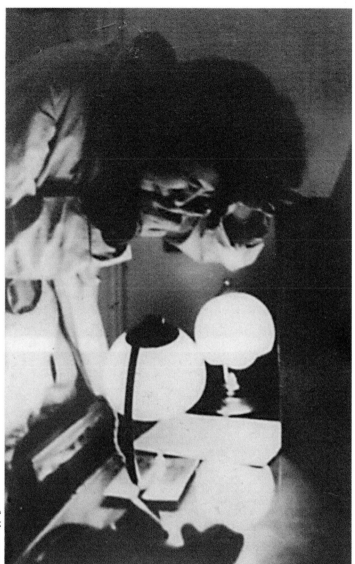

Above: Klop's agent 'Ecclesiastic' was photographed by her German lover copying supposedly secret British documents. In fact they had been supplied by Klop as part of a deception operation.

Right: An MI5 file picture of Klop in the coat with the distinctive Astrakhan collar that he wore on assignment in Lisbon.

Klop's girlfriends:
Top: Liz Brousson
painted by Nadia
Benois and, *below*:
Thea Struve,
photographed by
the surrealist artist
Roland Penrose.

Previously unseen sketches from Nadia's notebook: Klop in the 1930s, *above left*, and sporting a monocle in 1922, shortly after their arrival in London.

Above: Peter Ustinov as a child.

Above: On the brink of
triumph: Peter Ustinov at his
Chelsea home with Nadia
and Klop on 1 January 1953,
the year he won an Oscar
nomination for *Quo Vadis*
and the Critics' Award for
the Best Foreign Play for
the New York production of
The Love of Four Colonels.

Right: Klop and Nadia
outside their retirement
cottage at Eastleach.

appropriate person until mid-January 1945. It seems never to have been released in Britain but a copy does exist in United States archives.[199] The existence of Captain Basett, however, remains a mystery. He does not appear in wartime military service records and is presumably an alias. Despite Basett's doubts, John obtained his release from the interrogation centre thanks to Sefton Delmer, a *Daily Express* journalist whose role for the Political Warfare Executive involved creating demoralising black propaganda to broadcast to the enemy. Otto John became one of the announcers on Soldatensender Calais, a bogus station aimed at German troops. Working alongside him was Klop's old friend and informant Wolfgang zu Putlitz. Otto John was not allowed to use his real name, because it was not German enough, and instead was called Oskar Jurgens. And he was not allowed to broadcast, as he had intended, messages that might give hope and encouragement to the anti-Nazi resistance. Unconditional surrender remained the sole objective.

Otto John, Wolfgang zu Putlitz and other Germans who found refuge in Britain were frustrated at the political restrictions imposed upon them. Whether Communist, Social Democrat or Conservative, they saw themselves as the guardians of the future once Hitler had been defeated. At first the BBC welcomed their contributions, or at least consulted them. They were not keen on Jewish broadcasters, because they thought their accents would be suspect to German ears, and they discouraged politicians attempting to raise their personal profiles. Black propaganda was handled in the early stages of the war by a special department at Electra House run by Sir Campbell Stuart whose experience began with propaganda under Lord Northcliffe at the Ministry of Information in the First World War and then as a journalist at *The Times* and *Daily Mail*. He was invited to make use of Putlitz soon after his escape from Holland in 1939 and was utterly contemptuous of his abilities. He told Sir Alec Cadogan, permanent undersecretary at the Foreign Office, that he had nicknamed Putlitz 'William

Putter', and regarded him as an intellectual lightweight, possibly
a spy, who refused to look him in the eye and appeared to know
nobody in Britain, except for spending weekends with Sir Robert
Vansittart, and was of no use for broadcasting. It might be helpful
to pick his brains provided he was given no information in return.
Cadogan wholeheartedly agreed, which led to an explosion of rage
from Vansittart. He commented:

> He came over here hoping to help to win the war; and if the
> Germans had secured the services of one of our Counsellors
> they would no doubt have made good use of him. Sir Campbell
> Stuart's organisation has not known how to do so, and Putlitz
> long ago resigned himself to this disheartening experience. He
> and I have watched mistake after mistake being made, and a cast
> iron case simply being frittered away ... Putlitz has worked with
> me and MI5 for years; he has consistently risked his life in our
> interests and was only just got out of Holland with an hour to
> spare ... MI5 always referred to him as 'our most trustworthy
> source'. The sole reward for a man who has sacrificed everything
> in our cause is that Sir Campbell Stuart – without the slightest
> knowledge or justification – goes libelling him behind my back ...
> If we continue to reject his [Putlitz's] advice we shall continue to
> lose the propaganda war.[200]

Initially the German exiles were encouraged by the Labour minister
Hugh Dalton, who was head of the Special Operations Executive
and responsible for propaganda, and by Sefton Delmer, who had
worked in Germany for years. Events quickly changed Delmer's
priorities. The pact with Stalin meant that promoting democracy
was not the priority; propaganda was to be crude and demoralising,
holding out no hope to the German population of anything other
than crushing defeat.[201] Despite that, Delmer succeeded in recruiting
a team of émigrés to help prepare the material.

Some of them, including John and Putlitz, eventually returned to play a part in the rebuilding of their country but it was not always the role they wished for, or that those who had protected them expected. A significant number, including John and Putlitz, ended up on the wrong side of the Iron Curtain. It cast a shadow over the Intelligence services who sought to manipulate them during the Cold War. It may well have contributed to Klop eventually retiring from the service in circumstances of mutual suspicion and recrimination.

While Klop's involvement with Otto John remains unconfirmed by official sources, his links to another anti-Nazi German were recorded by Guy Liddell in his diary in March 1944: 'U35 has succeeded in making contact with Mariaux, a German journalist whom he knew formerly in Brussels. This ought to make a very profitable beginning.'

Franz Mariaux was a conservative-minded journalist, a critic of the Weimar Republic but also opposed to Hitler. In the early 1930s he worked closely with Edgar Jung, publicity adviser to Chancellor Franz von Papen who had tried to prevent Hitler replacing him. Under the circumstances, Mariaux was lucky to be alive. Towards the end of June 1934 he had been arrested by the Gestapo. He was suspected of being an intermediary to General Kurt von Schleicher, the army officer who had been behind the *Black Reichswehr* – the secret army constructed in defiance of the Versailles Treaty – and who briefly became the last Chancellor of Germany before Hitler. On 30 June, within days of Mariaux's arrest, Hitler had launched the Night of the Long Knives in which he purged the Brownshirts – the thuggish paramilitary force that had helped bring him to power. Its leader, Ernst Röhm, and his henchmen were murdered as were many more of Hitler's opponents, among them Schleicher and Edgar Jung. Goebbels accused Schleicher of treason for seeking the support of the French government against the Nazi regime and claimed that Mariaux had been his go-between. The outraged protests of the French ambassador may have saved Mariaux from execution and in due course he moved to

Paris, where he worked for most of the war. He was correspondent of the *Kölnischen Zeitung*, the daily newspaper of Cologne until it was suppressed for failing to toe the Nazi line, and an informant for the Abwehr. Simultaneously he worked for the Johannssen Service, a news outlet controlled by the German Foreign Office as a competitor to the Propaganda Ministry run by Joseph Goebbels. So he was potentially of immediate use to Klop as a double agent and he also had long-term significance.

One of Klop's old army friends from the First World War, Hans Speidel, had also been in Paris, arriving in 1940 with the invading army and becoming chief of staff to the military governor. Speidel would later claim that as an army officer he tried to mitigate the worst excesses of the Gestapo and that he helped maintain a cultural détente. In 1942 he was transferred to the Eastern Front but he left behind a group known as the George V circle, named after the luxury hotel where they met. A central figure was company commander Ernst Jünger, who was a renowned writer and philosopher in Germany and maintained social contacts with artists like Picasso and Jean Cocteau. Speidel had first met him during the First World War when Jünger was an officer in the 73rd Grenadiers who relieved the 123rd at Guillemont. It is likely, therefore, that Klop had also known him then. Jünger was a war hero who had been wounded three times in the earlier conflict. He was an anti-Nazi who referred openly and contemptuously to Hitler by the nickname Kniebolo – roughly translatable as kneel to the devil – and believed that he thrived on cult-worship. Even in 1941, at the zenith of Hitler's power, Jünger was working on an ethical peace manifesto that assumed German defeat and a Europe which had to be the homeland of the different mother countries. There were others in the George V circle who were of a like mind, among them Rolf Pauls who became Germany's first post-war ambassador to Israel.[202] A number of journalists were members of the group and it seems likely that Mariaux was among them. Although they were anti-Nazi, they were politically conservative or right wing, credentials which would have appealed to the Western Allied governments as they contemplated the future of Europe, after unconditional surrender by Germany, and the increasingly obvious aspirations of the Soviet Union to extend Communist control. They were a more attractive proposition than the likes of Otto John, whose co-conspirators were thought to have social democrat and left-wing sympathies.

Speidel returned to the Western Front in April 1944 when he was appointed chief of staff to Field Marshal Erwin Rommel, commander of Army Group B whose main task was to defend northern France against the expected Allied invasion. This was just at the time that Klop was having fruitful contact with Mariaux. Speidel, among others, was instrumental in persuading Rommel to lend his name to the conspiracy to depose Hitler, but not to assassinate him. All of them knew in advance of the 20 July bomb plot.

Rommel was apparently deeply impressed by Jünger's redrafted philosophy, first shown to Speidel three years earlier, which encompassed in its structural design a United States of Europe infused with a spirit of Christian humanism.[203] This vision was not too dissimilar from the various anti-Soviet pan-European movements which attracted MI6 support in the immediate post-war period.

Among Mariaux's pre-war contacts had been Konrad Adenauer, the mayor of Cologne until 1933 when he was forced out of office by Hitler, and the wealthy industrialist Paul Silverberg. Silverberg had been chairman of the Cologne Chamber of Commerce, a powerful figure in the coal industry and politically active in economic and union affairs. Mariaux, who edited his speeches and letters, described him as having the 'sharpest critical intelligence' among the business leaders of the period.[204] Despite having converted from Judaism to Christianity, Silverberg soon fell foul of the Nazis and fled to exile in Switzerland, renouncing his German citizenship. But he retained his loyalty to his old home town and to his friend Adenauer.

In 1945 the former mayor was reinstated and Mariaux returned to become his press spokesman. Adenauer had been imprisoned twice by the Hitler regime, narrowly escaped deportation to Eastern Europe and lost his home. Now he set about building a new political institution, the Christian Democratic Union, which sought to unite German Protestants and Catholics in an anti-Communist political party. His early efforts were made possible by Silverberg, who sent him gifts of food and medicine for his sick wife that were unavailable in post-war Germany. The Adenauer family spent holidays with Silverberg in Switzerland.[205] The CDU was an almost instant success and has been the dominant force in German politics ever since. Mariaux continued to work for Adenauer when he became Germany's first post-war Chancellor in 1949.

Clearly Mariaux could have had a valuable role to play, both in filtering British propaganda into his newspaper reports, supplying intelligence from occupied Paris or in putting Klop in touch with leaders of the German Resistance. Although his Resistance contacts did not have such a high profile within the 20 July conspiracy as Otto John's, they did continue to exert a long-term influence on Germany's future. And they fitted the profile that MI6 had already determined by 1944 was to be the foundation of its long-term strategy against Communism and the Soviet Union.

The Germans seem to have had no inkling of Mariaux's role. Under interrogation after the war, Walther Schellenberg, who replaced Canaris as head of the reformed Abwehr, described Mariaux as 'a priggish journalist who had only joined up as a collaborator in order not to have to join the Army'.[206]

When he returned to London in mid-July 1944, Klop went for an unofficial debriefing session with Liddell at Dick White's flat. He was less than complimentary about his new MI6 colleagues, painting a 'positively lamentable' picture. The head of station, Cecil Gledhill, was initially hostile, regarding Klop as a rival, and then bad-mouthing other members of the embassy staff, including the ambassador Henry Hopkinson. Klop in turn told Liddell that his male colleagues in Lisbon were very nice people but complete amateurs and pretty indiscreet. The best elements were the women. Liddell noted in his diaries:

> U35 is horrified by the way Gledhill and Charles de Salis go about their business. They do not appear to exercise any reasonable precautions and are obviously being led up the garden path in a number of cases. Attempts were made to put U35 himself in touch with all sorts of undesirable people who would have ruined all the work he was doing with Mariaux. He tactfully declined.
>
> The office itself is overlooked and no attempt is made to screen it. People can be seen from the other side of the street photographing letters and every sort of thing. The only part of the work that he seemed to think was any good was the facilities for examining air mail.[207]

Klop also voiced concern that the chief of Portuguese police was often taken into their confidence even though they knew he was receiving huge bribes from German intelligence and inevitably compromising any secrets they might tell him.

He was conscious that he risked betrayal from the dubious company he was obliged to keep and had been warned to beware of assassins sent to wipe him out. He would always stand nervously at the back of a lift, against the wall, hoping to avoid being stabbed from behind with a hypodermic needle, fretted that his food was poisoned, or that a honey-trap with a homicidal femme fatale might be set for him. [208]

But his duties in Lisbon also had a more agreeable aspect. Klop was running an attractive 22-year-old Czech agent codenamed Ecclesiastic. She was the mistress of an Abwehr officer in Lisbon, Franz Koschnik, an expert on air force technical information. MI6 set Ecclesiastic up with a job in an office staffed by RAF personnel and provided her with 'chicken feed', low-level intelligence she could use to tempt her lover into indiscretions of his own which were of use to MI6. Klop managed to have twenty-six meetings with her in the space of five months and even obtained a photograph, taken by Koschnik, of Ecclesiastic copying the supposedly secret documents for him. Guy Liddell, apparently amused by Klop's antics, suggested the photograph of Ecclesiastic would make a good frontispiece for his memoirs when he wrote himself up as a master spy. Klop found she enjoyed the game of mobilising her ample female resources against normal male instincts. Though he was very susceptible to such charms himself, he did find it necessary to reproach her that

> her appreciation of the role we are assigning to her is at present more romantic than practical and [that is] why her cohabitation with Koschnik has ... not yielded greater results so far. I made it clear that to live with the Abwehr is not quite helpful enough and that more concrete results must be achieved.[209]

He provided her with scraps of Air Ministry paper, apparently salvaged from waste paper baskets, containing disinformation about the effect of the V1 rocket attacks on London, and persuaded her to deploy her charms on another Abwehr officer, Rudolf Baumann, who failed to succumb despite 'two prolonged kissing bouts ... one of which lasted thirty-five minutes'.

Klop was frequently in touch with the head of the Abwehr's Lisbon office, Fritz Cramer, who in peacetime had been secretary of the prestigious Adlon Hotel in Berlin. He was a hearty, strongly built man with a florid, scarred face, living well beyond his means, with a mistress at the Atlantico Hotel and a fondness for beer, horses, gambling and women. Klop's task was to sow suspicion and dissent between him and his colleagues and their rivals in the German SS, by spreading black propaganda about the war crimes charges they would face when the war was over. Whether by accident or design, this led to Cramer being suspected by his superiors of working for the British and towards the end of the war he did in fact approach the Americans with a view to defecting.

One of Cramer's best agents caused continuous concern to MI5. Paul Fidrmuc, codename Ostro, kept up a steady flow of intelligence about Britain, and British activity in the Middle East. The code-breakers at Bletchley Park were able to monitor Ostro's reports as they were radioed back to Germany, and knew that most of his British information was hopelessly wide of the mark. Sometimes, though, he was too close to the truth for comfort, particularly about secret RAF operations, and his Middle East information was apparently reliable. The problem for British intelligence was not so much that a German spy appeared to be running agents in London, although that was bad enough, but that he was endangering their own carefully constructed and entirely bogus agent Juan Pujol Garcia, codename Garbo. Pujol had invented a fictional network of agents in Britain, which he used to supply the Abwehr with false information. He became the star of their network of double-cross agents; his greatest coup was to mislead the Germans about the date and place of the D-Day landings. He was awarded the British MBE and the German Iron Cross for his services. But what the Double-Cross team really did not need was a rival agent, Ostro, who was not under their control, feeding in contradictory intelligence which might lead the Germans to doubt Garbo's reliability.

MI5 and MI6 debated whether to assassinate him. Sir Stewart Menzies, head of MI6, was against the idea, on the grounds that the highly secret Enigma decrypts must never be compromised by revealing knowledge that could not have been obtained through another source. The Double-Cross committee disagreed and even after D-Day continued to press for liquidation. At one point, after Ostro revealed plans to move Canadian troops from Italy to France, they considered approaching the two supreme Allied commanders General Eisenhower and Field Marshal Alexander, to overrule 'C'.

Instead, a plan was hatched to compromise Fidrmuc in the eyes of his German paymasters by giving the impression that he was a double agent in the pay of the British. Klop must have been involved in this because the first step was to be an approach to Fidrmuc to change sides, made by Klop's agent Ecclesiastic.[210] That idea was dropped and when Fidrmuc was eventually captured, Klop and MI5 officer Joan Chenhalls were given the job of investigating him. They went to great lengths to establish how he had succeeded in running the only undetected spy ring in Britain.

The tall, powerfully built, blond agent was taken aback by Klop's announcement, at the start of questioning, that he already knew him well from his time in Lisbon. Fidrmuc had apparently been unaware of the existence of his opposite number. But he was quite unabashed about his role in feeding intelligence to the Germans. He was a German, born in the Czechoslovak Sudetenland in 1898, who had business interests in metal trading, dabbled in journalism and prided himself on his physical fitness. It was known that he obtained some of his information from Dutch airline pilots flying the London to Lisbon route. He named his best source in London as his distant relative, a Czech lawyer, Rudolf Ratschitsky, who worked in the economic department of the Czech government in exile at Princes Gate. Ratschitsky got information from his friend Air Vice-Marshal Karel Janoušek, head of the Czech air force, but his best, unwitting, contact was Maxmillian Lobkowitz, Czech ambassador in London during the war. Lobkowicz had been a member of the underground movement against the Nazis and would certainly not have provided them with information deliberately. Fidrmuc claimed that Ratschitsky managed to obtain the names of German cities that were about to be bombed by the RAF and left coded messages on the notice boards of Catholic churches around London which were collected by a Spanish Republican with a radio transmitter and relayed back to the Germans. In 1947 June Chenhalls tracked Ratschitsky down in the United States and went to interrogate him. He flatly denied the allegation and was able to demonstrate that many of the details provided by Paul Fidrmuc were incorrect. When confronted with this denial Fidrmuc stuck to his story. Klop came to the conclusion that he probably had recruited Ratschitsky before the war but had then invented his reports to win favour and admiration from his Nazi controllers.[211]

But there were still nagging doubts that they never managed to resolve. Agent Garbo's cover story had been that his reports were radioed from London by a Spanish Republican; it was a bizarre coincidence that Fidrmuc should invent the same story. Fidrmuc's supposed Middle Eastern agent, whom he named as Ahmed Isauri, a representative of the Yemeni royal family, was never traced. Fidrmuc, who was married, had indulged in the glamorous life of the secret agent, mixing with the dubious characters who gathered nightly at the El Galgo restaurant and nightclub run by Rosalinda Fox, a British informant with high-placed sources in the Spanish government. Fidrmuc even had an affair with a married MI6 agent, Denise de Lacerda, who had tipped off her employers about his activities. And whatever else he invented there was one espionage coup involving the veteran British ambassador in Portugal, Sir Ronald Campbell, which Klop and Miss Chenhalls were able to confirm. Fidrmuc told Klop how he had been sunning himself on a rock on the beach at Arrábida near Setúbal in August 1943 when he noticed two men and a woman having difficulty mooring a small boat. He went to their assistance and was amazed to recognise one of the party as the ambassador, who was with his wife and a friend. They gratefully accepted his help and Sir Ronald asked Fidrmuc to keep an eye on their clothes while the party went for a swim in the sea. While they were gone Fidrmuc went through the ambassador's pockets and found a notebook with a coded reference to a meeting with representatives of Pietro Badoglio, the newly installed Prime Minister of Italy, who had sent three generals to Portugal to negotiate a surrender. Fidrmuc tipped off the Abwehr, who refused to believe the story. But it was confirmed, in part, by Sir Ronald who had told the MI6 station chief Charles de Salis at the time about his surprise encounter with a German. Sir Ronald was no fool and it seems incredible that he would have been so careless, so it may be that Fidrmuc substantially embellished the story for reasons of self-aggrandisement. [212]

Klop was of the opinion that Fidrmuc stuck to his story because he had taken to writing spy novels and thought his own career would give his plots credibility. Guy Liddell came to the conclusion that Fidrmuc's vanity would not allow him to admit that his reports were fabricated. To do so would make life difficult for him as he attempted to rebuild a career in Germany. [213]

Fidrmuc was not the only troublesome Czech in Lisbon. They had their own intelligence branch there, run by Major Václav Pan, but once again German subversion was successful. Walther Schellenberg told Klop after the war that Fritz Cramer's greatest achievement in Lisbon had been to penetrate British intelligence through the Czechs. His mole was Pan's deputy Jean Charles Alexandre, a cover name for an Austrian agent of the Abwehr, Wilhelm Gessmann. His treachery, which included betraying a Resistance network in France, was revealed by intercepted Abwehr radio traffic and by tapping the Czechs' own communications. It was discovered by MI5 that Gessmann had handed over to Cramer a British radio intended for use by the Resistance and the Germans had used it to feed false information back to Britain. Klop briefed his Czech intelligence contact Václav Slama who set up a confrontation in London between Major Pan and their boss František Moravec. Pan tried very hard to defend his protégé and Klop was convinced that Pan and Gessmann had both been involved in some dubious business in Lisbon. Gessmann refused to come to London and was sacked but Stewart Menzies was so angered by his behaviour that he sought Foreign Office approval for a plot to lure Gessmann into fleeing Portugal on a neutral passenger liner which MI6 and the Royal Navy could intercept in international waters to arrest him. This would have been a breach of international law but fully justified, in Menzies's view, to deal with 'an enemy agent of quite extraordinary calibre'. In November 1946, after Klop completed his investigation, Guy Liddell recorded:

Gessmann was a high grade German agent whose penetration on the Allied intelligence service was extremely successful. He joined the Czech I S in Lisbon in 1940 and he was able to betray to the Germans the Czech intelligence network in Paris and Marseilles about November 1941. He was responsible for the death of many members of the French Underground. His treachery was discovered by our service and he left the Czechs but managed to gain the confidence of the Americans who employed him for some time afterwards.[214]

It would be surprising if the Americans had not been warned about Gessmann. One of Klop's jobs was liaison with FBI Special Agent Dennis A. Flinn, whose cover was as legal attaché at the US embassy. He was the first FBI man to take up a posting in Europe and unusually, given the rivalry between the two, worked simultaneously for his official boss J. Edgar Hoover and the head of the recently formed OSS, Colonel William Donovan. He reported on the Abwehr's leading personalities in Portugal and their technical capabilities – in cryptography and the use of secret inks for instance. He also played a role in identifying German agents sent to the US. Flinn went on to be director of the Office of Security at the State Department.[215]

CHAPTER 12: SCHELLENBERG

Walther Schellenberg, head of Hitler's foreign Intelligence service, was one of the biggest names in the Nazi hierarchy brought to Britain for interrogation at the end of the war. There had been intense competition between the British, Americans and Russians over who should benefit from his revelations. It fell to Klop to do the first examination. Extraordinarily, MI6 tried to block his participation, on the grounds that he was out of the country on a more important mission. What that was has never been explained. The result was that Schellenberg spent nearly all of May and early June 1945 in Sweden before being flown to Allied headquarters in Frankfurt on 17 June. Rather than allow him to be held at the American Oberursel interrogation centre, Dick White arranged for Schellenberg to be kept at a private house to await Klop's attentions. Apparently, therefore, Schellenberg had ten days of private contemplation before Klop arrived on 27 June to begin sixteen days of questioning. That rather defies belief, unless there was some compelling reason why Klop should conduct the interrogation in preference to anyone else.

Recently released documents in the United States suggest a sensational explanation. FBI Agent Frederick Ayer Jr had persuaded Schellenberg's captors to let him sit in on the interviews but was so in awe of Klop that he wrote to his director, J. Edgar Hoover:

After conferring with the Special Interrogator sent down from the War Office in London, a Mr Johnson [Klop's cover name] ...

I decided that it would be best if this were not so. Johnson is a man who has made a study of Schellenberg for the past five years and has had a penetration Agent in close contact with the man for some time. In fact he knows Schellenberg almost as well as he knows himself.[216]

The idea that Klop had someone inside Schellenberg's office in the *Sicherheitsdienst*, able to monitor his every move over a long period, would have been a hugely significant breakthrough. Yet it seems to have passed unremarked in Britain. Unlike the leaky Abwehr outfit run by Canaris, Himmler's SD and SS were a much more secure and dangerous proposition. The fact that Klop had been investigating him for the past five years means that he had been aware of his importance almost from the time of the Venlo fiasco. Human intelligence from Germany, as opposed to signals intercepts, was in short supply. Recently released files suggest that MI6 had an agent who was privy to military planning for the Eastern Front offensive in 1942 and that prior to that they had a source in Berlin who could find out how Allied plans were being leaked to the Germans. This unidentified agent was, unsurprisingly, difficult to contact so response times were inevitably slow.[217] It is believed that Polish intelligence, working alongside the British, had a source inside Hitler's headquarters who reported back via Switzerland.[218]

One clue to the identity of Klop's mole is buried in Nadia's memoir of her husband. She claims that after the war he was visited by his former secretary, who came over from Germany and told him that that Schellenberg had tried to send her to Portugal to poison him and that she had refused the mission. Who this secretary was is not explained, nor when she was Klop's secretary, nor how she came to be taking orders from Schellenberg.[219]

The SS man was the seventh child of a piano builder of modest means from Saarbrücken. He had worked his way through law school, joining the SS in 1933 partly because membership qualified him for grants to complete his education. He was an ascetic workaholic, who neither drank nor smoked, and that quickly brought him to the attention of the head of the Gestapo, Reinhard Heydrich. By 1939 Schellenberg was head of a Gestapo department of counter-intelligence, at home and abroad, and had formulated his goal of a single united German Intelligence service, with him at its head.

Whether he recognised his interrogator is not known. Answering questions, he referred to Klop by his cover name of Mr Johnson. Certainly their paths had run perilously close, if not actually crossed, in the previous six years. Schellenberg had played a leading role in the Venlo disaster; he had been behind the attempts first to flatter, then cajole, then bribe and ultimately kidnap the Duke of Windsor from Spain and he had spent some time undercover in Lisbon. He had risen under Heinrich Himmler's patronage to be SS-Brigadeführer in charge of all Nazi foreign intelligence, eclipsing the faltering Abwehr military intelligence operations of Admiral Canaris.

As Hitler prepared Operation Sea Lion, the projected invasion of Britain in 1940, Schellenberg had the job of flooding the country with secret agents and of drawing up the *Sonderfahndungliste GB* (literally Special Search List for Great Britain, inevitably called The Black Book). It was a hit list of 2,820 prominent people who were to be rounded up and handed over to the Gestapo. These included, obviously enough, Winston Churchill and other members of the War Cabinet, plus leaders of foreign governments in exile, prominent Jews, and writers including Virginia Woolf, H. G. Wells, Noël Coward and E. M. Forster, the psychologist Sigmund Freud – who had died in London in 1939 – and even the black American singer Paul Robeson. Klop and Wolfgang zu Putlitz were both on it, marked down as British agents for special attention by Schellenberg's counter-espionage department IVE4. Klop's cover name was given as 'Middleton-Peddelton'.[220]

Reinhard Heydrich had organised six *Einsatzkommando* for the major cities, terror groups whose role was to destroy all civilian resistance to the conquering German Army. Schellenberg's later knowledge of the slaughter of thousands of Jews in Eastern Europe by these groups would lead him into the dock at the Nuremberg War Crimes Trials, where he denied taking part in the planning of the atrocities and was acquitted of that particular charge. But he admitted being present when 120 members of the Czech Resistance were slaughtered by the Gestapo in the Karl Borromäeus church in Prague in May 1942.[221]

Schellenberg deluded himself in thinking that Hitler's security chief and Interior Minister, Heinrich Himmler, might be an acceptable alternative as German leader. In the last days and months of the Third Reich, Schellenberg persuaded Himmler to turn a blind eye as thousands of Jews were rescued from the concentration camps via Switzerland and Sweden. That much at least stood to his credit when Germany finally capitulated. He was by then acting as a peace emissary in Sweden with Count Bernadotte, whose humanitarian efforts on behalf of the Red Cross he had facilitated. He gave himself up to the Swedish authorities and it was through them that he agreed to return to Germany to face his inquisitors.

As FBI Agent Frederick Ayer Jr explained to Hoover, Schellenberg had been greatly surprised that he had not been brutally interrogated and shot. Instead he had a week in the safe house surrounded by books and with meals brought to him on a tray. Klop's interrogation technique did not come from the Gestapo textbook either. As Agent Ayer described it:

Johnson's approach to the man was to introduce himself and tell Schellenberg that he was proud to meet him and had studied his career as an intelligence operator and officer with great interest, and wished to talk to him as one professional to another. This manouver [sic] was eminently successful and Schellenberg has been furnishing almost too much information.[222]

Klop himself reported back to London that the first meeting 'left nothing to be desired and justified reasonable hope that complete answers will be received to all queries which Schellenberg is competent to answer'.

Klop's interrogation style continued to mirror his personality: conversational, inviting his subject to expand on subjects that fascinated him and about which he already knew a little. His opening gambit was to inquire about events in Spain and Portugal, which of course he knew well and might therefore spot very quickly whether Schellenberg was telling the truth. This must have been a relief to Schellenberg. Still only thirty-five, he was exhausted, chronically unwell and had good reason to expect and fear harsher treatment. That would come later. He responded well. In his preliminary report Klop, who was probably assisted by Patrick Milmo and Stuart Hampshire, was able to say:

> Walter Schellenberg is facing his present plight as a prisoner in Allied hands in a spirit of complete realism … The fact that Schellenberg seems to be possessed by a certain amount of good faith in Allied goodwill is due to his conviction that he has, ever since becoming conscious in 1940 that Germany had lost the war, been striving for a settlement with the Western powers and for an improvement of the lot of Allied nationals, soldiers and civilians in German hands.[223]

On 7 July it was time for Schellenberg to be taken to Britain. FBI Agent Ayer, watching him depart, wrote to Hoover:

> This whole case is regarded by the Allied Counter-Intelligence officers, and in particular by the British, as being the most important single case to come up in the history of Counter-espionage by the Allies. A thorough study is being made of the information obtained and a great deal of further interrogation will be done in London.[224]

On the journey to London an unidentified companion recorded in terms entirely redolent of Klop's imaginative prose:

> The plane which brought Schellenberg to England on a glorious summer day passed over Greater London. Schellenberg, who for the first time in his life flew *gegen Engelland*, stared spellbound down on the giant living city. His eyes sought anxiously for the wounds inflicted on the centre of the British Empire. He could find no wounds, nor even scars. Giving up the hopeless search, he whispered: 'I cannot understand – no destruction at all.'[225]

Schellenberg was taken to Camp 020 – actually not a camp at all but a rather plain Victorian country house, enclosed by a wooden fence and a double ring of barbed wire, on the edge of Ham Common woodland next to Richmond Royal Park in south-west London. Latchmere House had been the home of a wealthy marine engineer, Joshua Field, and then used during the First World War as a military hospital, treating officers for 'neurasthenia', a euphemism for shellshock. The thirty rooms that had once been used for patients were converted to cells, which were bugged. Staff lived in Nissen huts in the grounds. This had been the main interrogation centre for German agents under Lt Col. Robin 'Tin Eye' Stephens who had a reputation for uncompromising methods. Prisoners were required to stand during interrogation and there was to be 'no chivalry, no gossip, no cigarettes. Figuratively a spy in war should be at the point of a bayonet.'

Stephens supposedly forbade physical violence because it produced answers to please rather than the truth. He later faced a court martial for alleged mistreatment of Nazi prisoners in Germany and was cleared, although there was evidence that torture had been carried out by subordinates. But he was not averse to psychological pressure, including threats of execution or being subjected to the horrors of Cell 14, a mythical torture centre whose torments were planted in the minds of prisoners.

And Stephens certainly did not like Walther Schellenberg,

describing him as 'a priggish little dandy … [who] sulked peevishly until he was brought face to face with the reality of British contempt for him and his evil works'.[226]

Schellenberg later claimed at the Nuremberg Trials he had been subjected to bright lights, being hollered at, and cold water baths, adding: 'I was finished. Eight weeks in a lightless cell. I wanted to kill myself. It was not possible.'[227]

Unsurprisingly, there is no mention of this in the MI5 files, other than a slightly conscience-stricken concern that if the circumstances in which a confession had been obtained from him were made public at his trial it might be ruled inadmissible in court.[228]

It seems certain that Klop continued to be one of the interrogators because in August Schellenberg wrote, or dictated, a long statement clearing up various points that had been raised with him, including some details of the Coco Chanel operation 'for Mr Johnson'.

Some time before that, a preliminary report had been drawn up covering the period 27 June to 12 July. Once again, the conclusions have the hallmarks of Klop's florid style:

> For Schellenberg the puppet show has ended. The puppet show in which he pulled the strings and in which Grand Muftis, Balkan politicians, White Russian generals, French collaborators and other venal agents took his money and danced to the tune of the young SS General. Instead the tragedy has started. The tragedy which he foresaw and foretold early in the war but could not prevent because he and his betters, Himmler, Hitler and all the rest, lived in a world of their own making, i.e. a fool's Paradise. Their ignorance about the normal world around them, which had risen to crush the monster, staggers belief.[229]

He then recounted how Schellenberg and Himmler had discussed, apparently in all seriousness, in August 1942, a peace proposal under which Germany would give up most of its conquered territory, except parts of Poland, Czechoslovakia, Holland and Austria, in return for handing over France and the Low Countries to British rule.

The report itself, though, was extraordinarily wide-ranging. Schellenberg described his own role at Venlo; the existence of a private intelligence organisation, run by the IG Farben chemical conglomerate, which Schellenberg had used; the breaking of the *Rote Kapelle* (Red Orchestra), the Russian intelligence network in Germany and France, including the identity of high-ranking Germans who had collaborated with it; his views about the Max Klatt network which supplied him with intelligence from the Russian front; his honey-trap operations in Spain and Portugal, using girls supplied by a Berlin bar; and Himmler's Werewolf scheme to maintain an underground Nazi network after defeat and to aid the escape of its most wanted war criminals.

Schellenberg's close links with Roger Masson, head of the Swiss Intelligence service, would have been of particular interest to Klop. Masson's tactic had been to balance the very real threat of a German invasion against the value he could be as a conduit of information in both directions. He had regular contact with Schellenberg and eventually, under pressure from him, had rolled up the *Rote Drei* (Red Three), an incredibly productive, Geneva-based, Russian spy network which had penetrated the highest echelons of the German high command. Masson had known about them – indeed his own intelligence corps was suspected of being an unwitting source – and so had Britain. Klop and his old friend Nicholas Elliott, MI6 station chief in Berne, had already been investigating them and, as will be seen, had good reason to maintain their interest. Schellenberg had also been in contact with Eric Cable, the British consul in Zurich in 1943 and had put him in touch with Himmler about a possible peace deal. Hitler heard about it from Ribbentrop and vetoed it but it appears that Schellenberg kept up the contact.[230] As late as November 1944, Allen Dulles, the head of US intelligence in Switzerland, was told by the German consul Alexander von Neurath that he had been approached by Cable who wanted to be put in touch with representatives of the SS about a peace initiative in which the papal nuncio to Berne, Monsignor Phillippe Bernardini was also involved. Dulles was sceptical and telegraphed back to his HQ:

> Understand this matter caused some excitement in SS quarters in Berlin. Cable is an expansive person and has not given impression here of being particularly discreet. Difficult for me to judge whether this is his own initiative as consider unlikely he would have been used for highly confidential task. ... [In view of] possible capital Nazis could make out of this vis-a-vis Russians I have had nothing to do with it. [231]

The questioning of Schellenberg seems to have been largely forward-looking. Although it went over much old ground its purpose was to establish German methods, to identify German personalities who might still be active, and to understand the German intelligence perspective on the Soviet Union. The Cold War was already beginning. So, although Schellenberg gave a narrative account of Venlo, he did not clear up once and for all the extent to which a genuine possibility of a coup against Hitler had existed in 1939. The degree of treachery or complicity, if any, of the Duke of Windsor, was never explored and nor were the circumstances of Rudolf Hess's bizarre one-man peace mission to Britain in 1941, even though Schellenberg had the job of investigating his disappearance at the time and concluded that it had not been sanctioned by Hitler.

Maybe there was not enough time. The interrogators were under increasing pressure to hand over their star witness to the Nuremberg prosecutors and in the autumn of 1945 they were obliged to comply. Schellenberg's first appearance at the Nuremberg International Military Tribunal was as a witness against his former boss, Ernst Kaltenbrunner, who was hanged on 16 October 1946. Schellenberg then appeared in the 'Wilhelmstrasse Case', one of twenty-one defendants from different German government offices and organisations. Although acquitted of complicity in atrocities against civilians by Heydrich's special task forces, who murdered hundreds of thousands, he was found guilty of the extermination of Russian prisoners who had been forced to work as saboteurs and spies against their country, and of membership of a criminal organisation – the SS. He was eventually sentenced in 1949 to six years in prison but was already too ill to attend court. He was soon released and spent his last days receiving medical treatment in Switzerland and Italy. Coco Chanel, in voluntary exile in Switzerland to escape the opprobrium of her French countrymen for collaborating with the SS, paid his medical expenses. He died of liver and gall bladder problems in 1952.[232]

The questioning of Schellenberg about German intelligence assessments of the Soviet Union seems to have stirred something in Klop's memory. At the end of July 1945, sitting in Guy Liddell's office discussing future candidates for questioning, he asked Liddell if he knew the whereabouts of Gustav Hilger, his saviour in Russia in 1920.

Hilger had stayed in Russia and become Germany's most influential diplomat and leading Soviet strategist. When Hitler invaded in 1941 he returned to Berlin and became part of a small group of experts, known as the *Russland-Gremium*, on Foreign Minister von Ribbentrop's immediate advisory staff. He explained later:

> I spent the war years in Berlin watching with dismay the horror and
> muddle of German occupation policies in the conquered territories
> in the East … I had never believed that Russia could be defeated.
> My apprehensions turned into more concrete visions of utter defeat
> and destruction owing to our mistakes. [233]

In March 1945, Ribbentrop had suggested that Hilger should go to Stockholm to try to get in touch with the Soviet Mission to sound them out about a separate peace.

Klop's fellow interrogator Stuart Hampshire established that Hilger was being held in the American zone but it had not occurred to anyone to question him. It was only when Hampshire began trying to arrange for him to be sent to Britain that the Americans recognised the importance of their captive and refused to let him out of their clutches. It was decided that Klop should do a tour of Germany, under Dick White's direction, to capture the prevailing mood in the defeated country. White was based at Eisenhower's headquarters and involved in arranging interrogations of the major figures of the Nazi regime and investigating Hitler's last days in his Berlin bunker.

Klop was already in the process of interrogating Ernst Kaltenbrunner when White phoned on 24 August to say that the Americans were on the point of shipping Hilger back to Washington. Klop flew straight to Germany and managed to get three days' uninterrupted discussion with his old friend at Bad Oeynhausen, headquarters of the British zone of occupation.[234]

He reported back:

Gustav Hilger has probably more right than any other German today to speak with authority on German-Russian affairs during the last twenty-five years … a living encyclopaedia on Russia and Russians … the indispensable adviser of and interpreter to German Ministers and Ambassadors. Hilger's account and interpretation of events … deserve close attention. The fact that Hilger has been neither a soldier nor a member of the National Socialist Party adds to the soundness of his views.

He looks at the developments that led to Germany's downfall with the sad resignation of a man whose constant advice to his superiors: 'Do not underestimate Russian strength' was not heeded, who has lost his only son during Hitler's invasion of Russia and who, after passionate protests to his Foreign Office against the treatment reserved for Russian prisoners of war and civilians alike, knows [that] his wife, daughter and grandchildren [are] in Russian hands.[235]

Over fifteen close-typed pages Klop gave Hilger's account of the economic and military interdependence of Russia and Germany in the 1920s and 1930s, even after the advent of a Nazi regime that was ideologically totally opposed to Communism. There were eye-witness accounts of Ribbentrop's meeting with Stalin in August 1939 that led to the non-aggression treaty and Foreign Minister Molotov's return visit to Hitler, in November 1940, where it was clear the agreement was already beginning to unravel amid Russian territorial demands and Germany's increasing military prowess. Hitler had tried to divert Russia's military aspirations towards Iran and the Persian Gulf while he seized control of Western Europe. Hilger predicted that Stalin would see the destruction and subjection of Germany as vital to the Soviet Union's future security.

Hilger spent the rest of 1945 and part of 1946 at the US interrogation centre at Fort Meade, near Washington, but was returned to Germany in 1946 to help supervise the setting up of the Gehlen Organization, which eventually became the West German Intelligence service, under the command of Major General Reinhard Gehlen, Hitler's head of military intelligence on the Eastern Front. The Soviet Union were so keen to get Hilger over to their side that they held his wife, daughter and two granddaughters hostage until a successful CIA undercover operation succeeded in releasing them and bringing them to the West. Although Hilger was suspected of complicity in war crimes, through his knowledge of the death squads that operated in conquered territories in Eastern Europe, his expertise was considered invaluable and he continued to work for the CIA up until 1953 when he accepted a job in the German Foreign Office.[236]

The America-backed Gehlen, who recruited SS and German Army officers for his anti-Soviet operations, found himself in direct competition with the British-backed Office for the Protection of the Constitution led by Otto John, who had been a part of the anti-Hitler German Resistance.

Despite all this frantic activity, there is still the nagging question of what Klop was doing in early June 1945 that was so important that MI6 could not spare him to interrogate Walther Schellenberg. It is possible that Klop was deeply implicated in one of the most shameful incidents of the post-war era – the escape, via the Vatican, of a monstrous Nazi war criminal.

Ante Pavelić was the founder of the Croatian Liberation movement or *Ustashe* – meaning rebels – who were behind the assassination of the Serbian King Alexander of Yugoslavia in 1934. Pre-war they were backed by Fascist Italy and Hungary. When Germany seized control of Yugoslavia in April 1941, Pavelić was declared chief of an extended vassal state that included Bosnia-Herzegovina. He introduced a wave of ethnic cleansing against Jews, gypsies and ethnic Serbs who were terrorised, driven from their homes, raped and massacred. Some Orthodox Serbs were given the choice of conversion to Catholicism or death. Catholic clergy were implicated in the massacres and the Vatican has been accused of turning a blind eye. Estimates of the number of dead vary from four hundred thousand to one million. News of these atrocities had reached the Allies long before the end of the war and was certainly known to Marshal Tito's Communist Partisans who, with British support, had helped drive the Germans out of Yugoslavia. With the Russian Red Army advancing from the east, and the certainty that the Partisans would wreak terrible revenge, Pavelić and his Ustashe leaders decided early in May 1945 to flee westwards, taking with them the contents of the Croat Treasury and the proceeds of looted gold and valuables from their victims. US Intelligence estimates put the total of the Croat treasure at $80 million, some of which had already been transferred to Swiss bank accounts and more found its way to Spain and Argentina to facilitate the escape of Nazi war criminals. But a substantial part of it was with the Pavelić convoy which set out on 8 May from their temporary headquarters in the castle of Novi Dvor, near the Slovenian border, heading for the Austrian city of Klagenfurt with the intention of surrendering to the British and Americans.

They were still nursing the hope that they could continue the fight against Communism from there.[237]

No exact record of their surrender is available but an investigation into Nazi looted gold by President Bill Clinton's deputy Treasury Secretary Stuart Eizenstat in 1998 concluded:

> US Intelligence reports indicate that the fleeing Ustashe leaders carried at least part of the Croatian Treasury with them into the British zone of occupation in Austria where it was seized by the British authorities. The British occupation authorities in Austria acknowledged no recovery of any monetary gold or non-monetary gold originating with the puppet Croatian Ustashi regime, and no gold attributed to the Croatian regime was transferred to the Tripartite Gold Commission.[238]

Part of the basis of Eizenstat's conclusion was a five-page report by Special Agents William Gowen and Louis Caniglia of the US Army Counter Intelligence Corps, written in August 1947 but only released as a result of the 1998 Nazi War Crimes Disclosure Act in America. Quoting 'very reliable sources' they averred that when Pavelić fled into Austria he was 'protected by the British in British-guarded and requisitioned quarters for a two-week period'. Thereafter, to avoid the outcry that would be caused if their hospitality became public knowledge, Pavelić was allowed to find his own safe hideaway within the British zone of occupation in Austria. They went on to reconsider the many rumours surrounding the treasure that Pavelić and his entourage had brought out of Croatia and came down firmly on what they believed to be the version closest to the truth:

> British Lt Colonel Jonson was placed in charge of two trucks laden with the supposed property of the Catholic Church in the British zone of Austria. These two trucks, accompanied by a number of priests and the British officer, then entered Italy and went to an

unknown destination. This treasure is reputedly financing the Croat resistance movement in Yugoslavia. The resistance forces using the Croat Cross (similar to the Cross of Lorraine) as their symbol, go by the name of Krizari (Crusaders) and are under the command of former Ustashe General Boban.[239]

Jonson is not a common English name and there is no officer of that name, nor a Lt Col. Johnson, in the official British Army List for 1945-6. But we do know that Johnson was Klop's pseudonym and, according to his wife's account, he was permitted to use the rank of colonel and wear the uniform.[240] It wasn't unusual for members of the Intelligence services to be permitted a courtesy military rank: Dick White began as a major and rose to the title of brigadier during his service as a liaison officer with General Eisenhower's intelligence staff. Moreover, the timescale of mid-May to early June fits very closely with the period when MI6 was arguing that Klop was too busy to interrogate Schellenberg.

It was Helenus Milmo at MI5 headquarters who spoke to his counterparts at MI6 on 9 June, on instructions from Dick White, about arrangements for Klop to conduct the interrogation of Schellenberg. He recorded:

I undertook to put the matter up to Section V [of MI6] with the view to U35's recall from overseas for the purpose of proceeding to Frankfurt. I spoke to Major [Felix Cowgill] who felt that he could give no final decision ... but asked me to telephone Colonel White suggesting that U35 could be made available within a week to ten days, if this were acceptable to SHAEF [Supreme Headquarters, Allied Expeditionary Force]. He stated, however, that if a compromise of this kind could not be reached the Section V interest in allowing U35 to complete his present work before returning to the UK would have to give place to the major interest of ensuring that no stone is left unturned to make the exploitation of Schellenberg's case a success.[241]

Since there has never been any official British acknowledgement
of involvement in Pavelić's escape and disappearance it is
impossible to confirm Klop's involvement, if any. The extent to
which the Krizari, and their pro-Nazi predecessors in Croatia
led by Pavelić, had tacit support or even active encouragement
from the Catholic Church, in particular Archbishop Aloysius
Stepinac of Zagreb and the priest Krunoslav Draganović,
remains a hugely controversial subject. It became known that
the college and church of San Girolamo dei Croati in the Via
Tomacelli in Rome was being used by Draganovic as a holding
station for wanted Nazis escaping through the 'Ratlines' to
South America.

The two American agents remained very firmly of the view
that Britain was not only shielding Pavelić but deliberately
assisting the Krizari. This was considered to be part of a policy of
distancing Britain from the Communist President of Yugoslavia,
General Tito, despite having supported him wholeheartedly in
his guerrilla campaign against Nazi occupation of his country.

Gowen and Caniglia pointed out that Pavelić was certainly
getting help from someone and it was not the Russians or the
Americans. He was hardly likely to receive sympathy from
the French because he was held responsible for the political
assassination of the French Foreign Minister Louis Barthou along
with King Alexander of Yugoslavia before the war. And while the
Vatican might shield him they would not be able to support his
wife and family, whose whereabouts the British must surely know.
They pointed out that in August 1946 pamphlets, bearing Pavelić's
signature and pledging ceaseless warfare against the Communists,
were dropped over Croatia by aircraft apparently flying from the
British zone of Austria. They also accused Britain of an anti-
American propaganda campaign implying that the US authorities
were extraditing more people to face war crimes trials in Tito's
courts than was Britain.

Their suspicions would have been confirmed by a meeting in Rome on 11 August 1947 between Lt Col. George F. Blunda of US Army Intelligence and two British officials. An account of this meeting only emerged under US Freedom of Information rules in 2001. The British representatives were David Vere Bendall, Third Secretary at the Rome embassy, ex-Grenadier Guards, previously attached to Allied Forces HQ, Caserta, and Wing Commander Derek Hugo Verschoyle, pre-war literary editor of *The Spectator* magazine and appointed in 1946, without previous diplomatic experience, as embassy First Secretary. Blunda was in no doubt that Verschoyle was there to represent British Intelligence and both men were well aware, as was Blunda, that Pavelić was now being harboured by the Vatican.

Blunda was clearly irritated that the British had already missed an opportunity to arrest Pavelić during a search for war criminals in Genoa and acutely conscious that to arrest a man under the nominal protection of the Pope was a politically explosive operation. So he flatly refused the proposal by the two Britons that the Americans should go ahead and do the deed unaided. If there was going to be controversy then Britain could share in it, especially since he discovered that Verschoyle knew the exact location of the room within the Vatican grounds where Pavelić was holed up. He even had a report, from a month earlier, of their quarry being seen beyond the Vatican's protective cordon, walking in the Via Corso Umberto with a solitary bodyguard. His hair was cut short, he had a beauty mark on his left cheek and he was clothed in a monk's habit.

In the face of Blunda's obstinate refusal to go it alone, Mr Verschoyle proposed a splendid compromise: Italian police should carry out the arrest, without knowing exactly who their suspect was, with American and British agents on hand to ensure all went smoothly. Even better, Verschoyle agreed to devise a scheme to lure Pavelić from his lair and to make the phone call that would trigger the arrest.

As Blunda observed phlegmatically in a report to his superiors in November 1947, which he warned must not be seen by any British authorities:

To this day the British have not called on us to put this plan into effect. They have indicated that they are unable to get Pavelić out of the Vatican grounds.[242]

Pavelić remained in Italy, staying at a monastery near Castle Gandolfo, the Pope's summer palace, until November 1948 when he was smuggled away, by now disguised with a heavy beard and moustache, in an Italian merchant ship to Argentina. He continued his campaign on behalf of the Ustashe movement until his death in 1959.[243]

He remains one of the most notorious war criminals to escape retribution. He was the beneficiary of the dramatic realignment that was taking place in attitudes among British and American politicians towards the Communist menace that had preoccupied them before Hitler's rise to power. Behind the scenes, Allied Intelligence services were forging new alliances and re-establishing old ones in anticipation of that realignment. Pavelić had been smart enough to recognise that trend and as early as October 1944 had sent an emissary to Allied Command in Caserta in southern Italy pleading that Croatia could only exist with the support of Great Britain.[244]

Klop would have a part to play later in MI6's construction of a Cold War apparatus in Eastern Europe, particularly through his connections with the Czech secret service.

CHAPTER 13: MAX KLATT

The mystery of Max Klatt tested some of Britain's finest minds and found no convincing answer. Among those puzzling over its complexity were Gilbert Ryle, Waynflete Professor of Metaphysical Philosophy at Oxford University, the historian Hugh Trevor-Roper who officially investigated and recorded *The Last Days of Hitler*, and Klop Ustinov.

Professor Ryle, who had been recalled from Oxford in February 1946 to continue his wartime MI6 duties, teamed up with Klop to conduct the interrogations. They made an unlikely combination: the tall, slim scholar and the short, pugnacious spy. Ryle had taught himself German well enough to read the major philosophers in their own language but preferred to conduct the interviews in English with Klop adopting the more neutral role of interpreter, usually purporting to be a born and bred Englishman using his usual pseudonym of 'Mr Johnson' rather than giving away his original German nationality.

The existence of Max Klatt had been known to British intelligence since 1941, thanks once again to the cryptographers at Bletchley Park. In June that year, they began to decipher radio traffic picked up between the Klatt organisation in the Bulgarian capital of Sofia and the Vienna office of German military intelligence, the Abwehr.

It was immediately clear that this was a major intelligence asset for the German Army. Daily reports flowed in from all over the Soviet Union and British operations in the Middle East and

North Africa. By the end of the war Bletchley had dealt with more than 5,000 Klatt communications. Not only did they appear to come from many locations, they were extraordinarily up-to-date, sometimes reporting events on the day they happened. That implied that reports must be transmitted by radio yet the listeners could find no evidence of incoming radio messages from agents in the field to the collator at the centre of the web in Sofia. There was the additional mystery of why the network was based in Sofia, transmitting information huge distances, only to relay it back as a package to Vienna and then back to Berlin.[245]

The traffic was split into two main groups: Max and Moritz. Max appeared to have agents everywhere from Leningrad, 1,300 miles to the north, down to Batumi on the eastern edge of the Black Sea, on through Azerbaijan to the Iranian capital, Tehran, and then on to Baghdad in Iraq, 1,300 miles to the south. Initially MI5 and MI6 were more concerned with Moritz, whose sphere of operations extended from Syria and Palestine down through Egypt into Libya.[246] It appeared that the Germans had a mole inside General Bernard Montgomery's Eighth Army as he sought to turn the tide against the Panzer divisions of Field Marshal Erwin Rommel in the Western Desert.

Gradually the analysts came to the conclusion that the Moritz material was low-grade intelligence, often inaccurate and capable of being compiled by any well-informed observer.

The Max traffic, however, gave the appearance of being genuine, detailed and immensely valuable to the German high command. It provided information about shipping convoys and troop movements, planned offensives and situation reports from the siege of Stalingrad. With some trepidation, the Joint Signals Intelligence Committee, with representatives from MI5, MI6 and GC&CS (the Government Code and Cipher School) decided to alert the Russians to what looked like a horrendous security failure on their part. Their representative in Moscow, Cecil Barclay – Sir Robert Vansittart's stepson – was authorised to give a guarded account of the intercepts. This carried the risk that the Klatt operation would quickly realise the Russians had been tipped off. The codebreakers were not about to share the secret of Enigma, the German encryption method that they had broken, with their Communist allies. They were not to know that Russia's own double agents, Kim Philby and Anthony Blunt, were assiduously filing every detail back to Moscow anyway.

Additionally, a suspicion was forming in the minds of some in MI5 and MI6 that what they were seeing might be a huge deception operation by the Russians, deliberately feeding false intelligence, laced into genuine information, back to Germany. Britain was already doing the same thing. Cecil Barclay got a surprising response: bitter complaints that the British had been holding out on their allies. More surprising still, nothing happened. The Klatt operation carried on as before; apparently the Russians had done nothing to plug the leaks.

When President Yeltsin ordered the partial release of Russian Intelligence Service archives in the early 1990s it emerged that the NKVD and the counter-intelligence service Smersh had investigated Klatt but had not produced a final report until 1947. They concluded that the Klatt reports contained only 8 per cent genuine intelligence, that the agent names were fictional and that no radio network existed. They did not explain where the genuine intelligence had come from.[247]

Nevertheless, at the time the British concluded that the Klatt operation was genuine. This belief was fuelled by interrogation of captured German agents, in particular Mirko Rot, a Yugoslav Jew whose parents were among those massacred by the Hungarians in Novi Sad in 1942. He and his wife had narrowly escaped the same fate and he had trained as a German agent with the deliberate intention of getting sent undercover to an Allied country where he could defect. His opportunity came when he was posted to Lisbon and made contact with the First Secretary in the British embassy, Peter Garran. He was able to identify some of the Klatt agents, among them Willi Goetz, who was based in Turkey, and Elie Haggar, the 23-year-old son of an Egyptian policeman. Haggar had been recruited while studying chemistry at university in occupied France and was tracked by MI5 as he made his way home via Sofia, where he was briefed by the Klatt team. He was intercepted by the British in Palestine and interned. But the Moritz traffic continued. MI5 suspected that it might be the work of the correspondent of Tass, the Russian news agency, attached to the British forces.

More significantly, Mirko Rot gave MI5 Klatt's real name: Richard Kauder. He had met Kauder's mother, visited his flat at 15 Skobelev Boulevard, and knew about his mistresses in Sofia and Budapest. Klatt managed to operate independently of the local Abwehr office, which treated him with suspicion. Instead he made himself the most valuable supplier of intelligence to the Abwehr in Vienna. Rot was aware that the Klatt signals were highly valued. The Stalingrad reports had been of enormous help to the air force and led to the Russians suffering great losses. Rot also revealed that one channel of communication was a White Russian – someone who would be willing to see Germany triumph in his homeland to rid it of the scourge of communism.[248]

He identified this source as General Anton Turkul and was later able to describe how, in July 1943, Kauder had personally flown to Rome, accompanied by Turkul's head of intelligence Ira Lang, to persuade Turkul to flee to Budapest before the Allies invaded Italy.

Klop was briefed at an early stage on the Rot revelations so that he could run them past Agent Harlequin – the German Major Richard Wurmann – whom he had interrogated at his country home in Gloucestershire and who was now conveniently located in a neighbouring flat in Chelsea Cloisters. Wurmann could not help but Klop kept in close touch with developments and sought the help of his old friend Eugen Sabline for background on General Turkul.

Turkul, born in 1892 in Odessa in the Ukraine, was the son of an engineer and had enlisted as a private in the Imperial

Russian Army at the outbreak of the First World War, rising to the rank of captain. Promotion came even more rapidly with the 1917 Bolshevik Revolution. Turkul joined the White Russian resistance army in Poland and so distinguished himself that he was appointed general of an infantry division. When it became clear that the rebels were doomed to fail, Turkul, like 160,000 of his countrymen, fled to Turkey. As they then dispersed around Europe during the 1920s, he had eked out a living as a clerk in a sugar factory in Serbia, spent some time in Sofia and then become part of the exile community in Paris. He struggled to make ends meet, running a petrol station and a restaurant and taking in lodgers. He remained active in the many anti-Communist movements, wrote a book about his military experiences and, as he later confessed, was paid money by the Japanese – who were in constant conflict with the Soviets in the East – to infiltrate anti-Communist agitators back into Russia.[249]

All of this made some sense. Here was a right-wing White Russian intelligence organisation with extensive contacts still inside the Soviet Union. Their concern was not to rid Europe of Adolf Hitler; it was to rid Russia of Joseph Stalin, almost at any price. The opportunity to test this theory came with end of the war and the arrest of Kauder, Turkul and Ira Lang.

On 24 May 1945, Kauder was arrested by the Americans in their control zone in Vienna and the remains of his network were rolled up by the simple expedient of sending out a coded message to them in Kauder's name summoning them to a meeting. As they arrived they were arrested. British intelligence regarded him as a priority target but for more than a year they were prevented by the Americans from seeing him.

Kauder was questioned at length at the American interrogation centre in Salzburg. The master spy was only 5ft 6in. tall and weighed nearly 13 stone (82 kilos); he was stout, slow-moving, with a round, friendly face and smooth grey hair. He was Jewish by birth but had converted with his parents to Roman Catholicism under the pressure of rampant anti-Semitism in turn-of-the-century Vienna. His motivations for working for the Nazis were thought to be money and fear. He was paid large sums of money to meet the expenses of his supposed agent network but he still faced discrimination because of his background. At one point the Abwehr were forced to stop using him because of an order from Hitler that they should not employ non-Aryans. Kauder's mother was living in Vienna at the outbreak of war and he was anxious that she should be protected from persecution. His father, who had been a medical officer in the Austro-Hungarian Imperial Army, was dead.

There were plans to bring him to London but in March 1946 he attempted suicide and it was decided that he was not in a fit state to travel. It was July before Gilbert Ryle was able to see him in Salzburg but by then the Americans had provided a full background, running to more than seventy pages and listing all his Abwehr contacts and code names of his agents.

When Gilbert Ryle saw Richard Kauder he quickly came to the conclusion that the earlier suspicion that the Klatt organisation was a Soviet double-cross had been well founded. The key was Ira Lang, Turkul's intelligence chief. It became clear that he controlled virtually all the incoming traffic for the Klatt organisation and was extremely secretive about his sources. Lang was supposedly the son of a Czech father and a Russian mother and had grown up in Krasnodar in southern Russia, trained for the military at cavalry school but after the revolution had fought on the White Russian side under General Anton Denikin. Thereafter he had studied law in Prague, never qualified but worked for a Hungarian law firm. He had been jailed in Budapest for spreading anti-government propaganda and that was where he met Kauder, who was also briefly in jail because of irregularities in his travel documents. Lang led Kauder to believe that his intelligence sources were White Russians who had infiltrated the Soviet military command.

Ryle found it incredible that this network could have operated from 1941 to 1945, filing daily reports, without the Russians discovering it. And since he knew that the Russians had been told about Klatt, it was even more incredible that they took no action to close him down. He noted, too, that Turkul and Lang, who had not been under arrest in Salzburg in the immediate post-war period, seemed quite unconcerned that the Russians might try to kidnap them to answer for their duplicity. Yet the Russians had attempted to snatch Kauder from under the noses of the Americans and when that failed they tried to capture his mistress and hold her hostage. That too was thwarted. Ryle concluded that both Turkul and Lang knew they were safe because they had been working for the NKVD, the Russian secret police, forerunner of the KGB. He drew attention to the fact that Turkul had been expelled from France in 1938 after being implicated in the kidnap and disappearance of the White Russian leader in Paris, General Evgeni Miller. British intelligence had also been told, pre-war, by the Soviet defector Walter Krivitsky, that it was NKVD policy to infiltrate the rebel White Russian movement and control it from within.

Ryle concluded that far from running a network, Lang was being run by the NKVD. There had not been any two-way radio traffic, just a blind feed – a broadcast which Lang could pick up on any radio set and decode before recasting it in a series of 'headlines' to Richard Kauder who then recreated it as text to give to the Germans. Ryle suspected that the broadcast was powerful enough to be received by General Turkul in his Rome headquarters, and that Turkul had been selling it on to Mussolini, thereby doubling the income which kept him and his 'Anti-Communist Union' afloat.

That would explain why Kauder and Lang had to rescue Turkul from Rome before Mussolini was deposed. They feared that the whole operation would be exposed. Ryle was not convinced that the NKVD was deliberately feeding the Germans disinformation. He thought their sole objective was to control Turkul and through him all anti-Communist organisations. Turkul admitted, under questioning, that he had set out to undermine rival White Russian groups.

This was how Ryle explained his scenario:

It was no part of the concern of the NKVD to assist Russian generals to win battles or campaigns. Its business was to penetrate and tamper with anti-Communist organisations. Its enemy was not the Axis powers but, *inter alia*, the White Russians. Consequently while the Max system was indeed a double cross, it was not a method of leading the Axis General Staffs astray in tactical or strategic matters; it was a method of consolidating its agent, Turkul's control over White Russian activities...

It is also quite compatible with the single-minded ruthlessness of the NKVD that it should deliberately have issued Max-reports which were likely to lead to the sinking of a Russian convoy, the bombing of a new airfield or the destruction of a Russian division. When Lang confessed to Klatt that he hated to think of the thousands of Russians whose death he had brought about, the explanation may be not that Lang was beginning to swerve from his White Russian hatred of the Soviet regime but that he deplored the price paid by Russia for the build-up that the NKVD had given to him and Turkul.[250]

Ryle's hypothesis convinced his colleagues back in London and on 28 August a small group gathered in the office of Major Tar Robertson, who had coordinated Britain's Double-Cross operation which so successfully deceived the Nazis with disinformation. Robertson and his colleague Joan Chenhalls were hosts to Commander Win Scott and Sam Bossard of the OSS, the American forerunner of the CIA. They agreed that Turkul and Lang should be arrested and brought to London for questioning. Halfway through the meeting Kim Philby, head of counter-intelligence at MI6, rang to say new information was coming in from the French secret service lending credence to the idea that Klatt was a Soviet front.[251]

Turkul and Lang were to be held in Brixton prison but taken

each day for questioning at an MI5 safe house, Flat 19, Rugby Mansions, a red-brick four-storey block in Bishop King's Road, Kensington, a side street opposite the Olympia exhibition centre. It had previously been used to question Mirko Rot. Miss Chenhalls made the arrangements and explained to the housekeeper that the visitors were not prisoners, they were very important people who were visiting secretly and would be accompanied at all time by people 'who were looking after them'. Privately, she noted that the sitting room and dining room gave out on to a balcony and the guards would have to be careful that neither of their guests attempted suicide. Her biggest headache, though, was to get them ration cards so that they could be provided with food.[252]

It was agreed that Gilbert Ryle should conduct the interviews with Klop – 'Mr Johnson' – as interpreter. They would start in friendly fashion, seeking better knowledge of the Abwehr, and then turn up the heat. The interviews with Turkul took place on Thursday 19 September and the following day.

By the end of the questioning of Turkul and Ira neither man had broken down or confessed to being a Soviet agent but Ryle was confident that they had let slip enough to confirm that the Max/Moritz traffic was 'an up-to-date form of Trojan Horse'. He added:

> There is no room for doubt that the NKVD supplied Ira with military intelligence of as high veracity as could be achieved in order that he might secure from the Abwehr in return for these golden eggs the funds, the immunity from surveillance, the communications and the travel permits necessary for the prosecution of the covert-pro-Soviet operations of Turkul's organisation.[253]

Turkul had accepted under interrogation that Ira must have been foist upon him in 1940 by the NKVD. Questioned separately, Ira consistently denied the allegation, mocking it and offering to go on trial as a war criminal if they had enough evidence. The interview with him had started badly. He had a glass eye which was somehow damaged shortly after his arrival in London and the interrogators had to find a specialist who could replace it.[254] Ira's answers did nothing to illuminate the picture. He and Turkul confirmed that they had sought to undermine other White Russian groups working in Germany's interests. They attributed this to factional rivalry; Ryle put it down to NKVD instructions. He was firmly of the opinion that the principal object of the NKVD was to penetrate and control anti-Communist White Russian groups.

Klop agreed with the overall analysis but believed that there was two-way traffic, masterminded by Ira. He used the White Russians to supply the Germans with disinformation and to obtain intelligence on German responses which he could feed back to Russia. Turkul had been an insignificant figurehead who chose not to realise the obvious – that he was being used by Ira. In Klop's wonderfully mixed metaphor: 'The Trojan Horse had the head of an ostrich which it buried in the sands of the Campagna Romana.'[255]

There were other undercurrents that tended to confirm Ryle and Klop in their suspicions. According to Otto Wagner, head of the Abwehr office in Sofia, he had always regarded Klatt as a *'Nachrichtenschwindler'*, an intelligence fraud and a Soviet agent. Wagner reported that one wall of Klatt's office was covered with a map of the USSR west of the Urals, with a small light near each major city. Whenever Wagner or another Abwehr officer visited Klatt, one or more lights flashed repeatedly, whereupon Klatt would exclaim, for example: 'Ah! A report from Kiev has just come in.'[256] Wagner was unimpressed, and complained that Klatt was a Soviet plant, but he had twice been overruled by the head of the Abwehr, Admiral Canaris.

The SS General Walther Schellenberg, who replaced Canaris as head of the Abwehr, was another admirer of Klatt's network. In his memoirs he wrote:

The work of this man was really masterly. He was able to report large-scale strategic plans as well as details of troop movements ... usually two or three weeks ahead of events, so that our leaders could prepare suitable counter-measures – or, should I say, could have done so if Hitler had paid more attention to the information.[257]

Turkul also had connections with Claudius Voss, who had run a White Russian intelligence unit out of Sofia through the 1920s and 1930s. Voss, like Turkul, had been suspected of involvement in the kidnap and disappearance of the White Russian leader General Miller by agents of the NKVD. He had served in a German naval unit during the war. Post-war both Turkul and Voss had worked for the Americans in Vienna, purporting to identify Russian Communist infiltrators. And, as Klop no doubt knew, both had pre-war links to MI6. They had been recruited in the 1920s in Paris by Dick Ellis, whose brother-in-law was a White Russian. Ellis was later suspected of selling information to the Germans and the Russians.[258] Voss claimed to have carried on working for MI6 through the Gibson brothers, Alfred and Harold, who ran agents in Eastern Europe. He added that one of his men, Michael Skoblikov, had been executed in 1941 for spying for the British.[259] Not that working for the British and the Russians were mutually incompatible, as amply demonstrated by the MI6 officer overseeing Klop and Ryle's investigation – Kim Philby, KGB agent.

In October 1946, the decision to bring Turkul and Lang to London for interrogation was reported to Prime Minister Clement Attlee by the new director of MI5, Sir Percy Sillitoe.

Ostensibly, General Turkul, who was in control of many groups of genuine White Russians, was exploiting these forces in German interests. In actual fact he was controlling these groups on behalf of the Russian NKVD and betraying them to the Soviet, whenever it seemed profitable to do so. ... The case is of special interest, as it shows the total disregard of human life by the Soviet authorities when they feel that a major issue is at stake.[260]

Although the evidence that Klatt was a Russian front was mounting, it was still not conclusive and Klop was sent urgently to Switzerland to see Turkul's one-time secretary, George Leonidovitch Romanoff. This Rasputin lookalike had taken refuge in Geneva at the end of the war and entered Holy Orders. He was about to leave for a new life as a priest in Argentina. Klop was greeted in Switzerland by two old friends: the MI6 head of station Nicholas Elliott, who put him up in his apartment, and Paul Blum, Elliott's opposite number at the American Office of Strategic Studies. Klop and Blum had become friends as part of the Schellenberg interrogation team. He had already questioned Romanov and was keeping an eye on him.

Romanov had travelled all over Europe on Turkul's behalf, visiting the leading German expert on the Soviet Union, Gustav Hilger, in Berlin and the former Chancellor and wartime ambassador to Turkey, Franz von Papen. He freely admitted that his purpose was to advance the cause of White Russians through the Nazis and that was how he came to detest Ira. He denounced him to Turkul as a Soviet agent but in the ensuing power struggle it was Romanov who was forced out. He told Klop: 'Ira's main occupation was lying. Ira always lied, even when it was not necessary. He distorted everything, even lies.'

Klop, who had not expected to like Romanov, found himself warming to a man who had lived successfully for so long on his wits. By the end of the interview Klop was addressing him as '*mon père*' and Father George gave Klop a signed photo, acknowledging engagingly that he was bound to need it for secret service records. He also remarked that for a man who claimed he did not speak Russian, Klop's pronunciation of the names of people and places was remarkably fluent.[261]

Gilbert Ryle was pleased with Klop's efforts and there was a growing feeling that what they were looking at was an NKVD operation which would have continuing significance in the Cold War. Michael Serpell wrote an assessment for MI5's director general Percy Sillitoe, based in part on information provided by Wilhelm Flicke, head of the German equivalent of Bletchley Park. He had analysed the 'sensational' success of the *Rote Drei*, an NKVD 'ring of three' in Switzerland who consistently provided the Russians with accurate intelligence on German intentions on the Eastern Front. The Germans had gradually realised what was going on and a witch hunt against hundreds of their own people ensued as they tried to find the traitors. Serpell saw a direct parallel with the Klatt organisation. He believed that Klatt fed information to the Germans and used their responses to analyse their intentions and tactics. Serpell thought the fruits of their research were fed back to Moscow through the *Rote Drei*. He compared Klatt to Agent Garbo, Britain's most successful double agent who completely misled the Germans about the location of the D-Day landings. Garbo had been used in the same way: he fed information to the Germans, under British control, and his British controllers analysed the German responses for clues to their intentions. Britain had the advantage that it could track the German responses to Garbo's disinformation using the Enigma decrypts.

At the beginning of 1947 it was decided that Klop must have one more try at cracking the Klatt case. He was sent back to Camp King, the American military interrogation centre at Oberursel just north of Frankfurt and told to make 'a direct and unreserved attack on Klatt as a Soviet agent'.

He was to team up once more with the American interrogator Arnold Silver, who went on to a senior position in the CIA. Silver had already had several attempts at getting Kauder to tell the truth. He and his Hungarian mistress were under guard in a comfortable house on the camp's perimeter and appeared unaware that every room was bugged. Klatt's off-the-cuff remarks to his woman friend were often more revealing than his answers to direct questions.

Silver was not at first impressed by Klop's interrogation technique. He complained that Klop had tried to intimidate Kauder by leading him to believe that unless he told the whole truth immediately he would be handed over to the Russians. This, said Silver dismissively, made no impression on Kauder, who simply regurgitated stories he had already told. He and Klop subjected Kauder to hours of intensive questioning during which he refused to confess. Then, in a prearranged move, Klop ordered Kauder out of the room and he was marched away under armed guard, not to his mistress in their comfortable house but to a stark cell. The implication must have been clear enough. An hour later Kauder tried to hang himself. He had written a suicide note maintaining that he had told the truth and never suspected that Ira was a Soviet stooge. He was cut down and given a few hours to recover before being brought back the interrogation room. Still in a semi-coma induced by sleeping pills he had taken as part of the suicide attempt, finally he admitted that he had realised very early on that he was being fed Soviet disinformation but dare not admit it because his income would dry up and there would be terrible reprisals from the Germans. In this vulnerable state he was required to confront Ira and attempt to get him to confirm that he had been working for the Soviets all along. It didn't work, but it did serve to convince Klop and Silver that Ira was running rings round Kauder and had been for years. Klop then had another go at breaking Ira and got five different stories out of him in the space of an hour, all of which were dismissed as fiction.[262]

Silver was dismissive about Kauder's co-conspirators. He said later:

Turkul was a useless oaf who had lent his name to the Klatt network as the man who allegedly recruited sources in the USSR. He never recruited even one source … Ira Longin was an intelligent liar who could spin off sixty cover stories in as many minutes.[263]

Since there were no longer grounds to detain them, Kauder, Turkul and Ira Lang were released in mid-1947. Kauder continued to masquerade as a spymaster, offering his non-existent Soviet networks to visiting CIA men to no avail. Klop returned to London apparently full of admiration for the way Silver and his team were operating at Camp King. According to Silver, Klop told a colleague that the operation at Oberursel was the most professional intelligence and counter-intelligence interrogation centre he had ever seen.

And yet, whatever Silver's opinions really were, General Turkul continued to operate as a source of Soviet intelligence for the Americans. FBI special agents working in Germany had convinced themselves that Turkul was one of the few White Russians genuinely opposed to the Soviet regime. They complained about his arrest and interrogation, insisted he had their complete confidence, and re-employed him when he was released. Later investigation has confirmed that Turkul was supplying Mussolini, but more importantly in the longer term, he was an agent of Vatican intelligence in their behind-the-scenes determination to stem the tide of Communism. He had been involved in the 1930s in Intermarium, sponsored by MI6 among others, an organisation whose objectives included a Catholic alliance of East Europeans opposed to Communism.[264]

Post-war, the Americans attached Turkul to Reinhard Gehlen's espionage unit. Gehlen had been head of German military intelligence on the Eastern Front and a regular recipient of the Max Klatt organisation's traffic during the war. Now he was working for the Allies, recruiting many of his former comrades, in the Cold War offensive against the Soviet Union. He became effectively head of the West German Intelligence service until increasing evidence that his organisation had been penetrated by Soviet agents, including Turkul, led to his downfall in 1968.

It surely must have astonished Klop, as he observed the blunders that beset Western Intelligence services in the early stages of the Cold War, that such people continued to prosper when he had so comprehensively debunked their reputations.

CHAPTER 14: SWITZERLAND

In January 1946 Klop was in Switzerland, teaming up with his old friend Nicholas Elliott, who was MI6 head of station in Berne, to investigate Russian espionage. Elliott returned to London on leave and went to see Guy Liddell, still technically Klop's boss at MI5, to say that MI6 required Klop's services for another month because he was doing extremely useful work. Liddell was astonished to discover that MI6 had not briefed their own man on evidence that was emerging from interrogations of German intelligence officers about the extent of Soviet penetration, not only in Germany but in neutral and Allied countries. He explained to Elliott that corroboration had been obtained from a Soviet defector in Canada, Igor Gouzenko, and commented:

> This of course should really be a job for SIS but I have never been able to discover that anyone is taking an interest in following up all the various leads from the Kopkow case.[265]

Horst Kopkow was a major in the Gestapo who had investigated two Russian spy rings set up to infiltrate Germany, the *Rote Kapelle* and *Rote Drei*, but had also been responsible for the capture and death of many British agents. When he was captured his knowledge was considered so useful that he was brought to Britain and questioned at length. His interrogators produced a sixty-page report. Officially, Kopkow died of bronchopneumonia in 1948 but recent American investigations suggest that he was simply 'disappeared' by British Intelligence so that he could carry on supplying anti-Soviet information unrecognised. This investigation led to a statement by the German War Graves Commission that Kopkow had changed his name to Cordes and did not die until October 1996 in Gelsenkirchen.[266]

There was no shortage of work for Klop and new avenues kept opening for him. Agent Sloane was about to return to his native Czechoslovakia and hoped U35 might join him in Prague.[267] In February Klop told Guy Liddell that he was full of ideas of a short- and long-term kind, the details of which have been deleted from the published version of Liddell's diaries.[268] In September 1946 Dick White, presumably recalling that Klop had been brought up in Palestine, suggested using him as a cut-out man or intermediary to liaise with secret agents from the Jewish Agency. It was the time of the British Mandate when the Jewish terrorists of Irgun and the Stern gang were wreaking havoc in pursuit of the establishment of a Jewish state. The Jewish Agency pursued the same goal – and would eventually form the first government of Israel – but during the war they had established friendly links with British intelligence in combating the Nazis and this had continued once the war was over. Teddy Kollek, the future mayor of Jerusalem, was the main point of contact and by 1946 was based in London. MI5 was simultaneously suspicious, intercepting his mail and tapping his phone, and anxious for any help they could get in stemming the rising death toll from bombings and ambushes. They were particularly fearful that the terror campaign might be switched to London, with Foreign Secretary Ernest Bevin a prime target for assassination. While they were prepared to cultivate Kollek, they wanted to keep him at a distance, fearing that he might infiltrate their organisation or reveal the extent of his contacts at an embarrassing moment. Part of the bait he was offering was to give British intelligence access to the Jewish Agency's network

of spies throughout Europe and in Russia. Klop was proposed as
Kollek's contact on the grounds of his considerable experience
and maturity. As it turned out, Kollek had already struck up a
rapport with a counter-terrorist officer, Anthony Simkins, who
went on to be deputy director general of MI5.[269]

By December 1946 Klop was again discussing his future with
Guy Liddell but fretting that he might become 'an embarrassment.'
He was presumably concerned that his Russian ancestry, and
Russian wife, might make him suspect in the dawning of the Cold
War. Liddell did his best to reassure him that there was still plenty
of work and that he should continue with his interrogations and
gather new evidence of Russian methods of infiltration.

Klop returned repeatedly to Switzerland, spending weeks at
a time with Nicholas Elliott and his family, as the two of them
investigated the Russian *Rote Drei*. Elliott had been a diplomat at
the British embassy in The Hague after the declaration of war and,
as night duty officer, was the first to know of the German invasion
of Holland on 10 May 1940. He stayed on, with the British minister
Sir Nevile Bland, helping the Dutch royal family and the head
of Dutch intelligence, General van Oorschot, escape to Britain.
After his own return he joined the Intelligence Corps and was
posted to Cairo and then to neutral Turkey where he alternated
between Ankara and Istanbul. The embassy was overflowing
with intelligence officers, equally matched by their opposite
numbers from Germany and both constantly under surveillance
by the Turkish secret police. The British ambassador, Sir Hughe
Knatchbull-Hugessen, never lived down the embarrassment
caused by Agent Cicero, his valet, who photographed documents
from his safe while the ambassador was in his bath and sold them
to his German handler Ludwig Moyzisch. Despite that setback,
Elliott had scored a noteworthy success in handling the defection
of Dr Erich Vermehren, assistant to the head of the Abwehr in
Turkey, and his wife Elisabeth. They were both anti-Nazis and
Elliott found himself dealing with 'a highly strung, cultivated,

self-confident, extremely clever, logical-minded, slightly precious young German of good family'. He smuggled the couple out of Turkey in company with two other defectors. This triumph, in the summer of 1944, threw the whole German Intelligence service into confusion and led ultimately to the dismissal of the head of the Abwehr, Admiral Canaris. An internal MI6 assessment praised Elliott for handling the operation with 'consummate skill and sympathy, but with just the necessary touch of firmness'.[270] Klop had a peripheral role in the defection, monitoring the fall-out in Lisbon where Vermehren's mother worked as a journalist for German newspapers. Although every bit as much of an anti-Nazi as her son, she returned to Germany immediately when she heard of her son's defection, hoping that by doing so she would spare the rest of her family from persecution. Klop reported that there was a feeling among her friends in Portugal that Erich had behaved rashly and inconsiderately and that good Germans did not defect in times of war however much they opposed the regime.[271]

Later in his career Elliott was to be associated with two MI6 disasters. He was the duty officer who obtained authority for navy diver Buster Crabb's ill-fated attempt to spy on the warship that had brought President Khrushchev to Britain in 1956 when the Prime Minister had vetoed all spying activity. Crabb had an impressive wartime record as a diver but was a little past his prime and possibly not fit enough for this mission. He made one recce under the ship in Portsmouth harbour, looking for evidence of a new propeller design, but failed to return from a second dive and is presumed to have got into difficulties. Some of the Soviet crew reported spotting him in the water, which led to a diplomatic incident. Crabb's headless body was only found in nearby Chichester harbour a year later. And in 1963 Elliott was sent to Beirut, where he finally succeeded in getting his close friend Kim Philby to confess that he had been a Soviet agent. Incredibly, he then returned to London, allowing Philby to slip away to Moscow before he could be arrested or exposed.

But when he took over in Berne in the summer of 1945, Elliott's stock was high as he and Klop investigated a microcosm of the entire Soviet espionage network worldwide. The two men and their families had long been friends.

Elliott, a laid-back, witty character himself, gave full acknowledgement to Klop's talents as bon viveur, wit, raconteur, mimic, and linguist. He appreciated his delightful company and excellent cooking. Klop's signature dish was *rognons de veau liégoise*, veal kidneys cooked in their own fat with potatoes and juniper, which he would prepare in his tiny flat in Chelsea Cloisters and carry round to friends' homes in his father's leather top hat case.[272]

For his part Klop enjoyed the family atmosphere and made friends with the Elliott children, particularly four-year-old Claudia. Nadia and her sister made a 'klop' ragdoll for her. There is a certain irony in Klop showing affection for the Elliott children. In July of 1945 he was briefly in London, having returned from Lisbon, and accompanied Nadia to the hospital to see Peter and Isolde's first child, and their first grandchild, Tamara. He was not, according to Nadia, an enthusiastic grandparent, seeming to regard the onset of a new generation as a shock and a calamity that he had never expected to happen to him. Tamara, in hindsight, got the same impression, recalling him to be 'short and an odd character, not terribly fond of children'.

She was of the opinion that Nadia had been enormously involved in Peter's life and career, shaping his destiny, and that Klop may well have been jealous.[273] A remark of Nadia's, referring to Klop's return to London from Switzerland, in 1946, to find Peter's name in lights in West End theatre land, illustrates the point:

Klop said that he had never before felt so painfully self-conscious as when seeing his name staring at him in huge letters from all sides, but of course he was thrilled and happy for Peter. There was no doubt, Peter was becoming well known and our roles were interchanging. A few years earlier he had been my son (the son of

Nadia Benois) – now I was gradually becoming his mother (the mother of Peter Ustinov).[274]

Nadia visited Klop in Berne during that year and found little comfort there. One of the few pieces of personal memorabilia she left behind is an anguished fragment from a pocket notebook from that visit. She wrote:

> Splitting of hairs is just as dangerous as splitting the atom. What matters what the method is for killing as long as killing is regarded as a possible and sometimes a necessary action. Man is an animal first of all. The only thing which distinguishes him from other animals is his free will i.e. his ability to control instincts. If man would realise that he is nothing else than a beast he might find ways for improvement. Unfortunately man imagines that he is something quite special and therefore behaves like the lowest beast.[275]

Klop, on the other hand, was among friends; he was also assured of a welcome at the British embassy where his mentor Clifford Norton was head of mission from 1942 to 1946.

The investigation on which Klop and Nicholas Elliott now embarked into the *Rote Drei* was the most complex of Klop's entire career. Its subject matter is so full of intrigue that it continues to fascinate spy writers even now. It exercised the best minds of MI5 and MI6, the CIA and the FBI and the German Intelligence Service, who provided many of the early clues to its organisation. At its heart were two men codenamed Lucy and Dora and two women called Sissy and Sonja. None of them was Russian. Nor was their chief radio operator: Alexander Foote was British. Among the many unresolved questions is the extent to which MI6 knew the innermost workings of the *Rote Drei* at the time and how far they collaborated.

The *Rote Drei*, or Red Three, was so-called because the Germans knew the group had three radio transmitters, which they did their utmost to shut down. Wilhelm F. Flicke, the senior German cryptanalyst who worked on the case during the war, estimated that the three transmitters sent 5,500 messages to Moscow, averaging five a day, over a three-year period.[276] The Germans never succeeded in cracking completely the *Rote Drei* codes or identifying all their sources, some of whom seemed to have almost instant access to the Nazis' military plans.

But they did know that this Swiss-based operation had grown out of the much wider network they described as the *Rote Kapelle,* or Red Orchestra. Its tentacles spread across Europe and it had existed long before the outbreak of war. By 1945 the Abwehr and the SS had a good knowledge of its workings and had uncovered at least seven separate networks. Under interrogation by Klop and others, these German officers revealed the techniques and personnel of the Soviet organisation. The realisation dawned that this was an orchestra playing more than one tune. It spied on its supposed Allies every bit as much as its enemies and its soloists often responded to more than one conductor. Agents whom the Germans supposed to be theirs were not, just as agents whose loyalty to Britain went unquestioned turned out to be devoting their virtuosity to a Russian master.

The focal point of the *Rote Drei* was Sándor Radó, who used Dora as his codename. He was a Hungarian cartographer who had joined his country's Communist party and Red Army when it briefly held power under Béla Kun in 1919. In the 1920s he had run an anti-Fascist newsletter in Berlin and settled in Geneva in 1935, under Russian directions, using a map publishing business, Geopress, as cover. His work was overseen by Russia's most notorious woman agent, Red Sonja, real name Ursula Kuczynski, a Jewish refugee from Germany. Radó recalled her at their first meeting as 'a tall, slender, almost fragile looking woman in a closely fitting woollen dress. I put her age at about thirty-five. Her movements were smooth and a trifle languid.' She had learned her trade with the Russian agent Richard Sorge in China and moved from Switzerland to Britain with her English husband Leon Beurton. There she lived quietly in the Oxfordshire countryside while running the atom bomb spies Klaus Fuchs, who had been recruited by her brother Jurgen, and Melita Norwood. Her three sisters were also part of the network.

By the time Kuczynski left Switzerland, Radó's network was in full flow, mainly supplied by Rachel Dübendorfer, codename Sissy, another German-Jewish Communist, who had married and settled in Switzerland. She initially kept her best source, codenamed Lucy, secret even from Radó but he was later indentified as Rudolf Roessler, also German, who ran a publishing house in Lucerne. He had links to Büro Ha, a semi-official Swiss Intelligence service named after its director, Major Hans Hausamann.[277] For the neutral Swiss to supply a foreign intelligence network with information about an enemy was a dangerous game. It remains unclear to what extent Roessler used his contacts in Germany to brief the Swiss or vice versa.

The wartime MI6 officer and broadcaster Malcolm Muggeridge later claimed that Roessler was a friend of Foote and that some of Roessler's information had come not from Germany but from British intelligence. The theory was that Churchill was not prepared to initiate Stalin in the mysteries of the Enigma system that was enabling codebreakers at Bletchley Park to read the Germans' most secret radio messages. Apart from an unwillingness to share his prize asset, Churchill was concerned that the knowledge would leak back to the Germans who would immediately change all their codes. But in order to keep his conscience clear, Churchill is supposed to have authorised the leaking of Enigma intelligence, unsourced, via the Lucy network. The trouble was, even if that were true, Stalin didn't always believe it. Radó had radioed in a warning about the imminent German invasion of Russia in June 1941 but it went unheeded. It was only after he had been consistently proved correct in his predictions of German intentions on the Eastern Front that he gained acceptance. Muggeridge claimed to have had this theory confirmed by Alexander Foote after the war and commented:

> I found it highly appropriate that Stalin could only be persuaded to believe in the reliability of Allied Intelligence if it reached him from an undercover network on a dubious channel.[278]

Klop and Elliott's investigations were incorporated in a three-volume special report compiled by MI5 and MI6 and the CIA in 1949.[279] It summarised everything that was known about the *Rote Kapelle* and the *Rote Drei*, and included pen portraits and photographs of hundreds of agents. A chart drawn by Klop showed the links between them, including the route by which funds were transferred via Canada and New York through the Helbros Watch Company run by a Russian-born American, William Helbein. He specialised in selling Swiss watches to American troops.

The report was only declassified in Britain in 2008. It acknowledged that the Russians had agents operating in London pre-war, controlled from Paris by the *Rote Kapelle*'s two leaders, Henry Robinson and Leopold Trepper. And despite the assistance of the Soviet defector Walter Krivitsky, MI5 still could not identify who they were.

The report identified Maria Poliakova, codename Vera, as the founder of the Radó network. She had been recalled to Moscow and, while most of her family died in Stalin's purges, she had prospered and risen in the Russian Intelligence Service hierarchy so that Radó and Rachel Dübendorfer answered directly to her. When Sonja succeeded Poliakova in Switzerland she recruited Alexander Foote through the Communist Party of Great Britain headquarters in King Street, Hammersmith, and he in turn recruited Leon Beurton. They had fought together in the International Brigade against General Franco in the Spanish Civil War. The intermediary at King Street was fellow International Brigade member Fred Copeman who abandoned Communism before the outbreak of war and was awarded an OBE for his work organising London's air-raid defences. He passed his two colleagues on to Sonja's sister in London, Brigitte Lewis.

The whole operation had been jeopardised when Sonja divorced her first husband, Rudolf Hamburger, and married Leon Beurton, supposedly for purely ideological reasons. Sonja, despite her Communist credentials, continued to employ the old Kuczynski family maid from Germany, Olga Muth. She was so outraged when she discovered that Sonja's relationship with Leon was founded on passion as well as politics that she tried to turn them in to the British consulate as spies. Unfortunately the local official could not understand her limited English and ignored her. Leon was not popular with Maria Poliakova either, on account of his use of the secret radio network to try to keep in touch with his wife when she returned to England and he had to stay in Switzerland.

The report concluded that Sonja's mission had been principally concerned with sabotage operations, which were suspended on the signing of the Soviet-Nazi pact, and that Foote and Beurton had been chosen deliberately as English activists who could be disowned if caught. Even more extraordinarily, the authors thought that Sonja had ceased to be an active agent when she returned to Britain. Nothing could have been further from the truth but the investigators seem to have relied on a report by Roger Hollis of MI5 on the basis of surveillance and postal intercepts. Hollis was at the time the senior officer responsible for monitoring Communism and left-wing subversion. He later became director and had to face down suspicions that he too may have been a Soviet agent. In 1944 he wrote:

> Mrs Beurton appears to devote her time to her children and domestic affairs. She has not come to notice in any political connection, nor is there anything to show she has maintained contact with her first husband.

Months later, as a result of the Venona Project – American intercepts of Russian communications – the British atom scientist Klaus Fuchs was arrested as a Soviet spy and it emerged that Mrs Beurton, the housewife from Oxfordshire, had been his Soviet controller.

The report was remarkably circumspect about any British or American connections with the *Rote Drei*. It acknowledged that Sándor Radó had visited Britain in 1937 and may have been sent on an unspecified mission by his Soviet controllers. Yet MI5 had had a file on him and his wife, Helene Jansen, since 1929. Helene had come to notice working for the German Communist Party in Berlin and Sándor was known to be an associate of one of Germany's Communist leaders, Willi Münzenberg. Helene's two sisters, Emma and Maria, both Communist supporters, had moved to Britain and were under surveillance. Emma was married to the Communist trade unionist Ernest Woolley. MI6 also knew in 1940 that Sándor was running Geopress from Geneva.[280]

MI5 had warned the Home Office as early as April 1940 that German exiles, mostly Jewish refugees fleeing persecution, had to be regarded as potentially subversive and that there was often an overlap between German and Russian intelligence operations. Particularly suspect were supporters and sympathisers of the banned KPD, the German Communist Party.[281] Klop's Czech intelligence source, agent Sloane, wrote him a lengthy report on Ernst Meyer, a musician specialising in early English music who fled to London and was a founder member of the *Freie Deutsche Kulturbund*, a cultural haven for musicians, artists and writers but strongly suspected of being a Communist front.[282] Another leading light was Heinz Kamnitzer who worked with the Czech refugee Peter Smollett in the wartime Ministry of Information. Kamnitzer was also connected to the Association of Scientific Workers, whose chairman was the Communist Jurgen Kuczynski, the man who recruited the atom bomb spy Klaus Fuchs to the Soviet cause.[283] Thirdly there was the artist and photographer John Heartfield, who had anglicised his name from Helmut Herzfeld and had been identified by the Soviet defector Walter Krivitsky as an agent of OGPU, the secret police whose duties included targeting Russian dissidents abroad. Surveillance of his mail revealed that in 1948 he was in contact with Helene Radó, wife of the leader of the *Rote Drei*, and her British sisters.[284]

The report had little to say about what ensued when the Swiss authorities closed down the network. In late 1943 they had arrested Foote and the other radio operators. Radó had gone into hiding. Rachel Dübendorfer and Roessler were still functioning but had no means of communicating with Moscow Centre.

It has since emerged that when the network was infiltrated by the Germans Radó made contact with MI6 and wanted to seek refuge in the British embassy but was refused permission by Moscow.[285] Instead he went into hiding and later fled to Paris. Dübendorfer also approached MI6 in Switzerland and delivered some of Roessler's intelligence reports to them, on condition that they did not reveal this to the Russians. They were passed on to London and described as 'Captain X's flimsies'. This was also the codename for reports supplied by Karel Sedlacek, an agent of the Czech Intelligence Service, who was reporting to his boss František Moravec in London. Sedlacek had been given cover and a passport as a British businessman with the name Charles Simpson.[286] According to Moravec, his man had been in touch with Roessler throughout the war and had been feeding back to London the same material that Dübendorfer and Radó sent to Moscow. Moravec in turn handed it over to Stewart Menzies at MI6. Roessler's motivation was financial rather than political.[287] According to Alexander Foote, Roessler was paid 7,000 Swiss francs a month by the *Rote Drei* for himself and his sources.

In his post-war investigation Klop concluded that Sedlacek had been a member of the *Rote Drei* and this appeared to be confirmed when Swiss police rearrested Roessler in 1953 and charged him with espionage. He admitted that he had resurrected the spy ring in 1948 at Sedlacek's request.

It is also clear that MI6 was kept fully informed by Roger Masson, head of Swiss military intelligence, about his investigation of the *Rote Drei* and the eventual arrest of some of its members. When Alexander Foote was arrested, Masson had checked with Menzies that his prisoner was not working for the British and warned Menzies that there was a general crackdown on illicit radio transmissions. As a result Menzies placed a severe restriction on the use of the MI6 transmitter in Berne.[288]

Menzies had two other sources of direct information from the Abwehr, one of them provided by its leader Admiral Wilhem Canaris, personally. When the Germans invaded Poland, Canaris arranged for a close friend, Halina Szymańska, wife of the former Polish military attaché to Berlin, to move to Berne with the idea that she should establish contact there with the British secret service and convey messages from Canaris. She travelled to meet him in France and Italy, using false papers supplied by MI6, and passed on a warning from Canaris that Hitler was about to invade the Soviet Union. She maintained contact with the deputy head of MI6 in Berne, Andrew King, who later helped her to resettle with her family in England, and acted as a go-between for the Abwehr's agent in Zurich, Vice Consul Hans Bernd Gisevius. He is also acknowledged to have been one of the most likely sources of information supplying Rudolf Roessler and the *Rote Drei*.[289]

Foote was not held by the Swiss for long and on release broke his bail conditions and fled to Paris. After the Allies had liberated France, both Foote and Radó approached the Russian military mission in Paris and agreed to return to Moscow to be debriefed about their wartime network and its eventual collapse. They were given false identities as Russian prisoners of war and in January 1945 were put on a plane taking a circuitous route to Moscow via the Middle East. En route, it seems to have dawned on Radó that he might not receive a hero's welcome and that the penalty for the *Rote Drei*'s disintegration would be execution. During a stopover in Cairo he walked into the British embassy and asked for asylum. He showed officials his bogus Russian passport in the name of Ignati Koulicher and explained that he was a Hungarian national. Interviewed by officers of SIME, British Security Intelligence Middle East, he gave a modest, understated explanation of his role as a Soviet agent in Switzerland but claimed to be in fear of his life. By now the Russians were making official inquiries as to his whereabouts and, to complicate matters further, Radó tried to commit suicide by slashing his wrists and throat with a razor blade. The Foreign Office in London advised the embassy that they had no standing in the matter and recommended that he be handed over to the Egyptian authorities. This was done on 5 February and it was only two weeks later that MI6 suddenly woke up to who he was and declared him to be a person of 'considerable interest'.[290] Yet he remained in Egyptian custody for the next five months with no apparent attempt by the British to persuade the usually compliant Egyptians to hand him over. It is tempting to see the hand of Kim Philby, head of MI6's Soviet section, behind this inactivity. When Radó eventually left in July he needed a British visa for a transit stop in Palestine. He was under Russian guard and manifestly reluctant to make the journey.[291]

This became more embarrassing for the British when Helene Radó, who was still in Paris, started asking for news of her husband and it transpired that her sisters in Britain had influential friends, among them the Labour Education Minister Ellen Wilkinson and party chairman Professor Harold Laski. MI5 was keen to bring Helene to London for interview, if she were prepared to reveal more about the *Rote Drei*, and complained bitterly that a heavy-handed interview by Section IX of MI6 in Paris – Philby's department – had convinced her to remain silent.

By that time Alexander Foote had been interrogated in Moscow by Maria Poliakova. She was by then about forty-years-old, and described by Foote as good-looking, tall, with blue-black hair, high cheekbones and 'quite good porcelain artificial teeth'. She spoke fluent English and German. Poliakova accused Radó of embezzling $50,000, feeding the Russian Intelligence Service false information and selling information to the British through one of his journalistic sources, Otto Pünter. The service was even more suspicious of Radó's disappearance in Cairo, speculating that he was being held by the British to prevent him exposing Foote as a double agent.[292] When he eventually arrived in Moscow, having been put on a plane by Egyptian security police, he remained the object of suspicion and spent the next nine years in prison, only being released after Stalin's death. In his memoirs he confirmed the suspicion that Pünter had been supplying Britain with information during the war and named his contact as Elizabeth Wiskemann, who had been acting as assistant press secretary at the legation in Berne as cover for intelligence gathering.[293] Miss Wiskemann was of German descent but her outspoken criticism of the Nazis in newspaper articles during the mid-1930s had caused Klop, with whom she was friendly, to warn her that she was causing consternation in the German embassy in London. She had been arrested by the Gestapo and expelled from Germany in 1936.

In Switzerland she was in contact with members of the German Resistance, particularly Adam von Trott du Solz, an aristocratic German lawyer who was executed for his prominent part in the 20 July plot against Hitler, and Klop's close friend Albrecht Bernstorff, whom she met clandestinely several times. She said of him:

> Albrecht was intelligent and upright and he continued to be well-informed. He suffered from the drawback that people regarded him as what they termed a lightweight; he seemed wildly indiscreet and indeed, once the Nazi Reign of Terror had begun, absurdly foolhardy ... I think that he had to some extent calculated the risks and felt it to be important that so Nordic and aristocratic a man as Albrecht Bernstorff should defy the Nazis as openly as possible; in other words I think he was careless on principle.

Like Rudolf Roessler, she had contacts in the German theatrical world who were still able to visit the theatre in Zurich, and she met Swiss and German journalists who were able to travel between the two countries. A Jewish banker with a German wife told her in the winter of 1940–41 of the liquidation of incurables and others in Germany and by the end of 1941 had reported to her the intended slaughter of Jews in the Final Solution.

She later recalled that from Christmas 1944 onwards the Russians had become more and more suspicious that the British and Americans were intending to make peace with the Germans behind their backs. The Germans had done everything possible to nurture Russian suspicion. Messages had poured into Switzerland from Nazis asserting that they were prepared to come over to the British side in order to fight with the Western Allies against the Russians. She had been personally approached by representatives of the Croat Ustashe dictator Ante Pavelić and Himmler's head of Reich security, including the Gestapo, Ernst Kaltenbrunner.[294]

After satisfying his interrogators in Moscow, Foote was briefed to undertake a new mission in South America on behalf of the KGB, instead of which he handed himself over to the British in Germany in June 1947 and later published a memoir, *Handbook for Spies*, which had been ghost-written for him by Courtenay Young of MI5. Foote confirmed that in 1943 he had put a radio request to Moscow Centre on behalf of Radó to be allowed to seek refuge in the British legation. Radó told Foote that the legation had not only agreed to give him sanctuary but said they would allow him to continue despatching intelligence to the Russians. MI6 later denied any knowledge of this arrangement. But decoded intercepts of Foote's radio messages at the time seem to partially confirm it. The German investigator Wilhelm Flicke had cracked some of his codes and his files fell into British hands after the war. A message from Moscow via Foote in October 1943 rebuked Radó for making contact with the British military attaché in Berne, Col. Henry Cartwright, and ordered him to sever all connections. A month later, after further analysis, Moscow decided that Radó was exaggerating the danger of German or Swiss intervention and instead blamed British intelligence for trying to disrupt their network.[295]

Foote claimed that the Swiss police investigators knew of links between him, an arms dealer called Gerald Chamberlain who had managed to arrange $100,000 in finance for the *Rote Drei*, and MI6's air intelligence officer in Berne, Air Commodore Freddie West. In 1947 the Swiss put other members of the *Rote Drei* on trial and a police witness, Inspector Charles Knecht, told the court that the Radó network had spied for Britain as well as Russia.[296]

More light was shed on the British connection to the *Rote Drei* by Hans Rudolf Kurz, a lawyer who joined the Swiss defence ministry in 1946 and became its deputy director. In 1972 Professor Kurz published a review of Swiss intelligence operations during the war in which he stated that Otto Pünter, one of Elizabeth Wiskemann's sources, had begun building up a private intelligence network during the Spanish Civil War and supplied both the French and the British. He remained in contact with British intelligence during the Second World War, supplying microdot copies of German documents that found their way to Britain attached to postcards and letters sent by air mail to Portugal. His greatest success was to obtain details of the German V1 and V2 rocket research at Peenemunde from an Austrian scientist who had fled to Switzerland.[297]

Constantine Fitzgibbon, an Irish-American who served in the British Army and then with US military intelligence during the war, has argued that the *Rote Drei* saved Russia from defeat at the hands of Germany in 1942. He maintains that such was the level of distrust by the Russians of intelligence emanating from Britain that the only way to convince them of its veracity was to supply it surreptitiously via the Lucy network. Fitzgibbon had been initiated into the Enigma secret at Bletchley Park as part of his intelligence training. He implies that if the Lucy network continued to operate after the war it was because it suited Britain and America for it to do so. It was a means of feeding into the Soviet machine intelligence that they would trust and not recognise as emanating from the Western Allies. This raises interesting questions about the role of Klop and Nicholas Elliott. Were they on the outside, looking in, or had they effectively infiltrated it?[298]

Klop's Cold War duties in Switzerland also covered fears of undue Communist influence within the fledgling United Nations organisation.

With the help of one of his Czech contacts, George Simunek, he kept a particular eye on the Swedish economist Gunnar Myrdal, executive secretary of the UN Economic Commission for Europe. Myrdal had been a Social Democrat MP and his country's trade minister from 1945 to 1947, when he came under fire for his close relations with the Soviet Union. He went on to win a Nobel Prize for economics. Klop also reported on Myrdal's Russian special assistant, Evgeny Chossudovsky. He came from a Jewish merchant family who had fled the Soviet Union in 1921 when their property was confiscated after the revolution. He had studied at Edinburgh University and married Rachel Sullivan, an Ulster Protestant, shortly before the outbreak of the Second World War. Some of his family had died in Auschwitz. His wife was believed by MI5 to have Communist sympathies.[299]

Klop also played a part in the defection of the Czech chargé d'affaires in Berne, Dr Ivan Glaser-Skalny, who had been President Beneš's wartime aide-de-camp. He had strong connections with Britain – his brother Erik and stepsister Mila were British subjects. He resigned early in April 1948 following the coup in which the Communist Party seized control of his country, with Soviet backing, thus heightening the tension of the Cold War. Dr Glaser-Skalny publicly announced that he refused to support a government which 'suppressed man's most sacred rights', and added: 'I could not look decent people in the face if I represented such a Government.'[300] Behind the scenes he had discussed with

Klop the possibility that most of the staff of the legation, including the minister Dr Jindrich Andrial and his wife Juliana would also defect. The prospect was particularly difficult for them because they faced leaving their children behind in Czechoslovakia. The response from the Foreign Office was distinctly offhand. They were not interested in Czech refugees and offered no encouragement to East Europeans wanting to escape their Communist regimes. The most they would do was grant temporary access to refugees who had visas for travel to the United States. Skalny was able to take advantage of this offer, married Mary Isabella Weir, daughter of Sir Cecil Weir, economic adviser to the Allied Control Commission in Germany, and then emigrated to America. His parents, Karol and Ludmilla were granted British citizenship.

It was during this period that Klop met the seventeen-year-old Elizabeth Brousson, who was working as a children's nanny for the Swiss Foreign Minister Max Petitpierre while improving her French. They sat next to each other at a dinner party hosted by the British military attaché Norman Fryer, and the incorrigible Klop, making light of a nearly forty year age difference, asked her out. She recalls:

I didn't have much of a social life and if I got invited to anything I just said yes. I was so anxious for experience outside the little island of my life. I was still very young. He was charming and all sorts of people imagined all sorts of things that weren't happening [about their relationship]. I was used as a sort of decoy. He took me to meet all sorts of peculiar people and I realised later that they must have been German or Russian spies. I was just an acceptable normal healthy English girl. People didn't know who I was. It was an excuse.

I didn't understand about spies and that sort of thing and I always had a question mark in my mind as to what was going on. A lot of the conversation was in Russian. I just looked vague and benign and enjoyed the good food when I was with him. It was

only later when I read things about Klop that I wondered whether
I was part of the set up.[301]

It was a relationship that endured, and blossomed as she became
a close lifetime friend of Nadia too. When she returned from
Switzerland, Klop found her a job with MI5. She was also a guest
at one of his intimate dinners at Chelsea Cloisters where she
drank too many cocktails and fell asleep on his bed. She awoke
after midnight to find Klop waiting patiently to serve her dinner.
Or so she thought. Later he admitted he had locked her in the
flat and gone out for a riotous dinner party with the art historian
Francis Watson and friends, returning just in time for her to
regain consciousness.[302]

CHAPTER 15: MOURA

As the Nazi threat receded, Klop and his joint masters at MI5 and MI6 became increasingly preoccupied with the menace of Soviet Communism. The investigations in Switzerland had demonstrated that the Russian Intelligence service had never allowed the immediate danger from Germany to deflect them from the wider imperative of long-term conflict with Western capitalism.

There had been an embargo on British agents spying on their Soviet allies during the war so it came as a devastating blow to discover how widely the forerunners of the KGB had infiltrated the highest levels of the British diplomatic, scientific and intelligence communities.

The shock of betrayal caught MI5, in particular, at a moment of weakness. Sir David Petrie retired as director general in 1946, well regarded by political masters and colleagues. His last act had been to fight a rearguard action against those who wanted to subsume his organisation into MI6. The new Labour government, with some justification, nursed deep suspicions of the security services in peacetime. The leaking of the Zinoviev letter, which had helped bring down the first Labour government more than twenty years earlier, still rankled. MI5 brought in an outsider, Sir Percy Sillitoe, chief constable of Glasgow, to replace Petrie. He had no real experience of intelligence work but was thought to be a safe pair of hands who would keep his agents noses out of places they had no need to be poking. For Guy Liddell, the deputy director who had appeared to be a shoo-in for the job, it was a bitter disappointment. For Dick White and Klop Ustinov it was an ominous precedent. They had previous form with Sir Percy.

On the eve of the outbreak of war one of Klop's surveillance tip-offs had led to the arrest under the Official Secrets Act of a suspected German agent. It was hardly a significant coup and caused barely a ripple at the time. William Brand, a 27-year-old electrician, was seized by police at a Perth post office in Scotland on Saturday 23 August 1939 and in a closed session of the local magistrates was accused of offering to communicate secrets that might be useful to an enemy. He was remanded in custody but by the following day needed hospital treatment and on the Monday was released 'to take a holiday'. No more was heard of the case.

Behind the scenes, Klop had warned several months earlier that the German consul in Glasgow, Werner Gregor, was a suspicious character. Like Klop, Gregor had served in the German Army in the First World War and then entered the diplomatic service. He had been shunted into a dead-end job in Glasgow after making derogatory remarks about Hitler, but Klop, for some reason, thought he was up to no good. MI5 began intercepting his mail and discovered a letter, which they traced back to Brand, purporting to pass on naval intelligence. Under questioning Brand confessed that the intelligence was entirely the product of his own imagination. The only noteworthy aspect of the case was the difficulty Dick White had encountered in getting it investigated. The Glasgow Chief Constable, then Captain Percy Sillitoe, was a personal friend of Werner Gregor and took some convincing that he could be mixed up in espionage. Gregor in due course returned to Germany, where he remained in the diplomatic service throughout the war, and in 1948 wrote to his old friend asking for a reference to help him get a job. By that time Sir Percy Sillitoe had been two years in the job of head of MI5 and duly provided Gregor with a letter confirming his anti-Nazi credentials and omitting any reference to the espionage allegation.[303]

That demoralising incident was as nothing to the furore when the atom bomb scientists Alan Nunn May and Klaus Fuchs and the diplomats Guy Burgess and Donald Maclean were exposed. Between them they had given away the secrets of nuclear weapons that granted the West a commanding military advantage over the Soviets and exposed the innermost workings of the Intelligence services and the Foreign Office. It was obvious they had not acted alone so suspicions spread like a virus among their friends and colleagues. One figure, who seemed to stand at the heart of it, innocently clutching a large gin and tonic, gossiping and flirting for all she was worth, was Klop's old friend Moura Budberg. In terms of colourful antecedents, amorous adventures, devious plots and dubious friendships, she was at least his equal.

Moura was born in the Ukraine around 1893, the daughter of Ignaty Zakrevsky, a Russian diplomat and former Attorney-General. Her sister Alexandra was great-grandmother to the British Deputy Prime Minister Nick Clegg. At the age of seventeen Moura married Johann Benckendorff, a diplomat at the Russian embassy in Berlin and a relative of the tsarist ambassador to Great Britain. When her husband was called away to fight in the First World War she returned to St Petersburg and led the life expected of a wealthy aristocrat, ingratiating herself particularly at the British embassy where she befriend the ambassador's daughter Meriel Buchanan. They would spend long weekends together on the Benckendorff estates at Yendel, in Estonia, where they would be joined by naval officers from British submarines in port at the capital Reval (now Tallinn). Among them was Captain Francis Cromie. When Meriel and her father were obliged to leave St Petersburg after the revolution a tearful Moura was the last person waving them off from the rail station platform.[304] She stayed on, as did Captain Cromie, who had been appointed naval attaché. He was killed on the steps of the embassy as he tried to obstruct members of the Cheka, the Russian security police, who were intent on breaking in to discover what Britain's secret service agents were up to. Moura knew full well what they were up to. She had begun a passionate affair with the British diplomat Robert Bruce Lockhart who was implicated in a plot to assassinate Lenin. As a result Lockhart and Moura were arrested and it was only her feminine wiles that persuaded the head of the Cheka, Felix Dzerzhinsky, and his deputy, Yakob Peters, to release her lover.

He ungratefully abandoned her, returning to his wife in Britain, although they resumed their friendship in later life. In the meantime her husband had been murdered by revolutionaries on his estate and Moura turned for consolation to the writer Maxim Gorky. She became his lover and his secretary at around the time he was running the House of Arts where Nadia and Klop used to go to dance and it is entirely conceivable that this is where they first met. It was at this time too that the British author H. G. Wells travelled to meet Gorky. Wells later recalled his first sight of Moura in Gorky's flat in 1920. She wore an old khaki British Army waterproof coat, a shabby black dress, and had a black stocking tied in her hair for decoration. He thought her magnificent, gallant and adorable:

> I fell in love with her, made love to her, and one night at my entreaty she flitted noiselessly through the crowded apartments in Gorky's flat to my embraces. I believed she loved me and I believed every word she said to me.[305]

She saw little of Wells for several years thereafter, but when they were reunited his affection for her developed into a lifelong passion which she never fully reciprocated, refusing his frequent proposals of marriage.

Moura had two children being raised by relatives on her late husband's Estonian estates. She was unable even to visit them, since she lacked the necessary travel documents, so Gorky, who was on good terms with the Communist regime, intervened with Dzerzhinsky of the Cheka to get her permission. Once there, the ever-resourceful Moura managed to make ends meet by dealing in gold and jewels on behalf of the immensely rich Urvater family, diamond dealers from Antwerp.[306] Her longer-term expedient was to marry another Estonian, Baron Nikolai Budberg, in 1922. She helped him pay his gambling debts and he enabled her to obtain a legitimate passport and travel documents which she very soon used to return to her lover, Gorky. By 1926 she and the baron had divorced and he had left to start a new life in South America. She continued to live in exile with Gorky, in Germany and Italy, but when he was persuaded to return to his native land she chose instead to migrate to Britain, setting up home with her two children and her niece Kira Engelhardt in Cadogan Square, Knightsbridge. Her affair with H. G. Wells granted her an entrée into London society and introductions that would enable her to earn a living as a literary translator and film studio adviser.

Through Wells she met other literary luminaries such as George Bernard Shaw, Somerset Maugham, Ernest Hemingway and Graham Greene. She worked with Alexander Korda on the film adaptation of Wells's novel *Things to Come*. Korda had close links to Claude Dansey, the deputy director of MI6 and Greene worked for the intelligence agency during wartime.

She settled in a flat at 68 Ennismore Gardens, Knightsbridge, where her almost nightly cocktail parties attracted a range of mainly left-leaning socialites, from the former Russian Prime Minister Alexander Kerensky to the exiled Jewish psycho-analyst Sigmund Freud, philosopher Bertrand Russell, politician and writer Harold Nicolson and the poet Robert Graves. She was a regular house guest at the home of the libidinous young MP Duff Cooper and his wife, Diana Cooper, acclaimed in the gossip columns as the most beautiful woman of the century. It was there that Moura met the pre-war Foreign Secretary Antony Eden.[307]

It had long been suspected, by writers such as Nina Berberova, who was part of the Gorky household, and by H. G. Wells, that Moura had been recruited by the Cheka as far back as her association with Robert Bruce Lockhart and that the price she paid for his freedom was to be a lifelong informant for the Soviet authorities. Berberova maintained that Moura betrayed Gorky by handing over Gorky's private archive to Stalin when the writer died.[308]

MI5's publicly available records on Moura date back to 1921 when they spotted her name while monitoring the correspondence of Prince Pierre Volkonsky. He was related to Moura's first husband and had been a leading diplomat in the tsarist regime before being jailed by the Bolsheviks. His wife, Princess Sophy, a successful surgeon, pilot and published poet, was a direct descendant of Catherine the Great. She had escaped from Russia in 1917 with the few surviving close members of the tsar's family, but returned secretly to enlist Gorky's help to get the prince released. The Volkonskys spent their impoverished exile in Paris: Princess Sophy became a taxi-driver and her daughter became a member of the Communist Party of Great Britain.[309]

Much of MI5's information about Moura came from the shipping magnate Sir Lionel Fletcher, whose Russian wife, Liuba, had previously been married to Captain William Hicks, Bruce Lockhart's right-hand man when they were all arrested in Moscow over the Lenin assassination plot. Fletcher described her as an attractive person to meet though by no means good-looking. He added:

> She is intimate with the Duff Coopers at whose house she meets, inter alia, our Foreign Secretary [Anthony Eden]. My wife warned me at the very outset that the Baroness was not really a clever woman, but she liked to be considered the best-informed woman in Europe; that she talked a great deal, knew an immense number of people, and I was advised to watch my step when talking to her. The Baroness has certainly heard things which should not have been repeated in her presence by ministers.[310]

Moura's character was further damned by the First Secretary at the French embassy in Moscow, Maurice Dayet, who assured Conrad Collier, the British air attaché, that Moura had three meetings with Stalin while in Russia to attend Gorky's funeral, and took him an accordion as a present. Many years later the Russian newspaper Pravda claimed that Moura had poisoned Gorky while working for British intelligence and many years after that a former KGB agent claimed she poisoned him on Stalin's orders; two stories that even by the standards of Moura's extraordinary life seem equally preposterous.

MI6, as usual, was playing devious games. When Moura's daughter Tania applied for a job with the Hungarian travel bureau in London in 1934 and needed security clearance, MI6 spoke up on her behalf, pointing out that MI5's head of counter-espionage, Guy Liddell, knew the family well. The manager of the travel bureau was under observation and MI5 went to considerable trouble to ensure Tania got the job; the implication being that either she, or perhaps Moura, would be a source of information about him. A year later, after Maurice Dayet's claims that Moura was 'a letter box in the Russian interest' and possibly a German agent as well, Liddell himself contacted MI6 and was reassured by Valentine Vivian, their Russian expert, that the stories were 'the result of spite and vindictiveness on the part of monarchist White Russians'.[311]

Vivian sent Liddell some notes on Moura compiled by one of his agents, probably Ernest Boyce who had been with Bruce Lockhart in Moscow in 1918 and was then appointed head of station in Helsinki and Tallinn from 1920.

During the war, the suspicions of Russian espionage continued to be voiced by Scotland Yard's Special Branch, based on surveillance which showed Moura in frequent contact with the gregarious Soviet ambassador Ivan Maisky. Yet her social circle extended to Winston Churchill and his personal assistant and propaganda minister Brendan Bracken. Duff Cooper described her as 'a tiresome old woman' who was nevertheless a prominent person in official circles.[312]

Despite the rumours, Moura was recruited at the start of the war to a secret radio propaganda unit, the Joint Broadcasting Committee, run by the former BBC director of talks, Hilda Matheson. She found herself working alongside Guy Burgess. Special Branch reports claiming that she was a Soviet agent, who had meetings with Communist agitators, led to her being disbarred from this work, yet she somehow managed to act as an adviser to the BBC on its Russian coverage. MI5 asked Klop to keep an eye on his old friend and report regularly. Within weeks he wrote a supportive note saying that Moura was highly intelligent, shared H. G. Wells's political views, and that both had been dumbfounded by the Russian pact with Hitler. It was out of the question that she would be pro-Nazi. Late in 1940 she went to work for the left-wing journalist André Labarthe on his magazine *La France Libre*, which was financed by the Intelligence services. Robert Bruce Lockhart had a hand in the appointment and required Moura to be the eyes and ears of the Foreign Office inside Labarthe's organisation.[313] He and his comrades were the driving force of a rival faction to General de Gaulle's leadership of the Free French, regarding de Gaulle as right-wing almost to the point of fascism. Among the magazine's contributors were Wells and George Bernard Shaw. Military articles were written by Stacho Shimonchek, a Pole married to Marthe Lecoutre. Among the financial backers were Cecil and Marie-Alixe Michaelis of Rycote Park, Thame, friends who lived close to Moura's daughter Tania in Oxfordshire.[314]

The rivalry between the left- and right-wing factions of the Free French led to a series of farcical confrontations which sucked in MI5 and MI6 and caused ever deepening rifts between de Gaulle and Churchill. The left's rallying point was Admiral Emile Muselier, leader of the French naval forces. Late in 1940 MI5 obtained documents from members of his staff which appeared to show that he had betrayed plans for the unsuccessful Free French raid on

Dakar in West Africa in September to the Vichy regime, puppets of the Nazis, who held the port. According to Guy Liddell of MI5, he personally took the evidence to Churchill's security adviser Desmond Morton while warning him that it was not conclusive. But on Morton's advice Churchill ordered the immediate arrest of Muselier and his entourage and intended to have Muselier executed. In the police raids that followed, two women were found in bed with their lovers. One, celebrating his birthday by sleeping with her for the first time, ended the night in police cells; the other claimed diplomatic privilege and was released. The admiral was also entertaining a lady friend, somewhere out of town, and could not be arrested until the following morning.[315] De Gaulle had also been out of town – on official business – and was outraged that the action had been taken behind his back, quickly denouncing the evidence as fake and accusing British intelligence of planting it. MI5's source, a disgruntled member of Muselier's staff, admitted soon after that he had forged the documents. Churchill was forced into a humiliating apology and MI5 had to take the blame for the precipitate arrests. That did not stop Muselier's supporters, André Labarthe, Marthe Lecoutre and Moura among them, plotting to supplant de Gaulle with their man. They had a good deal of British sympathy. Harold Nicolson recorded in his diary a dinner with Juliet Duff in December 1941 at which the guests were Moura Budberg and André Labarthe. He felt that Labarthe was a passionate and brilliant man, loved by the French people and representing their country far better than de Gaulle.[316]

Churchill's security adviser Desmond Morton, the man who had come close to getting Muselier executed at the beginning of 1941, had been paying close attention to the Muselier–Labarthe machinations, to the extent of attending a meeting at the Savoy Hotel in September 1941 where Muselier, Labarthe and others discussed how de Gaulle might remain as a figurehead while they democratised the Free French movement. Muselier had already handed de Gaulle a note to that effect. Churchill had been urging

de Gaulle for some time to agree to a ruling council and was in
favour of Muselier's move. De Gaulle was not, and effectively
scotched it. Muselier, however, did not give up and in March
1942 tried again to form a breakaway movement, once more with
support from the Labarthe faction and from the British. De Gaulle
sacked him, placed him under house arrest, and denounced him to
the British as 'morally unbalanced', accusing him of 'indulging in
drugs'.[317] The latter was no surprise to MI5 who had found opium-
smoking equipment in his flat when they arrested him.

MI5 was aware of Moura's involvement in this latest escapade
but do not seem to have thought any the worse of her for it. One
MI5 officer, Kenneth Younger, commented that there were half
a dozen women and scores of men who deserved a reprimand
for their part in the quarrel but he did not believe Moura would
deliberately do Britain harm.

Downing Street was less sanguine. Without alluding to his
own role in the previous conspiracy, Desmond Morton wrote to
MI5 director Sir David Petrie complaining about 'this appalling
woman' who was a perfect terror at intrigue in Free French affairs
and a violent enemy of de Gaulle. Lord Winster, private secretary
to the First Lord of the Admiralty, had complained to Morton
that Moura had tried to involve him in the Muselier conspiracy,
having accosted him at a dinner party. Winster remarked that
Moura was a friend of Victor Cazalet, the Conservative MP who
had fought the Bolsheviks in Siberia in 1919 and became liaison
officer, the Polish leader General Wladyslaw Sikorski, and of
Lady Ravensdale, daughter of the former Foreign Secretary Lord
Curzon. Her extraordinary range of social contacts also included
the veteran MI6 officer Sir Leonard Woolley who had run agents
throughout the Middle East during the First World War, worked
with Lawrence of Arabia and directed archaeological excavations
of the ancient Mesopotamian city of Ur.

Others, including Harold Nicolson, retained their admiration
for Muselier and Labarthe. In the space of a week in April 1942,

immediately after de Gaulle had sacked his naval commander, Nicolson lunched with Muselier and then Labarthe, whom he found brilliant and difficult to disagree with when he complained that de Gaulle was untruthful, treacherous and unbalanced yet still treated as the embodiment of France. He held further talks with Muselier in June of that year but by then de Gaulle had fully asserted his authority.

It only emerged long after the war that Labarthe's group at *La France Libre* had been working for Russian intelligence as early as 1940, at a time when the Soviet Union was still observing its peace pact with Hitler. The Venona transcripts were the result of a joint American and British project to decipher Soviet secret messages from the Second World War. Although the results started to flow in the 1950s, and were instrumental in unmasking many of the KGB's best agents, their existence was kept secret from the general public until the 1990s. Among the decoded traffic from London to Moscow in 1940 is a series of messages from an unknown agent describing his (or her) work with André Labarthe and Marthe Lecoutre. They in turn were putting together a network of agents and among the intelligence they supplied was news of the planned Dakar raid a month before it happened; details of a conversation with Churchill's private secretary; and figures for RAF aircraft production and losses. At one point Labarthe and Lecoutre proposed trying to steer de Gaulle into leftists' politics and were warned by their Soviet handler to leave de Gaulle alone and concentrate on keeping up the flow of intelligence.[318]

The novelist Rebecca West, who worked for MI6, insisted that Moura was working for the Russians while pretending to help the British, and that H. G. Wells and his family knew it. Her opinion may not have been entirely objective, since she had been H. G.'s lover, and had a son by him, before being supplanted by Moura. Her doubts about Moura's loyalty were not universal. When she applied in 1947 for British citizenship her proposers were Robert Bruce Lockhart and the former Labour Lord Chancellor Lord Jowitt.

Guy Liddell, head of counter-intelligence at MI5, took a passing interest in Moura in October 1946. Over drinks at his London club, the Travellers, he took the opportunity to ask Count Constantin Benckendorff, whose father had been Russian ambassador in London before the revolution, what he knew of Moura, 'whose true colour has always been a matter of some speculation in this office'. Benckendorff, who had remained in Russia until 1924 before settling in Britain, does not seem to have been able to enlighten him. The real irony of this inquiry, though, is that it was prompted by Guy Burgess, who had mentioned to Liddell that he often met Constantin at Moura's cocktail parties. Very soon the real question would become apparent – what was Burgess doing mixing in such company?

The suspicions intensified as the Cold War gradually engendered a kind of paranoia against all Communist sympathisers and fellow travellers. It would take decades to show how much of that paranoia was justified but at the time MI5 resorted to telephone taps, bugging devices and the bonhomie of Klop the little bedbug at Moura's soirées. They learned more than enough to cause alarm, and yet surprisingly, with hindsight, reacted not with panic but almost casual indifference.

In August 1950, at a time when questions were being asked about Guy Burgess, he was seen by Klop at one of Moura's parties in company with the publisher James MacGibbon. In a report to their legal adviser Bernard Hill, MI5 referred to the frequent accusations that Moura was a Soviet agent and made the point that while they had never been proved, it was fair to say that she was 'a dangerous woman and a born *intrigante*'. The report continued:

There is no evidence that Burgess was in any way indiscreet at this party, or that he notably exceeded the standard of conviviality common at such an occasion. On the other hand I am inclined to think that Budberg is not a desirable acquaintance for someone of his character and in his position and you may therefore like to have this note for your information.[319]

MacGibbon was already under investigation by MI5, who were certain he had been engaged in espionage for the Russians. He was another Communist recruited to the Intelligence services during the war and both he and Burgess had been stationed in New York at a time when secret telegrams were known to have been leaked. An MI5 telephone tap on the Communist Party headquarters in King Street, Hammersmith, had revealed that MacGibbon had performed such valuable service for the Russians that they had secretly rewarded him with a high military honour. A bug planted at his home produced further evidence that he was still under pressure from his Russian handler to provide further intelligence in the post-war period and that his wife Jean was begging him to drop the contact.

MI5 unleashed its best interrogator, Jim Skardon, on MacGibbon in 1950 but despite catching the suspect unawares, turning up at his home at 8:15 a.m. while MacGibbon was taking a bath, he could not extract a confession. He reported:

> During the interview he maintained a pose of carefree abandon, but he was in reality more than a little worried. However, he made no attempt to disguise his enthusiasm for Communism. Midway through the interview Mrs MacGibbon entered the room looking very much like my conception of Lady Macbeth, and in a very tense manner produced coffee for our refreshment.[320]

After Burgess and Maclean defected in 1951, Moura told Klop that Burgess had on occasions met Soviets in company with MacGibbon. She added: 'MacGibbon could tell you more about Burgess than almost any other person.' MacGibbon stayed on the suspects list and was questioned at least once more but apparently maintained his innocence.[321] His firm was suspected of being subsidised by the KGB and published Kim Philby's memoirs after he defected. It was noted that an American director of the firm had been linked to a KGB spy ring which infiltrated the US Treasury.

Shortly after the heavily censored MI5 files on MacGibbon were released in 2004, four years after his death, his friend Magnus Linklater revealed that he had made a deathbed confession.[322] It has since been claimed that among the secrets he handed over was the entire order of battle for the Normandy landings.[323]

Klop's observations also revealed Burgess's close friendship with the Russian refugee Salomea Halpern, who was considered to have pro-Soviet sympathies. She and her husband Alexander were often among Moura's guests. Alexander Halpern was a Russian-born lawyer who had been Alexander Kerensky's private secretary before the revolution and served with British Security Coordination – MI6's intelligence and propaganda arm in New York – during the war.

At the end of August 1951, Klop questioned Moura further about her knowledge of the defection of Burgess and Maclean and reported back:

> The most startling thing Moura told me was that Anthony Blunt, to whom Guy Burgess was most devoted, is a member of the Communist Party. When I said: I only know about him that he looks after the King's pictures; Moura retorted: Such things only happen in England.[324]

An unidentified senior MI5 officer issued orders that this information was not to be added to Blunt's file. A month earlier, a secret source had told MI5 that Blunt was even closer to Moura than Burgess. Blunt was questioned repeatedly over the ensuing twelve months but only confessed in 1964, in return for immunity from prosecution, after MI5 had already confirmed his guilt by the admission of one of his recruits, the American Michael Straight. He was only publicly unmasked by Prime Minister Margaret Thatcher in November 1979.

Blunt seems to have known rather more about Klop than Klop knew about Blunt. He had reported on his wartime activities to his Soviet controllers, in particular an investigation into a Czech intelligence officer named 'Brochbauer'. The investigation was done in conjunction with another of Blunt's contacts, Susan Maxwell, widow of the Tory MP Lt Col. Somerset Maxwell who had been killed in the fighting at El Alamein. She had obtained a job as a secretary at the Swedish embassy in London and kept Blunt informed of any pro-Nazi activity that went on there. Brochbauer appears to be a misspelling for Karl Bloch-Bauer who was the son of a wealthy Czech businessman who owned sugar refineries in Austria and had been one of the great patrons of the arts in the turn-of-the-century Vienna. Karl had been Swedish consul there until 1938 when he and many of his Jewish family were forced to flee, losing most of their possessions. He maintained his Swedish diplomatic connections during the war both in Paris and in London, where he joined the Czech Resistance army. There were question marks over his attempts to rescue some of the family fortune, but the most likely reason for MI5's suspicions was that he had fallen head-over-heels in love with the glamorous German film and cabaret star Rita Georg. According to Blunt he was being utterly indiscreet and using methods which were 'quite impossible'. Bloch-Bauer later married Rita and they settled in Canada. In 2006 the Bloch-Bauer family finally recovered the most precious part of their fortune – five paintings by Gustav Klimt, including two portraits of Karl's aunt Adele. The first of them later fetched a world record price for a painting of $136 million.

Blunt would have certainly known of the family. He explained to his Soviet handlers that he had not seen much of Klop since the Bloch-Bauer investigation. He had already filed a full report on him and would get an opportunity to update it when Klop's boss, Dick White, went away for a few weeks. He could, he said, always see him on personal grounds – a reference, presumably, to Klop's interest in art dealing since Blunt went on to reveal Klop's link to the Dutch art dealer and secret agent Daan Cevat.[325]

In October 1950, under Klop's insistent questioning, Moura had pledged 'to report everyone moving in her sphere whom she suspects of being a traitor to this country – actual or potential'. She duly regurgitated every piece of tittle-tattle which came her way at cocktail parties. They talked about the celebrated war photographer Lee Miller, employed at *Vogue* by Klop's friend Harry Yoxall, her Communist sympathies and relationship with the surrealist painter Roland Penrose, a friend and biographer of Picasso.

At the meeting where she denounced Blunt, Moura also passed on to Klop some gossip from the historian Philip Toynbee suggesting that Burgess and Maclean were lovers, who had sneaked away on a yachting trip in the Mediterranean, and that no Iron Curtain country was involved. A telephone tap also revealed that she was trying to contact Dick Ellis on behalf of a Russian friend, three months after Burgess disappeared. He was identified as a Russian mole within MI6 by Peter Wright when he reinvestigated the Cambridge spy ring of Blunt, Burgess, Philby, Maclean and John Cairncross twenty years later.

Klop and Moura became a kind of cocktail-hour double act, she playing the hostess and he mixing the drinks. Moura could, by all accounts, consume prodigious quantities of gin without impairing her mental faculties. She went out of her way to invite guests she thought might be of interest to Klop and enable him to tell his superiors how helpful she had been. He maintained that it was only his gallant assurance of her integrity that saved her from a Security Service grilling. The defections of Burgess and Maclean did not deter her guests from attending her salon or being indiscreet. In one week in July 1951, guests included the MI5 man Kenneth Younger, whom she described as her 'special pet', the scientist Julian Huxley, magazine editor Kingsley Martin, film director Carol Reed, author Rose Macauley, actress Vera Poliakoff, and Sir Christopher Warner, Soviet specialist and Foreign Office undersecretary, who apparently assured Moura that Burgess and Maclean had fled to escape prison for homosexual offences and not for political reasons. As an expert in anti-Soviet propaganda he presumably relished the opportunity to spread a little personal disinformation.

Confusingly, another of Moura's guests was Fred Warner, also of the Foreign Office, who had worked with Burgess when they were both in the private office of junior minister Hector McNeil and with whom he had become drinking buddies. He was regarded with deep suspicion when Burgess disappeared and took years to live down the association.

Moura was more than capable of catching Klop unawares. He attended one of her soirées in August 1951 where, apart from the usual suspects, like Communist sympathisers Alexander and Salomea Halpern, he discovered an 'old friend' George Simunek. He was a Czech diplomat who had been seconded to the United Nations in Geneva and had helped Klop arrange the defection of a fellow Czech to the West. He revealed enough of this story to his fellow guests to make Klop feel very uncomfortable.[326]

While Klop took a benign and indulgent interest in Moura, he was far less tolerant of one of her frequent party guests, fellow Russian Vera Traill. She was the daughter of a minister in the short-lived Kerensky government of 1917 who had fled to Paris after the revolution. She married Robert Traill, a committed British Communist who died fighting on the Republican side in the Spanish Civil War. Traill came from a 'respectable' British family who knew nothing of the marriage, or the birth of a daughter, until after his death when Vera came to claim her inheritance, a small annual income. They strongly suspected it had been a marriage of convenience, enabling Vera to claim British nationality. Vera latched on to Klop at one of Moura's parties, explaining that her Russian first husband had worked for Sergei Diaghilev and therefore knew Alexander Benois, Nadia's uncle. She invited herself round to drinks with Klop and Nadia. But when Klop studied a Special Branch report on Vera he found that she was associated with Roland Abbiate, a Russian secret service assassin responsible for the murder in Switzerland of Ignace Reiss in 1937. Reiss had been one of Stalin's best agents until he turned against the Russian dictator, denouncing his murderous purges and defecting to the West. What horrified Klop was that Vera Traill, despite this severe doubt about her character, had been assigned as interpreter to a more recent Russian defector, Victor Kravchenko, who had sought asylum in the United States in 1944. Shortly before Klop and Vera met, Kravchenko had launched a highly publicised libel action against a French Communist magazine and the Soviet government had despatched a host of party faithful as witnesses to try to discredit him. How had Vera been put in such a position of trust? Klop wondered. Did no one fear another assassination? MI5 appears to have been dumbfounded by the question, apparently unaware of the risk that had been taken.

Opinions about Moura's own loyalty remained divided. Her daughter, Tania Alexander, who scarcely saw her while she was growing up in Estonia but formed a closer bond after she moved to London in her late teens, says of her:

> Those who knew Moura testify at once to her courage, her charm, and her self-confidence: even her sharpest detractors do not deny her good humour, her warmth and her affection. And yet at the same time they also acknowledge the lack of scruple, the disregard for truth, the insatiable need for admiration and attention.[327]

She defended her mother against allegations that she betrayed Gorky to the secret police or that she had made some of kind of deal with the Cheka to act as their informant in return for Lockhart's freedom. Tania had visited Gorky's family shortly after he died in 1936 and met Genrikh Yagoda, who was by then head of Stalin's secret police and responsible for engineering the show trials and executions that purged the Russian hierarchy of Stalin's perceived enemies.

But it was only in 2010 that Moura's great-great-nephew, Dimitri Collingridge, discovered that the suspicions had been well founded. With the help of Colonel Igor Prelin, a former member of the KGB, he got access to secret police files from the 1930s which showed that Moura had been Yagoda's informant. Prelin told Collingridge:

As a former KGB operative I know how these things work. Of course Moura was asked to do certain things – to report about what was happening in Gorky's circle, to exert some influence over Gorky at the request of the Soviet authorities. Naturally she couldn't say no. She was compromised in connection with the Lockhart plot and could be arrested at any time. If Moura had refused she would have been denied permission to come to the USSR or she may have been prevented from leaving it and she was intent on seeing Gorky ... She was an informant for the secret service.[328]

Moura and Nadia Benois remained friends right up to Moura's death in 1974. They had already known each other for many years when Nadia asked her, in 1939, to help her translate a play by Alexander Blok from Russian into English. It helped to launch Peter Ustinov in his career as a theatre director.[329] He later gave her a walk-on part as Kiva the cook in the film version of his play Romanoff and Juliet.

Although Moura worked as a translator she was not hugely successful and often needed the help of friends to tidy up her work. So it was something of a coup in the 1950s when Nadia again turned to her for help and asked her to translate Alexandre Benois's autobiography. Moura's daughter regarded it as the most interesting and successful of the some twenty titles her mother worked on.[330]

Peter Ustinov remembered the indomitable Moura with special affection. She was, he said, a great intangible influence and when he was with her he felt 'deeply and serenely Russian.'[331]

Klop, having devoted the latter stages of his life to becoming most decidedly English, and trying to coax Moura along with him, might have found his son's spiritual association unsettling.

CHAPTER 16: DEFECTORS

One of Klop's post-war tasks was to keep an eye on Czechs in London. There had been a close relationship between British and Czech intelligence during the war and some of Klop's best contacts, including Josef Bartik and Václav Slama, chose to return home in 1945–46 to support the government of Edvard Beneš.

Beneš, who had led the Czech government in exile in London, returned as President in 1945, a position he held until 1948. He awarded Klop the Czechoslovak medal of merit, first class, and also gave a plethora of other awards, including the Order of the White Lion for Dick White, Guy Liddell and the directors of MI5 and MI6, Sir David Petrie and Sir Stewart Menzies.[332]

From 1947 Klop made a habit of spending Saturday afternoons with his old friends at the Czech Deuxieme Bureau office at 42 Wilton Crescent, Belgravia picking up the gossip on the exiles in Britain and the progress of the regime in Prague.

Czech refugees from the Nazi invasion had begun to arrive in Britain en masse in 1938–9 and been catered for by the Czech Refugee Trust, set up by Sir Walter Layton, chairman of the Liberal-leaning *News Chronicle*. It quickly became a matter of concern to MI5 that this organisation was being controlled from within by Communists, both British and exiles. They struggled to convince Sir Henry Bunbury, the retired civil servant responsible for administering the trust, that Communists were taking on positions of responsibility within the organisation with the intention of controlling it. Klop was drawn into this controversy and began working closely with Václav Slama who warned that nearly 90 per cent of the refugees taken in by the trust were socialists and Communists of German ethnic origin and therefore potential spies and infiltrators. He offered to draw up a list of the chief suspects. The director general of MI5, Sir Vernon Kell, warned the Home Office of this on at least two occasions and Klop's boss Dick White lamented:

> We estimate that we have here at least 100 Communists with long records of political activity in Central Europe in fully organised groups and still under the direct instructions of Moscow.[333]

One known Communist whose name cropped up in this connection was an American architect, Hermann Field, who married an English Communist supporter, Kate Thorneycroft. MI5 noted that he had been in Poland in 1939 when Germany and the Soviet Union both invaded under the aegis of their joint non-aggression treaty. Field had shown outstanding qualities of leadership and personal courage in bringing hundreds of refugees to the West. But he was known to have spent part of the 1930s on a collective farm in Russia and was believed to have trained as a Comintern agent for the purpose of infiltrating Western society and promulgating the Soviet creed. He was a known associate of William Koenen, the German Communist responsible for the London branch of the Comintern. His brother Noel, who shared his political convictions, worked during the war for the League of Nations in Geneva. These two brothers, and the Czech Refugee Trust, would now feature prominently in Stalin's Cold War purges of Eastern Europe.

As Poland, Hungary, Bulgaria and Romania fell increasingly under Soviet domination in the immediate post-war period, Czechoslovakia held out a glimmer of hope that an independent, reforming government, under President Beneš, might survive by negotiating a careful path between the might of the dominant power in Eastern Europe and the desire to benefit from the modernising influence of the Western Allies. Britain was anxious to see it succeed, feeling under some obligation for its abandonment of Czech interests at Munich in 1938 and the subsequent contribution that the government in exile in London and its armed forces had made to defeating Hitler. It was not to be. After elections in 1948, Communists increasingly controlled the main offices of state. Their influence, dictated by Stalin, led the country to reject American aid under the Marshall Plan. The Americans blamed the snub on the failure of President Beneš and his Foreign Minister Jan Masaryk to be sufficiently robust in their resistance to Stalin. Within weeks Masaryk died in a fall from a Foreign Ministry window; whether he committed suicide, fell accidentally, or was pushed, has never been finally established. But it marked the end of any pretence that Czechoslovakia was anything other than a Soviet satellite.[334]

Into this new regime in October 1948 stepped Noel Field, aged forty-four, British-born of an English mother and an American father. He was a committed Communist who had taken it into his head that his future lay in a career as a university lecturer in Prague. In his pursuit of this objective he would plunge his family into the nightmare world of secret police, incarceration without charge and treason trials where the verdict was inevitable and the death sentence a probability. The British-based Czech Refugee Trust would feature in the evidence as an alleged MI6 front operation.

Noel Field had worked as a senior economic adviser for the US State Department before taking a job in 1936 with the League of Nations in Geneva. When the Second World War broke out he stayed on in Switzerland as a member of the Unitarian Service Committee formed to offer relief to refugees from Nazi persecution. It was particularly active in Czechoslovakia where the Unitarian Church had many adherents. Noel Field was introduced to Allen Dulles, head of the Office of Strategic Studies in Berne, who realised that Field's refugee contacts were potential sources for US intelligence. As the war progressed, Field was also able to supply Dulles with contacts, many of them Communist sympathisers, in occupied Germany. It was never entirely clear in whose interests Field was working, Moscow's or Washington's, and in post-war years Dulles came to believe he had been duped. Equally, the Communist regimes of Eastern Europe regarded the Unitarians as a CIA front.

When the new Communist government in Prague came to carry out security checks in connection with Noel Field's application for a position at the Charles University, what they found was a man with many contacts, not only in Czechoslovakia but among members of the politburo throughout the Eastern Bloc; plus a highly suspicious association with Allen Dulles. As inquiries broadened, it became apparent that his younger brother Hermann had equally extensive contacts in Poland – pre-war he had been based in Katowice near the Czech border working for the Czech Refugee Trust.

In May 1949 Noel Field returned to Prague believing he was on the verge of getting his coveted university appointment. Instead, he simply disappeared. His German wife Herta, living in Geneva, chose not to mention this to the American authorities. In August she and Hermann went to Prague to look for him. They drew a blank and Hermann flew on to Warsaw … and vanished. Herta decided it was time to visit the US authorities in Prague. Twenty-four hours later she too had gone missing. The following year Erica Glaser Wallach, whom Noel and Herta Field treated as their daughter, also travelled behind the Iron Curtain in the hope of picking up the trail. She was neither seen nor heard of for many years.

Then the purges and the trials began. Klop's wartime contact in London, Josef Bartik, who had been promoted to the rank of general and head of Czech military intelligence in 1945, had already lost his job on the strength of forged documents.

Noel Field had been handed over by Czech security to their Hungarian counterparts. In September 1949 the trial began in Budapest of the former Foreign Minister László Rajk and accomplices. They pleaded guilty to belonging to an organisation dedicated to the overthrow of the state. They had been recruited, it was alleged, by Allen Dulles, Noel Field and British intelligence agents in Switzerland. This was the first acknowledgement that Field was in Hungarian custody. Similar trials followed in Czechoslovakia and Poland. These Communist enemies within the state were often accused of being Titoists, supporters of the Yugoslav Communist leader who had broken away from Soviet constriction. Stalin was purging potential dissenters.

MI6 did not officially exist in those days and since none of the missing individuals was British it was not too difficult for the Foreign Office to adopt the policy that serves them well so often: they sat back and awaited developments. The Americans made the obligatory inquiries about their absent citizens but did not quite raise the hullabaloo that might have been expected.

After Stalin died, on 5 March 1953, the gulags slowly began to give up their secrets. The following December, Lt Col. Józef Światło, deputy head of internal security in Poland, defected and began to reveal how the terror trials had taken place and how the Fields, and their East European friends, had been set up by the security police, including Światło himself, to satiate Stalin's lust for power and paranoia that he was being betrayed. He divulged some of the details on Radio Free Europe, the US-sponsored propaganda station whose broadcasts reached behind the Iron Curtain.

Extraordinarily, in October 1954 Hermann Field was freed from his Polish jail, given $40,000 compensation, and allowed to return to the US and his architects' practice, taking his English wife with him. While Hermann was en route, Noel and Herta Field quietly emerged from their separate prisons, were reunited, and astonished everyone by accepting the Hungarian authorities' apologetic offer of a villa on the outskirts of Budapest where they could live out their lives in a Communist sanctuary of which they apparently approved. It took another twelve months for Erica Glaser Wallach to find her way out of a Russian labour camp but she too returned to the West. Between them they offered little by way of explanation but the impression lingered that they had been part of a CIA mission which had been exposed and for which retribution had been taken. Britain was in no position to criticise: this was the era of Philby, Burgess and Maclean when any number of agents behind the Iron Curtain had been betrayed.

Klop, with his keen interest in Czech intelligence matters, must have followed it with interest. He may even have been involved but there is very little information in the public domain to address that point. It was not until twelve years after his death that a different interpretation began to be put on these events. It was argued that the whole thing had been an elaborate CIA charade, implemented by Józef Światło himself, on the instructions of Allen Dulles, who was by that time head of the CIA. Światło had been a double agent since 1948 when he had been recruited by MI6 and handed over to an American controller. The operation was codenamed Splinter Factor and its purpose was to win the Cold War by provoking antagonism between the nationalist sympathisers of the individual East European countries and the unflinching Soviet ideologues in their midst, laying the blame firmly at Stalin's door. Dulles, it was said, set out to alienate every East European country from the Soviet dictator and bring about the collapse of the Soviet Bloc from within.[335]

★

On 5 September 1945, Igor Gouzenko, aged twenty-six, a cipher clerk for the GRU – Soviet military intelligence – in Ottawa, walked into the Canadian Ministry of Justice with more than a hundred secret documents stuffed inside his shirt. Shortly afterwards he walked out again, still with the wad of paperwork bulging under his jacket, and tried his luck at the *Ottawa Journal*. He was the first important defector of the immediate post-war era. Unfortunately, nobody believed him. He had burned his bridges with his employers and had nowhere safe to go. He hid out in a neighbour's flat and it was not until the following evening, when Russian security men broke in and started ransacking his flat in search of the stolen secrets, that the Canadian authorities started to take notice. The documents soon revealed a network of agents stretching across the United States and Canada, linking back to Britain. The three countries had collaborated in the development of the atomic bomb, detonated over Hiroshima on 6 August. In particular, an Agent Alek was quickly identified as Alan Nunn May, a Cambridge-educated physicist with a long-standing association with the Communist Party, who had been working on the heavy water reactor at Chalk River, Ontario. He had handed information on the project and samples of its key uranium isotopes, U233 and U235, to his case officer, Pavel Angelov.

By 7 September news of the investigation began to filter back to Britain, straight into the hands of Kim Philby at MI6 who became the liaison point between Canada, MI6 and MI5, and the British government. Within a week Philby's Soviet controller in London, Boris Krötenschield, was able to confirm to Moscow what they must already have guessed about the extent to which their Canadian network was compromised. However, Philby was able to buy them some time, first by subtly impeding the flow of information and then by leading the chorus recommending that there should be no arrests until Nunn May returned to Britain. MI5 was initially opposed to this and the Foreign Office feared that Nunn May would realise the game was up and flee to Moscow, but Philby's view prevailed.

Among the stolen documents were the precise instructions from Moscow to the scientist laying down the procedure for establishing contact with his new Soviet handler in London. Since the documents could not be produced in court, catching the spy red-handed with a Soviet intelligence officer and possibly exposing a network in Britain was obviously an attractive option but it meant no action could be taken publicly against the ring in Canada. Philby and his masters had more time to wind up the operation and safeguard their best agents. With every day that passed Philby could tell them more about where the investigation was leading.

Nunn May was kept under observation on the plane from Canada and surveillance continued when he arrived at Prestwick at 6:15 a.m. on Monday 17 September and flew from there to Blackbushe Airport in Surrey. MI5's team of watchers were briefed to pick him up from there but they had a problem. He was not due to make contact with his new controller until 7 October at the earliest and round-the-clock surveillance over such a long period was impossible without being detected. His phone was tapped at King's College, London, where he resumed his old job as a lecturer, and at his digs, which he kept changing. He took precautions to make sure he was not followed, including jumping on to buses at the last minute and watching from the conductor's platform to see if anyone jumped on after him. He contacted hardly anyone, most days eating alone in restaurants near the college.

Nunn May's instructions from Moscow, as revealed by Gouzenko, had been that he was to attempt a clandestine meeting with his new handler at 8 p.m. on 7 October or on any date ending in seven thereafter. It was to take place opposite the British Museum, in Great Russell Street, near the junction with Museum Street. Nunn May was to approach from the direction of Tottenham Court Road and have a copy of *The Times* tucked under his left arm. The contact would come from the direction of Southampton Row, clutching a copy of *Picture Post* in his left hand, and say to Nunn May: 'What is the shortest way to The Strand?' Nunn May would reply: 'Well, come along. I am going that way.' The contact would then say: 'Best regards from Mikel.'

It was recognised from the start that there was a high risk

that he would be tipped off somehow that the ring in Canada had been broken and his own position jeopardised. It was at this point that Klop was brought in.[336] It was suggested that if Nunn May kept the rendezvous but his new handler failed to show, Klop should play the part of the Soviet handler, exchange signs and passwords with May and hope to persuade him to hand over secret documents which could then be used in evidence against him. If no documents materialised, Klop was then to warn Nunn May about what had happened in Canada and say that contact was being terminated. Nunn May would then be kept under close surveillance to see whether he tried to warn other traitors to lie low.[337]

When Guy Liddell first heard about it, talks were already going on at a high level and consequently, he complained, the whole thing was wrapped up in about four layers of cotton wool. He added: 'Most people have not realised quite that an atomic bomb has been dropped in Japan and that the world now knows quite a lot about it.'[338]

One of the first steps the security services had taken was to deny Nunn May access to his own work notebooks, recently shipped back from Canada, or any other reports relating to atomic weapons. Now Liddell proposed a dramatic reversal of this policy. Nunn May should be fed a couple of secret but relatively innocuous papers in the hope that he would be tempted to hand them over to his new controller at the first rendezvous. Sir Wallace Akers, director of the Tube Alloys project, as Britain's end of atomic research was known, was briefed to carry out the plan. Nunn May then confounded them by refusing to accept the papers on the grounds that he was not currently part of the research team and had no need of them.

As the date of the first rendezvous approached, Commander Len Burt of the Metropolitan Police Special Branch was brought in. He was on secondment to MI5 and, unlike their officers, he had powers of arrest. Burt was to watch over the rendezvous from the first floor of the Museum Tavern and use the pub telephone to call a telephone kiosk in Great Russell Street where one of the MI5 agents on the ground could take orders if they were to move in and grab either Nunn May, his contact, or both. Tommy Harris of MI5 was to drive around the museum area on the lookout for Russian secret service agents who might also be carrying out surveillance.

MI5 felt it had a number of options, none of them ideal: if the rendezvous took place and officers were sure secret papers had been exchanged they could arrest Nunn May and his contact; or they could let Nunn May walk away but remain under surveillance and arrest the Soviet agent once Nunn May was out of sight; or they could continue to keep both under surveillance pending a round of arrests at the Canadian end.

A decision had to be made at the highest level. Prime Minister Clement Attlee consulted the Canadian Prime Minister, Mackenzie King, and US President Harry Truman. Their first instruction, in mid-October, was that suspects in Canada and Britain should be discreetly interrogated without any publicity. MI5 felt constrained to point out the impossibility of such a policy. Recording it in his office diary, Guy Liddell indicated that serious consideration was being given to sharing the secret with the Russians in any case. He wrote:

> It was in our view better to wait for another two or three weeks until a decision had been reached about handing over the atomic bomb to the Russians. A memo has been prepared by the FO [Foreign Office] on these lines and the question will be submitted to Attlee and Mackenzie King.[339]

So the decision was to do nothing. To watch and wait and keep Klop in reserve in case an opportunity arose to use him.

Meanwhile, Kim Philby continued to keep Moscow abreast of the investigation, reassuring them on 18 November 1945 that neither Nunn May nor his Soviet controller had turned up for four scheduled rendezvous fixed for 7, 17, 27 October and 7 November.

He passed on MI5's opinion that Nunn May had not put a foot wrong: no suspicious contacts; no signs of being afraid or worried; and carrying on with his academic research. They had come to the conclusion that Nunn May was a tough customer who would not crack unless confronted with convincing evidence.

Philby also revealed that the matter was now a political decision at the highest level and that this involved consideration not only of maintaining friendly diplomatic relations with the USSR, but also of the future control over atomic secrets.[340]

In the event the watchers kept a thankless vigil in Great Russell Street throughout October, November and December without result. When the network was finally wound up in January, Nunn May confessed to Burt remarkably quickly, apparently shaken by the police officer's detailed knowledge of his rendezvous arrangements and passwords. It was only towards the end of his life that Nunn May actually admitted that he had been tipped off by the Russians that his cover was blown and all contact was severed. There had been no question of him keeping the rendezvous.

The Russians seem to have been aware of Klop's activities. He appeared in an undated document in NKVD files in a list of British agents who were reporting on individuals at the Soviet embassy in London and other Communist organisations. The list mentioned a number of journalists, among them Lady Listowel, daughter of a diplomat of the Austro-Hungarian empire, who published a post-war anti-Communist news sheet, *East Europe and Soviet Union*. Another writer, codename 'Brit' and identified as a journalist named Morton, had supposedly been keeping the Soviets' military attaché and intelligence *rezident* in London, Major General Ivan Sklyarov, under observation. Sklyarov and his assistant, Col. Simon Kremer, had been responsible for the recruitment of the atom bomb spy Klaus Fuchs, who was introduced to them by Jurgen Kuczynski. In MI5 files now available at the National Archives, Agent Brit is frequently referred to as a source on Russian activities but his identity is not revealed. Klop is described in the NKVD list as a White Russian officer.[341] Blunt had filed a full report on Klop during the war and Philby had plenty of opportunity to add to it. Klop for his part had warned Dick White in 1946 that Philby's first wife, Litzi Friedmann, was a Communist and Soviet agent. At the time, they were getting divorced and maybe because of that the information was discounted.[342]

Nadia's sister Olia had lived throughout the war in Berlin. She had divorced her first husband and married his cousin, Ernest Steiner, who was, like her, a Russian émigré. He worked for the German electronics giant Siemens. Somehow, Nadia managed to track them down in the British controlled zone of Germany and, with Peter's help, arranged for them to come to Britain. Quite how she achieved this at a time when thousands of displaced persons and refugees across Europe were being refused entry she never explains. It seems she got no encouragement from Klop, who was so angry about it he threatened to leave her. Nevertheless, he delivered the couple from London to Barrow Elm in October 1946, before returning to Switzerland. When he returned to find them still comfortably ensconced in his country home more rows ensued. Klop went back to Switzerland once more, returning in 1948 and this time his attitude to his sister-in-law and her husband completely changed. Nadia herself had been away in Italy, working on costumes and set design for Peter's film *Private Angelo* about a reluctant soldier in the Italian Army. She arrived to find Klop, Ernest and Olia working as a team looking after a couple of defectors who had been granted political asylum.[343]

It was an occasion for another of Klop's tall tales. He maintained that he had somehow procured enough lobster to concoct a lobster bisque, complete with cognac, cream and cheese, and had decanted it into a jar, which was travelling with him and his defectors on the train from London to Gloucestershire, securely contained in his father's old top hat box. Unfortunately Klop then placed the hat box upside down in the luggage rack and halfway through the journey observed, with a mixture of amusement and horror, that the bisque was dripping steadily on to the unwitting defector's Homburg hat.[344]

It has not been possible to identify the victim of this deluge with any certainty but the most high-profile case of that time was the Soviet scientific adviser on aircraft and jet propulsion Grigori Tokaev, who had been sent to Germany by Stalin to bring back scientists from the German rocket research programme, by kidnap if necessary. Instead he fled into the British zone with his wife Aza and young daughter Bella and sought sanctuary. He had to be kept in a safe house because it was assumed that the Russians would send an assassination squad to silence him.

Tokaev needed delicate handling. He had not wanted to come to Britain at all and was furious when he discovered that the Canadians with whom he had been in contact prior to his escape were going to hand him over. He objected to Britain's part in the Potsdam agreement under which Russia, America and Britain agreed the division of Germany into different control zones and he believed that Britain was in the habit of handing back defectors.[345]

Tokaev was able to give his interrogators some useful information about the state of Russian aeronautical research and was considered a prime asset for propaganda purposes. But his over-the-top denunciations of Stalin and the Soviet system, serialised in the *Sunday Express*, were considered by some to be counter-productive. He was then involved in an attempt to lure a second defector, Colonel J. D. Tasoev, from Germany. Tokaev had been taken to Germany secretly in an RAF officer's personal plane to persuade Tasoev to join him in Britain. The SIS officer overseeing the operation took a unilateral decision to bring the new man back immediately on the return flight. Tasoev was put up in MI5's safe flat in Rugby Mansions, Kensington, and promptly changed his mind and demanded to be taken home. News of the fiasco leaked out and questions were asked in Parliament.

MI5 was further alarmed when it discovered that one of Klop's former surveillance subjects, the White Russian Anatole Baykolov, was in touch with Tokaev. Baykolov was the subject of considerable suspicion that he was a plant by Russian intelligence, despite the fact that he was reportedly receiving covert funds from the Americans, through the Marshall Aid scheme, to finance an anti-Soviet campaign group.

As a result of the Tokaev case, Dick White, who was by then head of counter-intelligence at MI5, prepared a report on all twenty Russians who had defected since 1927. Only one, Vasilyi Sharandak, had chosen to come to Britain. He was a low-ranking translator and black marketer who fled from Hungary in July 1947. Like Tokaev, he told his interrogators that it was widely believed in Russia that Britain handed defectors back.

Although Dick White could not have known it at the time, this was probably the result of the botched defection of Constantin Volkov in Istanbul in the summer and autumn of 1945. Volkov was deputy head of Russian intelligence in Turkey and approached the British embassy offering what White described as 'a sensational catalogue of information' including a list of Soviet agents in Britain. The local representative of MI6 was dubious and referred the case back to London. During the inevitable delay Volkov and his wife were forcibly repatriated by the Russians and never seen again. It only emerged later that the delay had been largely the fault of Kim Philby, the case officer in London who would have known that he was likely to be exposed by Volkov's revelations. White's report was not declassified until February 2014.[346]

CHAPTER 17: OTTO JOHN

In October 1950, Dick White began setting up a German counter-espionage section of MI5. The deputy director, Guy Liddell, noted that this was necessary because the emerging West German state was to have consulates and diplomatic representation in foreign countries and could be expected to resume espionage activities. Klop had been given the job of establishing good relations with them which, it was hoped, would bear fruit.[347]

This coincided with the establishment of a West German equivalent of MI5, the Federal Office for the Protection of the Constitution, otherwise known as the BfV, short for *Bundesamt für Verfassungschutz*. Its first director was a controversial choice. Otto John had been proving himself useful to Britain since he gave up his duties broadcasting black propaganda for Sefton Delmer when the war ended. Like Klop, he had been employed in interrogating captured German officers, and with his legal background he had assisted at the Nuremburg War Crimes Trials. Latterly he had worked for a London law firm involved with cases involving German refugees and anti-Nazis. He contemplated taking British citizenship and was supported in that endeavour by Sir Robert Bruce Lockhart, who had been in overall charge of the Political Warfare Executive including Sefton Delmer's propaganda section. He felt that John was 'not getting a square deal' and lamented the fact that Peter Loxley, the Foreign Office liaison officer with MI6, who presumably knew as much as anyone about Otto John's contribution to the war effort, had died in a plane crash and was not around to lend his weight to the application. Others who had been involved with him were decidedly cool on the idea, despite an acknowledgement that in 1943 he revealed to MI6 in Lisbon the existence of the rocket development plant at Peenemunde, where the VI and V2 flying bombs were made; and the location of submarine building pens and an underground aircraft factory. The Air Ministry, which was thereby given the opportunity to bomb these facilities, candidly admitted that they had not really believed Otto John's tip-off. Sefton Delmer paid tribute to his hard work but did not consider that it merited special treatment. John Street at the Foreign Office commented that John's loyalties lay with the German Resistance movement rather than with the Allies, and Aubrey Halford-MacLeod, who had replaced Loxley as MI6 liaison, added that he doubted whether John merited special treatment on the basis of his services to MI6.[348]

But John had always hankered after a role in rebuilding a new Germany, and British officials tried, and failed, to ease him into a number of fairly insignificant positions. Then, to the enormous resentment of many of his fellow Germans, he suddenly landed a position that could be expected to be vital to his country's democratic future and rehabilitation in the civilised world. To many of them he was a traitor. It was not so much that he had participated in the 20 July plot to kill Hitler; it was the fact that he fled, and then worked actively for the enemy against German interests, that condemned him in their eyes. How had he survived when so many of the conspirators, including his own brother, had stayed behind and faced certain death? Although the British government has always denied it, the almost universal perception is that it was Britain that engineered his appointment as head of the BfV, purely in its own interests. Nine names had been put forward by the Germans, four of which were submitted to the Allied authorities that were still overseeing the government of West Germany. All were rejected, including Reinhard Gehlen whom the Americans preferred and who eventually became head of the equivalent of MI6. He had been in charge of military intelligence for Hitler on the Eastern Front. Then Otto John's name was submitted and the West German Chancellor, Konrad Adenauer, feeling he had been boxed into a corner, reluctantly authorised the appointment though he never fully accepted it.[349]

There is no doubt that the Intelligence services were in close touch with the new head of the BfV. Before taking up his appointment, Otto John came to London for a meeting with Dick White and the director of MI5, Sir Percy Sillitoe. The meeting had been set up by John Wheeler-Bennett, wartime assistant director of political intelligence, and General Kenneth Strong, who had been US General Eisenhower's chief intelligence officer during the war and subsequently became director of the British Joint Intelligence Bureau. Ostensibly this was a social call, at which Otto John was assured he would get any help he needed. He was then passed on to General Sir Sidney Kirkman, who was responsible for intelligence gathering in the British control zone of Germany, under cover of conducting an inquiry into military expenditure. Thereafter John reported regularly to Kirkman and his successors.[350] Gehlen told his American controller that Otto John had confirmed, after too much to drink, that he was a member of Britain's special services. Gehlen went on to claim that his opposite number was carrying out espionage operations on behalf of the British in East Germany, the Middle East and the Soviet Union, where he boasted of a contact in the immediate vicinity of Joseph Stalin.[351]

Klop used his German contacts to keep an eye on the way the new German government was developing and the appointment of former Nazis to positions of power and influence. In early 1951, his old friend, the former military attaché Leo Geyr von Schweppenburg, wrote to tell him that Fritz Hesse had become a member of the Senate for the Academy for Political Science and chief of the Institute of Public Opinion. Geyr added a Latin tag:

Dificile est satiram non scribere (It is difficult not to write satire). Klop reminded Guy Liddell:

> Fritz Hesse was an arch-Nazi and Ribbentrop's right hand man for press affairs in this country. After the outbreak of war it was he who ... demanded at a conference in the German Foreign Office ... the immediate bombing of the harbour of London predicting that the population of the East End of London would march in their thousands to Buckingham Palace demanding a peace with Germany. After the defeat of Germany Hesse was flown over to London and brought to my flat for interrogation.[352]

Klop and Geyr kept in touch. When the general became the first German to address the British Military Commentators Circle, in November 1954, on 'The Role of Germany in the defence of Western Europe', he invited Klop and his son as special guests. Geyr set up a similar discussion group in Germany but a year later he complained to the president of the British Circle, Basil Liddell Hart:

> It was yours and your friends' idea to form a corresponding circle in my country too. It is in being now, although it is fighting hard against more or less open and underground Nazi and Nationalist restoration.[353]

He explained that 'Nationalists' had been trying to cut him off from his international contacts. The concern that former Nazis were repopulating the new government of West Germany also weighed heavily on Otto John's mind. It was fomented by Klop's old friend Wolfgang zu Putlitz. Like Otto John, he had nursed hopes of playing a part in a new beginning for Germany. He could not return to his old estates in Laaske, because they had been expropriated by the Red Army despite his brother Gebhard converting to Communism, but he had at least been allowed to remain in his old home. With Dick White's help Putlitz had obtained a job in the Presidential

Chancellery in Kiel but, like Otto John, he found himself branded a traitor among his own people.

He wrote bitterly to Sir Robert Vansittart in 1946:

> I somehow resent being 'denazified' by people who probably did not do half as much against the Nazis as I did. But it is like that: For the British I am a German and therefore not trustworthy as a matter of principle. For the Germans I am – if not a traitor – at least a Junker with a title and therefore suspicious.[354]

Putlitz went on to complain that British attitudes to the occupation were choking off all attempts by Germans to build a new life and warned that if this continued Germany would collapse and France would follow, presumably into Communist hands. In a series of articles for *The People* he revealed his wartime spying and bemoaned the lack of opportunity that the peace had brought. This sense of rejection led him to take a step he had resisted throughout the war and assume British nationality. He tried teaching and commercial travelling without much success. His circle of homosexual friends, among them Guy Burgess and the Labour MP Tom Driberg, were politically left-leaning. Suspicions about Putlitz's own political loyalty began to be voiced by the Dutch secret service who questioned him about links with the pre-war Soviet spymaster Walter Krivitsky. Not long after, despite the death of his brother Gebhard in prison, Putlitz decided to settle in Communist East Germany and become an active advocate of their cause, contributing propaganda pamphlets attacking the 'rebirth of [West] German imperialism'.[355]

Not content with that, he sought out his old friend Otto John in West Berlin and began to berate him with the iniquities of the Adenauer regime and the perils of re-nazification. Putlitz encouraged John to believe that the only way to stop this was by exposing it from the sanctuary of East Germany. These contacts began in 1951, very soon after Otto John's appointment, and continued through to 1954. In March 1953 they met in a restaurant and, according to Otto John, Putlitz voiced all the arguments about a divided Germany, reunification, rearmament and peace negotiations that appeared daily in the eastern zone newspapers. John's account, written some time later in self-justification, describes Putlitz as a 'politically awkward' customer. John maintains that he drew Putlitz's attention to the fact that he was still technically a British citizen despite his adherence to his new political masters' doctrine.[356] Otto John apparently neglected to inform his superiors of these potentially treasonable discussions, although he kept his British handlers aware of them. He also briefed his old boss, Sefton Delmer, when he came to visit in 1954 intent on writing a series for the *Daily Express* entitled: 'How Dead is Hitler?' Otto John may also have been the source of an earlier Delmer article criticising his rival Reinhard Gehlen for being in the Americans' pocket. Delmer set up a meeting with Putlitz and then wrote a piece attacking him, while pursuing strongly the line that West Germany was in danger of falling again under the Nazi spell.

By 1954 British enthusiasm for Otto John was on the wane and a number of Germans were questioning his suitability. The week of the tenth anniversary of the 20 July plot to assassinate Hitler was the turning point. John attended a commemoration in Berlin and was clearly in an emotional state, possibly a little the worse for drink, as he reflected on the death of his brother and so many of his fellow conspirators. According to Sefton Delmer, John was due to meet two British intelligence officers for dinner that evening at the Maison de France restaurant and was dropped outside.[357] But, instead of going in, he walked to the nearby home and surgery of a physician who had treated his brother for war injuries, Wolfgang Wohlgemuth. He also had a practice in East Berlin and had been used by John as a conduit to Communist contacts. Two weeks earlier Wohlgemuth had spent the night at John's home, sitting up late and drinking together with Michael Winch, a former British agent who had worked in Portugal in 1943 and in Moscow in 1944.

On the evening of 20 July, he drove John to East Berlin, passing through checkpoints apparently without difficulty in the days before the Berlin Wall. Supposedly John was going to visit his brother's grave; in reality he ended up in a KGB safe house meeting Russian and East German intelligence officers. More drink was taken and John decided to stay. Whether he was drugged and abducted, went voluntarily and was forced to stay, or always intended to defect remains unclear to this day despite his later testimony and the accounts of witnesses from both sides. MI5 seems to have been in little doubt that Putlitz was behind the defection.

Initially the West German government tried to pass off this bombshell as an abduction but as John made radio broadcasts and held press conferences, at which he chatted amicably with Delmer and other journalists, without displaying signs of extreme duress, that version soon crumbled. In the broadcasts John attacked the re-nazification of West Germany and revealed delicate secret negotiations designed to admit the recently created state to a European Defence Community, thus paving the way for them to re-arm.

Previous links between John and other Communist sympathisers began to be uncovered. A newspaper drew attention to the fact that among John's former colleagues in Sefton Delmer's black propaganda unit were Baron Wolfgang zu Putlitz, Eberhard Koebel, Dr Honigmann and Karl von Schnitzler. Surely it was no coincidence that all were now in the Soviet-controlled part of Germany.[358] Otto John's deputy Albert Radke, who had previously worked for the Gehlen Organization, said it was apparent that he had no real experience of counter-intelligence and had a bad habit of conducting meetings behind his deputy's back. That included his conversations with Putlitz, although he had put a note on file saying that he rejected Putlitz's blandishments.[359] John was taken to Moscow and then to a Black Sea resort and questioned about his links to British intelligence and his 1944 escape to Britain. Then, just as unexpectedly as he had disappeared, he reappeared again in

West Berlin in December 1955, having slipped the attentions of his KGB minders while visiting a university campus.

This was no spur of the moment dash for freedom – it had been set up in advance in collaboration with British Intelligence – nor had John's disappearance come as a total surprise. In October 2013, as a result of a Freedom of Information request, the Foreign Office released a thick file of previously secret memoranda which shed new light on Otto John's defection. It maintains the convenient fiction that Britain was not responsible for John's appointment, attributing the nomination to the German politician Jacob Kaiser. Like Otto John, he had been a member of the 20 July plot and linked to the Cologne-based Nazi Resistance group. He was also a founder member of the CDU and therefore came from the same power base as the Chancellor, Konrad Adenauer. Yet the two men had significant political differences – Kaiser was a left-leaning trade unionist who had initially formed an East German branch of the CDU until forced out by the Soviet authorities. In Adenauer's West German government he was appointed minister for reunification.

It is clear that John was in regular contact with his handler from British Intelligence, Keith Randell of the British Services Security Organisation. He was also involved in running joint counter-espionage operations, as later alleged by Gehlen. But it was not until November 1952 that he revealed to Randell that Putlitz had contacted him eighteen months earlier. He had turned up unannounced and accosted John outside the headquarters of the BfV. John had invited him home to dinner where they had talked about old friends in Britain with whom Putlitz remained in contact.

John had then moved house but four months later Putlitz had turned up on his doorstep having done some detective work to track him down in Cologne. On 16 March 1953, the two men had lunch and twenty-four hours later John briefed Randell on what had happened but did not inform his own government. Putlitz had made a great play of his dislike for the Americans, vilified the British to a lesser extent, and stated that he would 'rather be a member of the proletariat under the Russians than a misused gentleman under the Western Allies'. He accused John of allowing himself to become the head of a new Gestapo. Then he came to his very important message: a senior Russian officer wanted to meet John, in West Berlin or Austria if necessary, and professed that this would be in Germany's best interests. John apparently declined the invitation and the conversation turned once more to old friends in Britain and what they were doing. Although Klop is not mentioned personally in Randell's report, Dick White, Vansittart and Malcolm Christie are. White and General Sir Kenneth Strong, who was also mentioned, were at that stage in the running to replace Sir Percy Sillitoe as director general of MI5.

One of Randell's colleagues pointed out to John that Putlitz had already fulfilled the classic early stages of a KGB sting operation against John – a target reconnaissance to establish where he lived, his family circumstances, opinions and reaction to what amounted to an offer to defect. He recommended putting Putlitz under surveillance and strongly advised John not to keep a rendezvous with Putlitz the following day. If he did meet Putlitz, he should make clear he 'had no interest whatsoever in his strange proposals and strange friends'. Randell recorded that John claimed not to have adequate resources for a surveillance operation, clearly did not like the advice he had been given and probably would not take it.

On 18 March, Randell saw John again to question him about his friendship with Wolfgang Wohlgemuth and revealed that Randell's boss, Edward 'Crash' Abbotts, was also in touch with Wohlgemuth. John confirmed that Wohlgemuth was a Communist. Randell was apparently concerned about John's associations and state of mind and he raised the subject again at a meeting on 15 July 1954, five days before John's disappearance. Randell made the point that Putlitz and Wohlgemuth were likely to find an opportunity to meet John during his visit to Berlin for the 20 July memorial and that dubious characters were bound to target him as head of the BfV. Once again John deflected the conversation and Randell was so suspicious that he recommended placing a tap on John's telephone at the *pension* where he would be staying: Haus Schaetzle in Seebergsteig (now known as Toni-Lessler Strasse) in the Grunewald area of Berlin.

It is apparent from the file that British Intelligence was already intercepting Wohlgemuth's communications. Internal memos on him and Putlitz have been withheld. They also had access to transcripts of a tap on John's home phone, although that may only have been imposed after his disappearance.

The Foreign Office in London had additional reasons to worry about John's intentions. He had written expressing his concerns to the Labour MP and future Cabinet minister Richard Crossman, who had been head of the Psychological Warfare Department during the war when John was broadcasting propaganda for Sefton Delmer. Crossman in turn discussed them with Sir Frank Roberts, a senior diplomatic adviser to the Foreign Secretary, before writing back to John. The contents of those letters are still secret but Crossman remained a supporter of John's after his defection and return, blaming Britain for his troubles. He wrote:

> We had used John as our tool during and after the war and therefore ought to accept a residual obligation to him. At the end of the war although John wanted to stay in this country he had been persuaded by the Foreign Office to undertake an important security post in West Berlin which led to his subsequent troubles.[360]

Crossman's letter to John was intercepted by the American postal censors in the Allied control area of Germany which caused considerable embarrassment at the Foreign Office. They were obliged to explain the circumstances in the hope of persuading the Americans that the left wing in Britain was not 'up to something' in connection with John's disappearance.

A damage limitation exercise followed. The consensus was that whatever John revealed under Soviet interrogation would not have serious consequences for Allied interests, other than revealing a secret memorandum of understanding which would allow Germany to re-arm as part of a European Defence Force. But there was a tacit acknowledgement that John's fears of the re-nazification of Germany had some substance and recognition that his appointment had been a mistake, leaving the BfV as a lame and ineffectual organisation.

Foreign Office official Peter Male, who had spent the last four years dealing with security issues at the Control Commission offices in Wahner Heide, near Cologne, minuted:

> The present BfV is useless and despondent. The danger is that the protagonists of a tough security service in Germany may win. Some of those German nationalists, including ex-Nazis, who are keen on such a centralised and powerful security service are now in influential positions.[361]

John's political superior, the Interior Minister Gerhard Schröder, had been a member of the Nazi party and was also a harsh critic of John's management of the BfV. His comments were believed to have been bitterly resented by John.

By mid-November 1956, British diplomats in London and Bonn were aware of the possibility that John would attempt to return to the West. These were backed up by a message from John to 'Crash' Abbotts delivered by a Danish journalist, Henrik Bonde-Henriksen, and a simultaneous approach by John's wife. It appears that Abbotts initially encouraged them to expect British assistance but this was very firmly stamped on by the ambassador, Sir Frederick Hoyer Millar, his colleagues in London and by MI6. Abbotts was told that if John turned up on his doorstep he was to be handed over immediately to the German authorities. As Peter Hope, counsellor at the embassy, explained:

Although John's re-defection might perhaps be claimed to be a minor triumph in the Cold War, we think here that the question of Anglo-German relations is much more important. We had a bad Press in the past over Otto John and his British connexion; we think it would be a great mistake if we were now to be involved in his re-defection. Moreover, I very much doubt whether the Federal government would relish John's return. ... All in all, therefore, we think we are probably better off with John being where he is and with all this in mind have made it clear to Berlin that Crash Abbotts should have as little to do with the John case as is possible.[362]

When John duly reappeared on 12 December he was arrested by the German authorities and tried for 'treasonable falsification and conspiracy', found guilty and sentenced to four years in jail, of which he served two. He had reverted to the defence that he had been drugged and kidnapped, subsequently going along with his captors' demands to avoid more intensive interrogation. He maintained that stance for the rest of his life although it was undermined by the KGB defector Vladimir Apollonowitsch in 1969. He claimed to have been the man John had gone to meet in 1954 and that he had been surprised by John's decision to defect.[363] Theories abound as to what really lay behind John's disappearance. After he died in March 1977 an obituary in *The Times* rehearsed various explanations, among them a suggestion that Kim Philby lay behind it. It would have suited KGB interests for John to get the job in the first place, and to defect in 1954 in order to denounce the secret European Defence Community. They speculated that John's return was calculated to create confusion in the mind of the new head of MI6, Dick White, who had begun to re-examine Philby's loyalties, an investigation which eventually culminated in his exposure as a KGB agent in 1963.

CHAPTER 18: PEACE

Sir Dick White's transfer from MI5 to head of MI6 preceded Klop's retirement by only a year. White was brought in to restore confidence after the fiasco of Buster Crabb's botched operation in Portsmouth Harbour, for which Nicholas Elliott bore some of the blame. Klop was approaching sixty-five and there is no reason to suppose that White did not still hold him in high esteem. But it must have been a miserable time to be a member of a service so riven by betrayal and botched operations, where technology was increasingly the king, and human enterprise, particularly of the type Klop had been used to, was bound to be suspect. What had once made him such a useful agent, his background knowledge of Germany and Russia, and close relationships to Germans and Russians, inevitably now attracted deep suspicion. Although Kim Philby had yet to confess his treachery, he remained under suspicion. Everyone who had been close to him, as Klop had been, had to be considered tainted and it was part of White's new role to clean up the mess.

Klop had been more or less estranged from Nadia, and at odds with his son Peter, for some time. Nadia seems to have taken the initiative to rescue the situation. Having left Barrow Elm for good in 1953, and with Klop's flat in Chelsea Cloisters being too small for both of them, she took on responsibility for finding somewhere larger for them to live. In the meantime she stayed with Peter at his Chelsea house. His marriage to Isolde had ended in 1950 but his career kept him constantly busy. He had enjoyed a huge stage success with his comedy, *The Love of Four Colonels*, and now attempted to replicate it with *No Sign of the Dove*, combining bedroom farce with a satirical rewriting of the story of Noah's Ark, condemning all the ills he perceived in modern Britain. Nadia designed the sets and went on the provincial tour which preceded its launch at the Savoy Theatre in the West End at the end of November 1953. Klop, feeling lonely and neglected, seemed to think that his wife and son were 'conspiring' to exclude him. The play was a massive flop, panned by the critics, booed by the audience on its opening night, and taken off within a week. It cannot have improved family relations that Klop sided with the critics. Peter should stick to what he was good at – making people laugh – he advised. Freed from her stage commitments, by the end of December Nadia had found a two-room ground-floor flat in Egerton Gardens, just off the Brompton Road in South Kensington. It was the first time for twelve years that they had lived together and there were clearly difficulties. Klop was suffering bouts of lassitude and depression. He was crotchety, objecting to her harmless pastimes, such as card games, and interfering in her painting. She began to take odd jobs, decorating houses and church interiors which took her away from the flat and helped to make ends meet.

Klop had remained friends with Rita Winsor, his MI6 colleague in Lisbon, and it led to an unusual commission for Nadia. Part of Rita's duties had been to make the complicated travel arrangements necessary for spiriting defectors like Otto John out of the country and ensuring safe passage for visiting intelligence officers like Ian Fleming, Somerset Maugham and Malcolm Muggeridge. She decided to put her skills to use in peacetime by opening an upmarket travel agency specialising in out-of-the-way places, among them trips to the moon scheduled to start in 2040. Nadia designed the poster showing travellers setting off.[364]

In 1954 Peter married the French-Canadian actress Suzanne Cloutier. They had three children, Igor, Pavla and Andrea. When

Igor was born in London in April 1956, Peter was unable to be present because it coincided with the first night of his play *Romanoff and Juliet*. Klop, showing a rare streak of sentimentality, went to the hospital and tearfully promised always to be around to care for Igor.

Visitors and pretty girls still sparked Klop's imagination but by now there was an air of desperation about it, including a passing interest in pornography. He was flattered when the former Soviet ballerina Galina Ulanova, by then in her forties, came to visit and played up to him. He spent occasional evenings with a Spanish air hostess at a local sherry bar and on one occasion managed to pick up a young French au pair who had rung his number by mistake and ended up being invited round to tea. But these fitful excursions down memory lane were interspersed with days when he fell asleep in his armchair while polishing his antique bronzes or suffered a panic attack after accidentally locking himself in the lavatory.

He was revived and immensely honoured when the German General Hans Speidel, who had been his commanding officer in the First World War, sought him out and spent a couple of days as his guest.[365] Speidel had recently been appointed commander-in-chief of NATO forces in Central Europe, and was doing the grand tour, meeting heads of state and senior military figures such as Lord Mountbatten and Field Marshal Earl Alexander but still found time for his former fellow lieutenant.[366]

Peter Wright, assistant director of MI5, visited Klop at home shortly after his retirement from MI6 in 1957, hoping to get some useful advice about a small operation he was planning against the Russian embassy. He expected to meet a hero of the secret world living in honourable retirement:

> In fact, Ustinov and his wife were sitting in a dingy flat surrounded by piles of ancient leather-bound books. He was making ends meet by selling off his fast-diminishing library.

As they spent the afternoon drinking vodka, Klop became bitter about the way he felt he had been abandoned, without a pension. He told Wright:

> When you work for them you never think about the future, about old age. You do it for love. And when it comes time to die, they abandon you … The gentlemen run the business and the gentlemen have short memories…[367]

Klop served for a brief period as a director of his son Peter's management company, along with Peter's cousin Julius Caesar Edwardes, who was also of Russian descent, and his literary agent Alroy Treeby. He acted as secretary, keeping notes of board meetings, but it was clear that business acumen was not among his talents. His chief virtue was fending off the many telephone inquiries that found their way to him at the Egerton Gardens flat because he was in the phone book and his son was ex-directory. Even that, in his son's bitter view, only served to remind Klop that Peter was not the failure he had always predicted he would be.[368]

As Klop tried to adjust to retirement he developed a hankering to live in the country. Once again Sir Thomas Bazley came to his aid. He had provided Barrow Elm during the war and later a place for Nadia's sister Olia and her husband to stay. Now he offered Klop and Nadia a large but dilapidated stone cottage, dating from Tudor times, at 49 Eastleach, a Gloucestershire village midway between Witney and Cirencester, not far from Barrow Elm. It needed renovation and they eventually moved from Egerton Gardens in October 1957. Nadia missed the colourful London scene more than Klop who, to her amazement, quickly settled into country ways once he had displayed his artworks, bronzes and sculptures, musical instruments and handblown black glass bottles. He even installed an old gravestone in the fireplace of his dark and overcrowded bedroom.

He befriended the locals, gossiping with them over large whiskies in the local pub, and took up bird-watching. But others saw a morose figure, not at ease in his tweed jackets and felt hat, more comfortable talking to his titled neighbours, Sir Thomas Bazley or Lord and Lady Howard, or Nadia's friends from the world of art and theatre. He was a bit of a snob, keeping up with the social scene in the pages of *Tatler* and *Queen* magazines. Nadia, on the other hand, was quickly accepted: helping out with harvesting and village bazaars, at once peasant and aristocrat, in woollen dresses, cardigans and slippers, puffing on a small cheroot.[369]

Peter Ustinov, observing these events more remotely as he sailed majestically between Hollywood, London and Paris celebrating success on stage and screen, was possibly more perceptive of their meaning. His father had always been an urban dweller, browsing in the shops for culinary delicacies, nipping through the streets by taxi, and this sudden conversion to the rural idyll smacked of the abandonment of all life's pleasures because what remained was the poignant echo of past excitement.[370]

Klop's mood cannot have been lightened by the publication that year of Wolfgang zu Putlitz's memoirs. The two men had kept in touch and indeed Putlitz maintained contact with Peter Ustinov even after Klop's death. While the book contained nothing that reflected adversely on Klop, it was an unwelcome reminder of how Communist agents had repeatedly duped British Intelligence. The English edition carried a particularly mischievous preface in which Putlitz explained that he hoped publication in London would restore old friendships damaged by his decision to make his home in East Germany. He singled out for special mention Lord and Lady Vansittart, Sir Colville Barclay, Colonel Graham Christie, Mr and Mrs Paul X and Mr Anthony Blunt, whose kindness and understanding he would never forget.[371]

Putlitz had been a frequent guest in the Vansittarts' home and they had done their best to make him welcome and comfortable in Britain; Col. Christie was the leading member of Vansittart's private Intelligence service; Paul X was the pseudonym Putlitz had used in the book to refer to Klop. His sensitivity in not naming a serving MI6 officer would have been more impressive had he not identified him clearly in the German edition. But the sentimental reference to Blunt must have been intensely irritating to the authorities, conscious that the book would have been vetted and probably orchestrated by the KGB. Although he had been under suspicion since the defection of Burgess and Maclean, Blunt did not confess until 1964, with a promise of immunity from prosecution, and was not publicly exposed until 1979.

Then there was Colville Barclay, Lord Vansittart's stepson, who had also fallen under suspicion of spying for the Soviets. He fitted the profile provided by the defector Walter Krivitsky when he was questioned by Guy Liddell and MI5's Russian expert Jane Archer in 1940. He told them of a mole with access to top secret government papers including the minutes of the Committee on Imperial Defence. This man, whom he was unable to name, was a Scottish aristocrat, artistic, educated at Eton and Oxford and wealthy enough not to want payment for his betrayal, which he justified on ideological grounds. His activities within the Foreign Office had begun around 1936.

Sir Colville was fourteenth baronet of a family whose noble Scottish roots could be traced back to the fifteenth century. He had indeed been educated at Eton, and Trinity College, Oxford, and he spent his post-war career as a painter and naturalist. He had joined the Foreign Office in 1937, left to serve with a naval unit carrying out covert operations in the run-up to D-Day, and was then recruited by Kim Philby to join his new Section IX anti-Soviet department at MI6. Sir Colville's younger brother Cecil had been their man in Moscow during the war. Jane Archer, who had interrogated Krivitsky and identified Sir Colville as a suspect, was also working for Section IX and queried his appointment. It was cleared by Philby after a trawl through MI5 files. In 1957, when the Putlitz book came out, Philby was also under suspicion but had not confessed. Sir Colville was only publicly identified as a suspect in 2003 when he told the author that he had never been questioned and had no idea the finger had been pointed at him.[372] Nevertheless, the KGB may well have known of it from Philby.

Once Klop and Nadia were ensconced in their rural retreat, guests began to come from London, among them one of Klop's old flames, an air hostess named Conchita who arrived one weekend with caviar from Moscow, vodka from Warsaw and chocolate from Madrid, supplemented by champagne and crumpets. Klop wrote euphorically to another of his girlfriends, Elizabeth Brousson, describing their gourmet weekend that had also included pheasant supplied by Lady Carmen Bazley, their landlord's wife. Nadia wrote to Elizabeth separately, telling her that Conchita was a very sweet girl and that Elizabeth must not be jealous.

Elizabeth, whom Klop had befriended during his time in Switzerland, also visited along with Moura Budberg whose unchanging lifestyle meant that she rose at lunchtime, having spent the morning in bed making phone calls, writing and receiving visitors. The three women got on famously but Elizabeth Brousson recalls that life was not easy for Nadia and Klop:

I used to go and spend weekends with them – they were sort of surrogate parents for me. They were the kindest people in the world. They made their life in the village and got to know all the villagers. I don't know how they managed to live. Klop used to find things in antique markets and have good luck through his sense of discernment. They never spent any money on themselves and when there was nobody about they lived on pretty much bread and cheese and saved everything for the weekends. Klop did cook beautifully and it was quite rich but it was only when he was entertaining. I think they were pretty short and the Bazleys were very good to them.

He used to tell these amazing stories. He was a terrific raconteur. People were very happy to sit and listen to him. Nadia had heard them endlessly. She really was an example of someone who really just loved him and smiled benignly at his little peccadilloes. He used to parade his girls around and make it very obvious. People didn't approve but Nadia was not a jealous woman. She knew in the end of it Klop would always come back to her even if he did have little flirtations on the side. They had been through a lot together coming back from Russia and they were totally necessary to each other. She didn't have to worry because there was no threat to their relationship. He probably needed a bit extra.[373]

There were still friends locally from their days at Barrow Elm, among them David and Tamara Talbot Rice and Phyllis Sorel-Taylour who, since Klop and Nadia did not have a car, often acted as chauffeurs for trips to the theatre or Klop's frequent forays to local antique shops and country house sales. Mrs Sorel-Taylour had been secretary to the eccentric archaeologist Alexander Keiller, who owned Avebury Manor and the ancient stone circle nearby.[374]

Tamara, a Russian exile like Nadia, and her husband had worked during the war for the Ministry of Information and military intelligence respectively. Two old friends from MI6 maintained their connection. Dick White, by now head of the service, and Nicholas Elliott would visit with their wives and children.

The country idyll had lasted only a few months when Klop's previously hedonistic lifestyle caught up with him. As a clap of thunder broke over the cottage he implored Nadia to run to the nearest phone box and summon the doctor. He liked to boast that he had not consulted a physician in more than forty years but at the age of sixty-five he needed one urgently. The diagnosis was not good: a serious heart condition, high blood pressure and liver problems. The remedy: a low-fat diet, complete rest and medication. To Nadia's surprise Klop submitted meekly to the regime and the benefits were soon apparent. On 17 July he got out of bed for the first time in weeks to celebrate their thirty-eighth wedding anniversary. With Peter's help, new home comforts were added to the cottage – a fridge, a television and, more vitally, a telephone.

By the following year life had returned to normality, with Nadia trying to enforce a more sedate pace. It was enlivened by a visit from the art historian Peter Ward-Jackson, who had been Klop's driver during his post-war investigations in Germany. His old friend arrived with a case of champagne and a new bride, Joan Schellenberg (no relation to Walther of the German Intelligence services). Klop and Nadia had introduced them.

It was followed by an excursion to Paris to see Peter, recently returned from America after eighteen months away, and to meet for the first time their latest grandchild, Andrea, who was four months old. It was an opportunity for Nadia to visit her uncle Alexandre, now aged eighty-nine and in failing health. He died the following February, shortly after publication of his memoirs, which Moura Budberg had translated into English.

Paris in the summertime revived Klop's spirits and his interest in cooking and pretty girls. But the euphoria did not last. He was becoming unsteady on his feet, self-conscious about his infirmity and less willing to be seen in public. There were interludes of enjoyment, when friends came to visit, but Klop and Nadia increasingly had only each other for company and though they were drawn closer by the experience it was a period of forlorn sadness. Peter was leading a hectic show business lifestyle. He arranged visits for them to the film studios and put them up in hotels while he was in London, even had them chauffeured from Eastleach to Montreux in 1961, to spend Christmas with him in his suite at a grand hotel. They seem to have found the surroundings uncomfortable. Klop fell several times in the bathroom and needed Nadia constantly within calling distance. An introduction to Suzanne's parents was not a success. Yet Klop couldn't resist the old lure of the showman. He dressed up as Santa Claus for the grandchildren. Igor, only five years old, remembers it well. He shyly presented this strange bearded figure with a little handkerchief which he had embroidered at school. About a week later he saw Klop blowing his nose on the handkerchief and that was how he came to realise that Father Christmas did not really exist.[375]

Klop and Nadia were driven back to Eastleach in March but very soon Klop's condition deteriorated and he became increasingly bedridden and feeble. Towards the end of November Nadia summoned Peter from Paris and he spent a night at Klop's bedside. The following evening at 8 p.m., while Peter was briefly away from the cottage, Klop died with Nadia at his side. He had always abhorred the thought of old age. It was 1 December 1962, the eve of his seventieth birthday.

He had eventually received a pension, but he left no will and an estate, which passed to Nadia, of only £1,124 7s 5d – less than £20,000 at current prices. Nadia lived on at their cottage until her death on 8 February 1975. She left £21,691, after tax, all of which, apart from some small personal bequests, went to her son.

Klop's death was announced in the Personal Column of *The Times*, curiously with the old German spelling of Jona Ustinow, but the funeral was private, followed by cremation and interment of his ashes in the local churchyard at Eastleach. The limelight in which he had played his finest roles had long ceased to glow but one of those who remained – probably Dick White – at least paid him this generous tribute:

He served the cause of freedom with devotion and courage and this country owes him a considerable debt of gratitude.[376]

Nadia included it in a personal memoir that she began writing in the summer of 1963. As she cast her mind back over their lives together she wrote to Elizabeth Brousson:

Sometimes it seems to me that I have been put into this world for this particular job. I am doing it with love and pleasure – it is like being with him. Mind you, our life together has not always been as harmonious as all that. We had many squabbles and we've been miserable at times, even hating the sight of each other! But when he left me I had the definite feeling, no more than that, – an absolute knowledge – that I've lost the very best friend I've ever had or am likely to have again.

She attributed their happiness together to an inner faith, that they shared, and to the circumstances that ensured they were far away from interfering relatives.[377]

It had been a period of film and theatre success for Peter Ustinov. His play *Photo Finish* ran for seven months in the West End and his film *Billy Budd* was acclaimed as a flawed masterpiece. His show business career continued to blossom; he became the ideal raconteur on television chat shows, with his gift for mimicry; and he began to take a new, more political direction. In 1968 he became a goodwill ambassador for UNICEF, devoting a great deal of time and energy travelling the world to promote their causes. That led in 1999 to the inauguration of the Ustinov Foundation, devoted to worldwide improvements in the lives of children through better education, medical care and social environment. He became the president of the World Federalist Movement and a globetrotting acquaintance of world leaders, among them Mikhail Gorbachev. Shortly before Gorbachev assumed control of the Soviet Union in 1985 as general secretary of the Communist Party, Peter published his book *My Russia*, which celebrated his own ethnic origins but also contained an almost total disavowal of British espionage in the Cold War, and by implication part of his father's career. He more or less exonerated the Cambridge Five, on grounds of their emotional attachment to Communism in the face of the 'crippling ineffectiveness' of Chamberlain's appeasement policy and blindness to the obvious menace of fascism, describing the Soviet Union at that time as the last bastion of hope. He described the allegations of espionage against Anthony Blunt as 'tiny scraps of dirt' redolent of the constant suspicion of Russia which 'retained its freshness at all times in the refrigerator of Western consciousness' and added:

> It is difficult for me to understand how anybody can become a spy, even for a financial consideration. I wouldn't know a secret if one came my way.[378]

This intemperate outburst is surely unfair if it applied in any sense to Klop. It was only towards the end of Peter's life that MI5 began to release its files and it may be that he knew more of his father's flamboyant escapades than the serious achievements that lay behind them. The extent of Klop's work, sometimes at the heart and sometimes on the periphery of so many of the crucial episodes of the Second World War and the Cold War, mark him out as a very special kind of agent. It is not a role that is ever likely to be replicated, given the far greater dependence on specialists and electronic surveillance.

Peter Ustinov's son Igor, a successful sculptor, based in Switzerland, and a director of the Ustinov Foundation, feels a certain affinity with his grandfather. Klop collected bronzes and antique bottles; Igor frequently casts in bronze and occasionally used bottles in his work. And he sees Klop in quite a different light:

> The way I see him is as a man who lost everything at the end of the First World War. He was in the Luftwaffe, his brother was killed. One of his younger brothers went to Canada and the other to Argentina. This is a man who was left totally alone. He hadn't died but his life had disappeared. His father had wasted all the family money. He gave more away than he invested. His whole life was blown to pieces. Instead of belonging to a wealthy, noble family he ended up with nothing. He is somebody who found strength in life after that period by belief in things, in values, and, in a way, fighting for them. He had lost all the other things in his life. That

is why, when he saw the Second World War coming, he started handing over documents from the German embassy and giving them to Chamberlain.

He even finds in this aspect of Klop's character an explanation for his infidelities:

> He was a womaniser, definitely. I think if Nadia was not an artist it would have blown her to pieces. It was not an easy set up for a family, to have a man who likes to wander around and have adventures. He probably had a feeling that having lost everything he would not get emotionally involved anymore. He doesn't want to live on the level of his feelings. He keeps them at the back of his intimate thoughts. I believe Klop was keeping a distance between himself and Peter and Nadia in order to protect them. He was doing fairly dangerous activities and wanted to avoid making them emotionally dependant on him.

Igor Ustinov sees Peter Ustinov's Foundation as a contribution to the same peaceful aspirations that originally prompted Klop to betray Nazi secrets to Britain. He believes that his father did come to recognise, very late in his own life, Klop's virtues and to understand some of his apparent failings as a husband and father:

> He was for the first time feeling a great respect for his father, who was a very secret person.[379]

GLOSSARY

FAMILY

Ustinov, Jona 'Klop': Former German journalist and diplomat, agent of MI5 and MI6.

Ustinov, Gregory: Klop's younger brother.

Ustinov, Grigori: Klop's Russian grandfather and notorious libertine.

Ustinov, Adrian: Klop's great-great-grandfather, founded the family fortune in the Siberian salt trade.

Ustinov, Igor: Klop's grandson, now a sculptor based in Switzerland.

Ustinov, Magdalena: Klop's mother, daughter of Moritz Hall and Katarina, Ethiopian aristocrat.

Ustinov, Mikhail: Klop's great-grandfather, owner of vast estates in southern Russia.

Ustinov, Peter: Klop's younger brother, killed in action when his German plane was shot down by British guns.

Ustinov, Peter: Klop's son; actor, director and raconteur named after Klop's brother.

Ustinov, Platon: Klop's father, Russian aristocrat who lived in exile in Palestine.

Ustinov, Platon: Klop's younger brother

Ustinov, Suzanne (née Cloutier): Peter's second wife, mother of Igor, Pavla and Andrea.

Ustinov, Tabitha: Klop's sister, married to Palestinian businessman Anis Jamal.

Ustinov, Tamara: Klop's first granddaughter, from Peter's marriage to Isolde Denham, now an actress.

Hall, David: Klop's uncle, son of Moritz and Katarina, later counsellor of state to the Emperor Haile Selassie of Ethiopia.

Hall, Katarina (aka Wayzaru Walatta Iyassus): Klop's grandmother, Abyssinian aristocrat and wife of Moritz.

Hall, Moritz: Klop's grandfather, of Polish extraction, missionary and armament maker to Emperor Theodore of Abyssinia.

Metzler, Peter: Evangelical pastor who converted Klop's father Platon to Protestantism.

Metzler, Maria: Pastor's daughter and Platon Ustinov's first wife.

Benois, Nadia (Nadezhda Leontievna): Klop's Russian wife, artist and theatre designer, daughter of architect Leontij and niece of Alexandre.

Benois, Alexandre: leading light of the World of Art movement and Ballet Russes.

Benois, Leontij (Louis): Nadia's father, architect and professor at the Academy of Arts.

Benois Albert: Nadia's uncle, successful water colourist.

Cavos Alberto: Nadia's great-grandfather, architect and designer of Mariinsky Theatre, home of the Imperial Ballet.

Edwardes, Matthew: British businessman married to Nadia's aunt Camilla. The family went into exile in Britain and Matthew's grandson Julius became Peter Ustinov's business adviser.

Horvath, General Dmitri: Married to Nadia's cousin Camilla. Leader of the White Russian rebellion in Vladivostok against the Communist revolution, with British support.

Krohn, Hugo: London-based wine dealer and husband of Nadia's relative Olia.

Rowe, Miss: Nadia's childhood English governess.

Steiner, Olia: Nadia's sister and companion in later life.

Steiner, Ernest: Second husband of Nadia's sister Olia.

Frieda: German cook and occasional nude model for Nadia at their London flat.

BRITAIN

Akers, Sir Wallace: Director of the Tube Alloys project, Britain's atomic weapons programme.

Archer, Jane (née Sissmore): Soviet expert at MI5 then MI6.

Attlee, Clement: Labour, Deputy Prime Minister 1942–45, Prime Minister 1945–51.

Baldwin, Stanley: Conservative, Prime Minister 1923–29 & 1935–37.

Barton, Susan: Cover name of MI5 agent Gisela Ashley, working with Klop in Holland in 1939 and on the interrogation of German agents during WWII. Member of team running Double-Cross agents.

Bazley, Sir Thomas: Gloucestershire landowner and MI5 officer who provided property for Special Operations training and homes for Klop and family members.

Best, Sigismund Payne: Long-serving MI6 officer in Holland, captured at Venlo.

Beurton, Leon: Husband of Soviet agent Ursula Kuczynski (Red Sonja).

Blunt, Anthony: Wartime MI5 officer publicly unmasked in 1979 as a member of the 'Cambridge Five' Soviet spy ring.

Bristow, Desmond: MI6 officer working with Klop in Lisbon.

Bruce, Henry: First Secretary at the British embassy in St Petersburg at the time of the revolution. Married Nadia's friend, the ballerina Tamara Karsavina.

Buchanan, Sir George: British ambassador to St Petersburg during First World War.

Buchanan, Meriel: Daughter of Sir George and friend of Moura Budberg.

Burgess, Guy: Member of 'Cambridge Five' Soviet spy ring, defected 1951.

Burt, Commander Len: Metropolitan Police Special Branch officer responsible for liaison with MI5.

Cadogan, Sir Alec: Appointed permanent undersecretary at the

Foreign Office in 1938, in place of Vansittart whose vehement opposition to appeasement had become unacceptable.

Chamberlain, Neville: Prime Minister 1937–May 1940, architect of appeasement.

Chenhalls: Family friends of Klop and Nadia. Joan worked with Klop at MI5, her brother Alfred was a showbusiness accountant and agent, sister Hope also had film star connections.

Christie, Group Captain Malcolm: Vansittart's foremost intelligence agent and peacebroker.

Churchill, Winston: Conservative, vociferous opponent of appeasement. Prime Minister, May 1940–45, 1951–55.

Cooper, Duff: Secretary of State for War 1937–38, wartime Chancellor of Duchy of Lancaster, friend of Moura Budberg.

Dalton, Hugh: Labour minister initially in charge of the Special Operations Executive.

Dansey, Claude: MI6 assistant chief, controller of the Z organisation of agents.

Delmer, Sefton: Journalist, head of black propaganda unit during WWII, friend of Otto John.

Dukes, Sir Paul: MI6 officer in Russia at the time of the revolution, closely linked to the Mariinsky Theatre.

Eden, Anthony: Foreign Secretary 1935–38, 1940–45, 1951–55, Prime Minister 1955–57.

Edward VIII: King, 1936, thereafter Duke of Windsor. Abdicated to marry American divorcee Wallis Simpson. Suspected of Fascist sympathies.

Elliott, Nicholas: Fellow MI6 officer and friend of Klop and Nadia.

Foote, Alexander: Radio operator for the Soviet *Rote Drei* network in Switzerland.

Fuchs, Klaus: German refugee, naturalised British, convicted of betraying atom bomb secrets to the Russians.

Gledhill, Cecil: MI6 station chief in Lisbon.

Halifax, Lord: Foreign Secretary 1938–40, ambassador to USA 1940–46.

Hampshire, Stuart: Philosopher, MI6 analyst and interrogator working alongside Klop.

Hoare, Sir Samuel: Former MI6 officer and Cabinet minister, WWII ambassador to Spain.

Intelligence services:

GC&CS (Government Code and Cipher School): Signals intelligence including Bletchley Park, Enigma, Ultra and ISOS decrypts.

MI5 (aka the Security Service): Domestic counter-espionage, including the Colonies.

MI6 (aka SIS – Secret Intelligence Service): Foreign intelligence.

SOE (aka Special Operations Executive): Responsible for sabotage behind enemy lines and Resistance operations.

Kell, Sir Vernon: Founder and director general of MI5, 1909–40.

Kerby: Captain Henry 'Bob': Russian-born member of MI5 and MI6, friend of Klop and of Russian royal family. Latterly a Conservative MP.

Korda, Sir Alexander: Hungarian-born film director with links to MI6.

Kuczynski: German-Jewish refugee family, most of whom were committed Communists and Soviet agents. Jurgen recruited atom spy Klaus Fuchs and his sister Ursula (codename Sonja). Ran Fuchs and other agents worldwide.

Liddell, Guy: Head of counter-intelligence, later deputy director of MI5. Recruited Klop.

Lockhart, Robert Bruce: British diplomat involved in plot to assassinate Lenin. Lover of Moura Budberg. Later friend and supporter of Klop in London.

Loxley, Peter: Senior Foreign Office liaison officer with MI6.

MacDonald, Ramsay: Labour, Prime Minister 1924, 1929–31 then as leader of National Government 1931–35.

Maclean, Donald: Member of 'Cambridge Five' Soviet spy ring, defected 1951.

Trevor-Roper, Hugh (later Lord Dacre): Historian and analyst for MI6.

Vansittart, Lord (Robert): Permanent undersecretary at the Foreign Office and vociferous opponent of Hitler's Germany. Obtained British nationality for Klop.

Venlo: Place on the Dutch-German border where MI6 officers Best and Stevens were captured in a Gestapo sting operation.

Vivian, Valentine: Head of the anti-Comintern Section V of MI6, and later deputy director.

White, Sir Dick: Klop's case officer in MI5, later director of MI5 and then MI6.

Willert, Sir Arthur: Head of News Department at the Foreign Office.

Windsor, Duke of: See Edward VIII.

Winsor, Rita: MI6 colleague of Klop's in Lisbon.

GERMANY

Abwehr: See Intelligence.

Adenauer, Konrad: Leader of Christian Democratic Union (CDU) and first post-war Chancellor in 1949.

Banse, Felix: Klop's Wolff Bureau colleague in Amsterdam and London.

Bene, Otto: Leader of German Nazi party in Britain prior to WWII.

Bernstorff, Count Albrecht: Respected anti-Nazi diplomat who formed a social double act with Klop.

Brüning, Heinrich: Leader of the Centre Party and Reichs Chancellor, 1930–32, later exiled to Britain and US.

Bussche, Baron Axel von dem: Volunteered for suicide mission to kill Hitler. Related to Klop's godmother.

Canaris, Admiral Wilhelm: Head of the Abwehr, aloof from but not unsympathetic to anti-Nazi conspiracies.

Cramer, Fritz: Head of SS in Lisbon and one of Klop's main adversaries.

Fidrmuc, Paul (codename Ostro): Successful Abwehr agent in Portugal.

Gehlen, Major General Reinhard: Hitler's head of military intelligence on the Eastern Front, Cold War head of West German intelligence.

Gestapo: See Intelligence.

Geyr von Schweppenburg, General Leo: Military attaché in London 1933–37, informant of Klop's and organiser of secret pre-war peace talks.

Goebbels, Joseph: Hitler's propaganda minister.

Hess, Rudolf: Hitler's deputy who flew to Britain in May 1941 on an apparently unauthorised peace mission.

Hesse, Fritz: Klop's pro-Nazi replacement as press officer in the London embassy.

Heydrich, Reinhard: Director of RSHA Reich security service, assassinated in Czechoslovakia in 1942 provoking terrible reprisals.

Hilger, Gustav: German diplomat in Moscow, helped Klop and Nadia escape in 1920; instrumental in Treaty of Rapallo; interrogated by Klop at the end of the WWII; became a Cold War adviser to the US government.

Hitler, Adolf: Founder of Nazi party, Chancellor 1933–45.

Himmler, Heinrich: Interior Minister and head of the RSHA.

Intelligence services:

  Abwehr: Military intelligence responsible for foreign espionage until supplanted by the RSHA.

  RSHA: Reich Main Security Office *Reichssicherheitshauptamt* incorporating the Gestapo (security police) SS (political police) and SD (security service) under the command of Heinrich Himmler.

John, Otto: Lufthansa lawyer involved in the resistance movement and the July 10 plot against Hitler. Defected to Britain 1944. Cold War head of German intelligence section, defected behind the Iron Curtain and back again.

Jung, Edgar: Anti-Hitler propagandist murdered during Night of the Long Knives, close friend of Klop's contact Franz Mariaux.

Jünger, Ernst: Writer and philosopher, served with Hans Speidel in Paris during WWII.

Kaltenbrunner, Ernst: Director of RSHA under Himmler.

Kauder, Richard: Austrian behind the Max Klatt spy ring.

Klatt, Max: WWII spy network based in Bulgaria, later discovered to be a Russian double-cross operation.

Kuczynski: See under Britain.

Louis Ferdinand, Prince: Grandson of Kaiser Wilhelm II and supporter of German resistance to Hitler.

Maltzan, Ago von: Head of eastern department of the German Foreign Office. Sponsored Klop's 1920 visit to Russia.

Mariaux, Franz: Journalist contact of Klop's in Lisbon, linked to conservative political opposition to Hitler.

Max von Hohenlohe, Prince: Peripatetic German agent and peacebroker.

Oster, General Hans: Nazi-hating deputy head of the Abwehr executed for his part in the 20 July 1944 plot to assassinate Hitler.

Putlitz, Wolfgang zu: Aristocrat and diplomat, Klop's best pre-war source.

Rathenau, Walther: German Foreign Minister in 1922, assassinated in right-wing plot soon after signing the Treaty of Rapallo.

Ribbentrop, Joachim von: Ambassador in London 1936–38, Foreign Minister 1938–45.

Roessler, Rudolf: German exile in Switzerland, principal source of intelligence for the Soviet *Rote Drei* network.

Rommel, Field Marshal Erwin: Head of Army Group B responsible for resisting D-Day landings, supporter of 20 July plot.

Rot, Mirko: Yugoslav Abwehr agent who defected to Britain and revealed details of Max Klatt spy ring.

RSHA: See Intelligence.

Schneider, Willi: Valet and lover of Wolfgang zu Putlitz.

Schalburg, Vera: German agent captured in Scotland and interrogated by Klop.

Schellenberg, Walther: Intelligence officer, head of SS Foreign Intelligence from 1944.

SD/SS: See Intelligence.

Seeckt, General Hans von: commander responsible for re-establishing the German army in the 1920s.

Speidel, Hans: Fellow officer of Klop's in the 123rd Grenadiers during the First World War and lifelong friend. One of Hitler's generals but an anti-Nazi involved in the plot to assassinate him. The first German to hold a senior position in NATO forces after the Second World War.

Spiecker, Dr Carl: Anti-Nazi politician whose information led to the Venlo Incident.

Stauffenberg, Colonel Claus von: Planted the bomb intended to kill Hitler on 20 July 1944.

Wilhelm II, Kaiser: Abdicated as last emperor of Germany after First World War.

Wolff Bureau: German news wire service later absorbed into the state-controlled DNB, German News Bureau. Klop was their London correspondent from 1921–30.

Wurmann, Major Richard (codename Harlequin): Head of Abwehr in Algeria, captured and interrogated by Klop, revealing extensive details of German military and espionage operations.

RUSSIA

Alexandrovna, Xenia: Grand Duchess, sister of Tsar Nicholas II, figurehead of Russian exile community in Britain.

Baykolov, Anatole: Exile contact of Klop and Guy Liddell, of uncertain loyalty.

Budberg, Moura: Russian countess and socialite, whose lovers included the diplomat Robert Bruce Lockhart and authors Maxim Gorky and H. G. Wells. One of Klop's best informants.

Cheka: See Intelligence.

Dzerzhinsky, Felix: Director of the Cheka, 1917–26.

Feodorovna, Maria: Dowager Empress, mother of Tsar Nicholas II, sister-in-law of British King Edward VII.

Golitsyn (or Galitzine), Prince Vladimir: head of wealthy White Russian family and leader of British exile community.

Gorky, Maxim: Russian writer, friend of the Benois family and lover of Moura Budberg.

Gouzenko, Igor: Soviet defector who revealed the existence of the atom bomb spy Alan Nunn May.

Horvath, General Dmitri: See Nadia's family.

Intelligence services:

    Cheka: Military and internal security police formed by Lenin after the Russian Revolution.

    NKVD: Overall state security apparatus which at varying times included OGPU (secret police) and was also responsible for foreign intelligence gathering, initially through the Comintern. Mutated into the KGB during the Cold War and more recently known as the SVR.

    GRU: Military intelligence often running parallel spy operations to the NKVD.

    Smersh: Counter-intelligence service.

Karsavina, Tamara: Friend of Nadia, principal dancer of Imperial Ballet and Ballet Russes, married British diplomat Henry Bruce.

Kerensky, Alexander: Leader of provisional Russian government prior to the 1917 Bolshevik Revolution.

KGB: See Intelligence.

Kuczynski: See under Britain.

Lang, Ira: Principal supplier of the Max Klatt spy ring, later revealed to be a Soviet agent.

Maisky, Ivan: Soviet ambassador in London 1932–43 and reputedly a friend of Klop's from 1920.

Nicholas II: Tsar of the Russian Empire 1894–1917 when he was forced to abdicate in the wake of popular riots and the February revolution.

NKVD: See Intelligence.

OGPU: See Intelligence.

Poleschauk, Valeria: Secretary to Nicholas Schreiber, childhood friend of Nadia, introduced her to Klop.

Romanoff, George Leonidovitch: Spy turned priest, one-time secretary to General Turkul. Briefed Klop on Soviet penetration of White Russian exile groups.

Rote Drei (Red Three): Russian intelligence operation in Switzerland, principally directed against Germany.

Rote Kapelle (Red Orchestra): Russian intelligence network in Germany.

Sabline, Eugen: Chargé d'affaires at the embassy in London until 1917, thereafter semi-official diplomatic representative of the exile community.

St Petersburg: Capital of tsarist Russia, renamed Petrograd in 1914 and Leningrad in 1924, reverting to St Petersburg in 1991. With some exceptions, referred to throughout as St Petersburg.

Schreiber, Nicholas: Retired naval officer who rented a room in his apartment in St Petersburg to Klop – scene of his first meeting with Nadia.

Stalin, Joseph: Soviet leader (as general secretary of the central committee of the Communist Party) 1922–52.

Turkul, Prince Anton: Leader of various anti-Communist exile groups but strongly suspected of being a Soviet agent and member of the Max Klatt spy ring.

Vlasov, General Andrei: Leader of exile army prepared to fight for Hitler against Soviet regime.

Voss, Claudius: Soviet agent used to penetrate German navy. Also used by MI6 pre-WWII.

Wolkoff, Admiral Nikolai: Exile and former naval attaché at the London embassy. Daughter Anna was convicted of espionage on behalf of Germany during WWII.

UNITED STATES

Bedaux, Charles: Nazi-sympathising millionaire businessman close to the Duke and Duchess of Windsor.

Blum, Paul: OSS agent who worked with Klop in London and Switzerland.

Donovan, Col. Bill: Head of OSS Intelligence service.

Dulles, Allen: Swiss station chief for OSS, later head of the CIA.

Intelligence services:

OSS: Office of Strategic Services, forerunner of the CIA (Central Intelligence Agency).

FBI: Federal Bureau of Investigation, headed by J. Edgar Hoover and fiercely protective of its role in internal security.

CIC: Counter Intelligence Corps of US Army used for Nazi interrogations.

Roosevelt, Franklin D.: US President 1933–45.

Silver, Arnold: Interrogator working with Klop in Max Klatt case, later senior CIA official.

Simpson, Mrs Wallis: Mistress of King Edward VIII, married him after the abdication and given the title Duchess of Windsor.

MISCELLANEOUS

Alemayehu, Prince: Infant son of Emperor Theodore of Ethiopia, brought to Britain and raised under Queen Victoria's patronage.

Bartik, Major Josef: Czech head of counter-intelligence in London in WWII.

Cevat, Daan: Well-connected Dutch art dealer and secret agent who befriended Klop in the 1930s.

Chanel, Coco: French fashion designer, with a German lover during WWII, used her past friendship with Churchill and the Duke of Westminster to make peace overtures.

Freie Deutsche Kulturbund: German exile group in London with links to Soviet agents.

Garcia, Juan Pujol (codename Garbo): Spanish businessman, Britain's most successful double agent.

Labarthe, André: Editor of *La France Libre* in London during WWII and employer of Moura Budberg. Later exposed as Soviet agent.

Masson, Roger: Head of Swiss military intelligence.

Moravec, František: Head of Czech Intelligence Service in WWII.

Muselier, Admiral Emile: Left-leaning rival to General de Gaulle for leadership of the Free French. Connected to Moura Budberg.

Pan, Major Václav: Head of Czech intelligence in Lisbon.

Pavelić, Ante: Croat pro-Nazi Ustashe dictator wanted for war crimes but allowed to escape, apparently with British connivance.

Radó, Sándor: Hungarian controller of Soviet *Rote Drei* network in Switzerland; married to Helene Jansen whose two sisters were naturalised British.

Sedlacek, Karel: Czech agent in Switzerland who had access to *Rote Drei* network and fed its intelligence back to Britain.

Slama, Václav: Klop's main contact in Czech intelligence.

Szymańska, Halina: Wife of former Polish military attaché to Berlin, lived in Switzerland and acted as conduit between Admiral Canaris and Allied Intelligence services.

Theodore, Emperor (aka Tewodros): Leader who united the rival tribes of Abyssinia (Ethiopia) by conquest. He brought down the wrath of the British Empire by taking their representative and other Europeans hostage.

Victoire (codename of Mathilde Lucie Carre): Member of French Resistance, captured and escaped to London where she was suspected of working for the Germans. Interrogated by Klop.

BIBLIOGRAPHY

ARCHIVE SOURCES

AA: Auswärtiges Amt (German Foreign Office), Politischés Archiv, Kurstraße 36, 10117 Berlin

British Library, 96 Euston Road, London NW1 2DB – India Office Collection.

CA: Churchill Archives Centre, Churchill College, Cambridge CB3 0DS

L-H: Liddell Hart Centre for Military Archives, King's College, Strand, London WC2R 2LS

IWM: Imperial War Museum, Lambeth Road, London SE1 6HZ

LB-W(S): Baden-Württemberg Central State Archives, Konrad-Adenauer-Straße 4 D-70173 Stuttgart

LB-W(L): Baden-Württemberg State Archives, Arsenalplatz 3, D-71638 Ludwigsburg

TNA: The National Archives, Kew, Richmond, Surrey, TW9 4DU (Categories: FO – Foreign Office; HO – Home Office; HW – Government Communications Headquarters (GCHQ); KV – Security Service, MI5; WO – War Office)

USNA: United States National Archives, 8601 Adelphi Road, College Park, MD 20740-6001

* Currency conversions to 2011 equivalents were calculated using the 'real price' index compiled by Professors Lawrence Officer and Samuel Williamson of the University of Illinois at www.measuringworth.com.

BOOKS AND JOURNALS

(Published in London unless otherwise stated)

Aarons, Mark, and Loftus, John: *Ratlines: How the Vatican's Nazi Networks Betrayed Western Intelligence to the Soviets* (Heinemann, 1991)

Aldrich, Richard J.: *The Hidden Hand: Britain, America and Cold War Secret Intelligence* (John Murray, 2001)

Alexander, Tania: *A Little of All These, An Estonian Childhood* (Jonathan Cape, 1987)

Amort C. and Jedlicka I. M.: *The Canaris File* translated from the Czech by Roger Gheysens (Allan Wingate, 1970)

Andrew, Christopher: *Secret Service, The Making of the British Intelligence Community* (Heinemann, 1985)

Andrew, Christopher: *The Defence of the Realm: The Authorised History of MI5* (Allen Lane, 2009)

Benois, Alexandre: *Memoirs Vols I & II,* trans. Moura Budberg (Chatto & Windus, 1960)

Benois Ustinov, Nadia: *Klop and the Ustinov family* (Sidgwick & Jackson, 1973)

Berberova, Nina: *Moura: The Dangerous Life of the Baroness Budberg* trans. by Marian Schwarz and Richard D. Sylvester (New York Review of Books, New York, 2005)

Bormann, Martin: *Hitler's Table Talk* (Weidenfeld and Nicolson, 1953) English translation by Norman Cameron and R. H. Stevens of the *Bormann-Vermecke*, the notes kept on the orders of Hitler's secretary Martin Bormann of meal time conversations with Hitler.

Borovik, Genrikh: *The Philby Files, The Secret Life of the Master Spy – KGB Archives Revealed* ed. Phillip Knightley (Little, Brown & Co., 1994)

Bower, Tom: *The Perfect English Spy* (Heinemann, 1995)

Breitman, Richard (co-authors Norman J. W. Goda, Timothy Naftali, and Robert Wolfe): *U.S. Intelligence and the Nazis* (Cambridge University Press, 2005)

Bristow, Desmond (with Bill Bristow): *A Game of Moles: The Deceptions of an MI6 Officer* (Little Brown & Co., 1993)

Brown, Anthony Cave: *Bodyguard of Lies* (W H Allen, 1976)

Buchanan, Meriel: *Ambassador's Daughter* (Cassell & Co., 1958)

Carter, Miranda: *Anthony Blunt, His Lives* (Macmillan, 2001)

Churchill, Winston S.: *The Second World War, Volume 1, The Gathering Storm* (Cassell & Co., 1950)

Cockburn, Claud: *In Time of Trouble* (Rupert Hart-Davis, 1956)

Colvin, Ian: *Chief of Intelligence* (Victor Gollancz, 1951)

Costello, John: *Mask of Treachery* (Collins, 1988)

Delmer, Sefton: *Black Boomerang* (Viking Press, New York, 1962)

Doerries, Reinhard R.: *Hitler's Last Chief of Foreign Intelligence* (Frank Cass, 2003)

Dorril, Stephen: *MI6 Fifty Years of Special Operations* (Fourth Estate, 2000)

Dulles, Allen: *From Hitler's Doorstep: The Wartime Intelligence Reports of Allen Dulles,* ed Neal H. Petersen (Pennsylvania State University Press, Pennsylvania 1996)

Eisler, Ejal Jakob: *Peter Martin Metzler (1824-1907): Ein christlicher Missionar im Heiligen Land* (Haifa University, 1999)

Elliott, Nicholas: *Never Judge a Man by his Umbrella* (Michael Russell, Norwich,1991)

Elliott, Nicholas: *With My Little Eye* (Michael Russell, Norwich, 1993)

Enssle, Manfred J.: *Five Theses on German Everyday Life after World War II* (Central European History, Vol 26, No 1, 1993, Cambridge University Press)

FitzGibbon, Constantine: *Secret Intelligence in the Twentieth Century* (Hart-Davis, MacGibbon, 1976)

George, Arthur & Elena: *St Petersburg, A History* (Sutton Publishing, 2006)

Geyr von Schweppenburg, General Freiherr Leo: *The Critical Years* (Allan Wingate, 1952)

Glees, Anthony: *The Secrets of the Service, British Intelligence and Communist Subversion 1939–51* (Jonathan Cape, 1987)

Goldring, Douglas: *Odd Man Out, The Autobiography of a "Propaganda Novelist"* (Chapman and Hall, 1935)

Graaff, Bob de: *The Stranded Baron and the Upstart at the Crossroads: Wolfgang zu Putlitz and Otto John* (Intelligence and National Security, Vol 6, No 4, 1991)

Hesse, Fritz: *Das Spiel um Deutschland* (Paul List, Munich, 1953)

Hilger, Gustav & Meyer, Alfred G: *The Incompatible Allies* (Macmillan, New York, 1953)

Hirschfeld, Gerhard (ed): *Exile in Great Britain: Refugees from Hitler's Germany* (Berg Publishers, for The German Historical Institute, 1984)

Hoare, Oliver (ed): *Camp 020: MI5 and the Nazi Spies* (Public Record Office, 2000)

Holtz, Avraham & Holtz, Toby Berger: *The Adventuresome Life of Moritz Hall* (Orbis Aethiopicus, ed. Piotr O. Scholz, Karl Schuler Publishing, Albstadt, Germany, 1992)

Hughes, Owain: *Everything I have Always Forgotten* (Seren Books, Bridgend, 2013)

Jeffery, Keith: *MI6, The History of the Secret Intelligence Service 1909–1949* (Bloomsbury, 2010)

Joeres, Neils: *Der Architekt von Rapallo* (PhD dissertation, Ruprecht-Karls-Universität, Heidelberg, 2006)

John, Otto: *Zweimal kam ich heim* (Econ Verlag, Düsseldorf, 1969)

Joll, James: *Europe Since 1870* (Penguin, 1980)

Jones, Wordsworth E.: *A brief account and description of an important collection of archaeological treasures & antiques brought from Palestine by Baron von Ustinov, after 35 years research* (British Museum Department of Greek and Roman Antiquities, 1913)

Kersaudy, François: *Churchill and De Gaulle* (Collins, 1981)

von Klemperer, Klemens: *German Resistance Against Hitler* (Clarendon Press, Oxford, 1992)

Knightley, Phillip: *Philby: The Life and Views of the KGB Masterspy* (Andre Deutsch, 1988)

Korbel, Josef: *Poland between East and West* (Princeton University Press, 1963)

Kurz, Hans Rudolf: *Nachrichtenzentrum Schweiz* (Verlag Huber, Frauenfeld and Stuttgart, 1972)

Lawrence, D. H.: *Reflections on the Death of a Porcupine and Other Essays* edited by Michael Herbert (Cambridge University Press, 1988)

Lewis, Flora: *The Man Who Disappeared, the Strange History of Noel Field* (Arthur Barker, 1965)

Lockhart, Sir Robert Bruce: *Friends, Foes and Foreigners* (Putnam, 1957)

Lockhart, Sir Robert Bruce: *The Diaries of Sir Robert Bruce Lockhart, Volume One* Edited by Kenneth Young, (Macmillan, 1973)

Liddell, Guy: *The Liddell Diaries 1939–1945* (TNA, KV4/185-196, 2002)

The Liddell Diaries 1945–53 (TNA KV 4/466-475, 2012)

Lincoln, W. Bruce: *Sunlight at Midnight: St Petersburg and the Rise of Modern Russia* (Perseus Press, Oxford, 2001)

MacDonald, Callum: *The Venlo Affair* (European Studies Review Vol. 8 No. 4, 1978)

Macintyre, Ben: *Double Cross, the True Story of the D-Day Spies* (Bloomsbury, 2012)

Marshall-Cornwall, James: *Wars and Rumours of Wars* (Secker and Warburg, 1984)

Meier, David Aaron: *A Cold War Catastrophe: The Defection, Investigation, Trials, and Fate of West Germany's Counter-Intelligence Chief: Otto John* (CreateSpace, United States, 2009)

Milne, Tim: *Kim Philby, The Unknown Story of the KGB's Master-Spy* (Biteback, 2014)

Moravec, František: *Master of Spies* (Bodley Head, 1975)

Mosier, John: *The Myth of the Great War* (HarperCollins, New York, 2001)

Mueller, Michael: *Canaris: The Life and Death of Hitler's Spymaster* translated by Geoffrey Brooks (Chatham, 2007)

Muggeridge, Malcolm: *Chronicles of Wasted Time* (Collins, 1972)

Murray, Lynda J.: *A Zest for Life: the story of Alexander Keiller* (Morven Books, Swindon, 1999)

Neebe, Reinhard: *Großindustrie, Staat und NSDAP* (Vandenhoeck & Ruprecht, Göttingen, 1981).

Nicolson, Harold: *Diaries and Letters 1930–1939* edited by Nigel Nicolson (Collins, 1966)

Oxford Dictionary of National Biography (Oxford University Press, 2004 and online)

Payne Best, Sigismund: *The Venlo Incident* (Hutchinson & Co., 1951)

Pedersen, Kirsten: *The History of the Ethiopian Community in the Holy Land from the time of Tewodros II till 1974* (Tantur Ecumenical Institute, Jerusalem, 1983)

Penrose, Antony: *Roland Penrose, The Friendly Surrealist* (Prestel, 2001)

Philby, Rufina, with Mikhail Lyubinov and Hayden Peake: *The Private Life of Kim Philby: The Moscow Years* (St Ermin's Press & Little Brown, 1999)

Prokofiev, Sergey: *Diaries 1915–1923 Behind the Mask* translated and annotated by Anthony Phillips (Faber & Faber, 2008)

Putlitz, Wolfgang zu: *The Putlitz Dossier* (Allan Wingate, 1957)

Radó, Sándor: *Codename Dora*, translated by J. A. Underwood (Abelard, 1977)

Ritter, Nikolaus: *Deckname Dr Rantzau* (Hoffman und Campe, Hamburg, 1972)

Rose, Norman: *Vansittart, Study of a Diplomat* (Heinemann, 1978)

Schellenberg, Walther: *Invasion 1940: The Nazi Invasion Plan for Britain* (St Ermin's Press, 2000)

Schellenberg, Walther: *The Schellenberg Memoirs* (Andre Deutsch, 1956)

Sebba, Anna: *Enid Bagnold, The Authorised Biography* (Weidenfeld & Nicolson, 1986)

Service, Robert: *Spies and Commissars, Bolshevik Russia and the West* (Macmillan, 2011)

Shirer, William L.: *The Rise and Fall of the Third Reich* (Arrow Books, 1998)

Silver, Arnold M.: *Questions, Questions, Questions: Memories of Oberursel* (Frank Cass: Intelligence and National Security, Vol. 8, No. 2, April 1993)

Skupinska-Løvset, Ilona: *The Ustinov Collection: The Palestinian Pottery* (Universitetsforlaget, Oslo, 1976)

Soltikow, Michael Graf: *Ich war mittendrin, Meine Jahre bei Canaris* (Paul Neff Verlag, Vienna, Berlin, 1980)

Speidel, Hans: *Aus unserer Zeit: Erinnerungen* (Verlag Ullstein, Berlin 1977)

Stanley, Henry Morton: *Coomassie & Magdala: The Story of Two British Campaigns in Africa* (Samson Low, Marston, Low & Searle, 1874)

Steven, Stewart: *Operation Splinter Factor* (Hodder and Stoughton, 1974)

Stone, Norman and Glenny, Michael: *The Other Russia* (Faber & Faber, 1990)

Stutterheim, Kurt von: *Die Majestät des Gewissens* (Hans Christian Verlag, Hamburg, 1962)

Sütterlin, Ingmar: *Die 'Russische Abteilung' des Auswärtigen Amtes in der Weimarer Republik* (Duncker & Humblot, Historische Forschungen Bd 51, Berlin, 1994)

Talbot Rice, Tamara: *Tamara: Memoirs of St Petersburg, Paris, Oxford and Byzantium*, ed. Elizabeth Talbot Rice (John Murray, 1996)

Tittenhofer, Mark A.: *The Rote Drei: Getting Behind the Lucy Myth* (CIA Historical Review Programme, Washington 1993 & online)

Tolstoy, Aleksey: *Road to Calvary* trans. Edith Bone (Hutchinson, 1945)

Trevor-Roper, Hugh: *The Philby Affair* (William Kimber, 1968)

Ustinov, Peter: *Dear Me* (Arrow, 1998)

Ustinov, Peter: *My Russia* (Macmillan, 1983)

Waller, John H.: *The Unseen War in Europe, Espionage and Conspiracy in the Second World War* (IB Tauris, 1996)

Wells, H. G.: *H. G. Wells in Love: Postscript to an Experiment in Autobiography,* ed. G. P. Wells (Faber & Faber, 1984)

West, Nigel: *Historical Dictionary of British Intelligence* (Scarecrow Press, Oxford, 2005)

West, Nigel and Tsarev, Oleg: *The Crown Jewels, the British Secrets at the Heart of the KGB Archives* (HarperCollins, 1998)

West, Nigel and Tsarev, Oleg: *Triple X, Secrets from the Cambridge Spies* (Yale University Press, 2009)

West, William J.: *Truth Betrayed* (Duckworth, 1987)

Wheeler-Bennett, John W.: *The Nemesis of Power* (Macmillan, 1953)

Wiskemann, Elizabeth: *The Europe I Saw* (Collins, 1968)

Wolfe, Robert: *Gustav Hilger: From Hitler's Foreign Office to CIA Consultant* (Online Essay by US National Archivist)

Wright, Peter: *Spycatcher* (Bantam Doubleday Dell, New York, 1988)

Zinoviev, Sofka: *Red Princess: A Revolutionary Life* (Granta, 2007)

ENDNOTES

1   Tom Bower: *The Perfect English Spy* p. 29.

2   Nicholas Elliott: *With My Little Eye* p. 15.

3   Peter Ustinov: *Dear Me* p. 11.

4   Sir Robert Napier's despatch, 12 May 1868, British Library India Office collection: IOR/L/ MIL/17/17/22; Henry Morton Stanley: *Coomassie & Magdala*.

5   Avraham & Toby Holtz: *The Adventuresome Life of Moritz Hall*.

6   Peter Ustinov: *Dear Me* pp. 8-11. Ejal Jakob Eisler: *Peter Martin Metzler (1824-1907)*.

7   Avraham & Toby Holtz: *The Adventuresome Life Of Moritz Hall*.

8   Peter Ustinov: *Dear Me* pp.10-11.

9   Nadia Benois: *Klop* pp. 29-35.

10 Nadia Benois: *Klop* p. 37. *passim*.

11 Peter Ustinov: *Dear Me* p. 46.

12 Wordsworth E. Jones: British Museum archive

13 Ilona Skupinska-Løvset: *The Ustinov Collection: Palestinian Pottery* p. 17.

14 John Mosier: *The Myth of the Great War* p. 158.

15 Hans Speidel: *Aus unserer Zeit* pp. 22-24.

16 *War Budget Magazine* 13 July 1916

17 LB-W(S) M411 Bü813

18 Hans Speidel: *Aus unserer Zeit* pp. 25-26.

19 LB-W(S) M430/3 Bü11668

20 Nadia Benois: *Klop* pp. 57-63.

21 Robert Service: *Spies and Commissars* p. 227.

22 D. H. Lawrence: *Reflections on the Death of a Porcupine and Other Essays* p. xxix introduction.

23 Neils Joeres: *Der Architekt von Rapallo* pp. 141-144.

24 Ingmar Sütterlin: *Die 'Russische Abteilung' des Auswärtigen Amtes in der Weimarer Republik* p. 155.

25   Josef Korbel: *Poland between East and West* p. 76.

26   Alexandre Benois: *Memoirs Vol II* pp. 59-61.

27   W. Bruce Lincoln: *Sunlight at Midnight* pp. 197-200.

28   Sergey Prokofiev: *Diaries 1915-23* pp. 25-31, 72, 204.

29   Arthur George: *St Petersburg* pp. 373-375.

30   Tamara Talbot Rice: *Tamara: Memoirs of St Petersburg, Paris, Oxford and Byzantium* p. 20.

31   W. Bruce Lincoln: *Sunlight at Midnight* p. 229.

32   Tamara Talbot Rice: *Tamara: Memoirs of St Petersburg, Paris, Oxford and Byzantium* p. 52.

33   Aleksey Tolstoy: *Road to Calvary* p. 199.

34   Alexandre Benois: *Memoirs Vol I* pp. 146-151.

35   Alexandre Benois: *Memoirs Vol I* pp. 163-164.

36   Arthur George: *St Petersburg* p. 458.

37   Nadia Benois: *Klop* pp. 87-89.

38   Nadia Benois: *Klop* pp. 85-90.

39   Personal interview, February 2014.

40   Nadia Benois: *Klop* pp. 67-68.

41   Nadia Benois: *Klop* pp. 75-82.

42   Gustav Hilger: *Incompatible Allies* p. 31.

43   Peter Ustinov: *Dear Me* p. 29.

44   Peter Ustinov: *Dear Me* p. 29.

45   Nadia Benois: *Klop* pp. 110-122.

46   AA PAIV Band 2, Russia Po 5, R83457

47   AA PAIV Band 2, Russia Po 5, R83457

48   John H. Waller: *The Unseen War in Europe* pp. 28-31.

49   Nadia Benois: *Klop* p. 125.

50   Nadia Benois: *Klop* pp. 126-134.

51   Personal interview, February 2014.

52   Nadia Benois: *Klop* pp. 144-146.

53   Nadia Benois: *Klop* p. 246.

54   *Daily Mirror*, 29 June 1929 p. 6.

55   Kirsten Pedersen: *The History of the Ethiopian Community in the Holy Land* pp. 79, 96, 118.

56   Peter Ustinov: *Dear Me* p. 48-49.

57   Nadia Benois: *Klop* p. 174.

58   Nadia Benois: *Klop* p. 178.

59 Peter Ustinov: *Dear Me* p. 45-46.

60 Peter Ustinov: *Dear Me* p. 351.

61 TNA FO 395/336 P1456

62 TNA FO 395/372 P2129/P2131

63 TNA KV 2/347 & GFM 33/4127

64 TNA FO 371/12885 C3226

65 TNA FO 371/14366 C9223

66 Robert Bruce Lockhart: *Diaries Volume One* pp. 81, 98, 200.

67 Robert Bruce Lockhart: *Friends, Foes and Foreigners* p. 144.

68 Martin Bormann: *Hitler's Table Talk* p. 276.

69 Norman Rose: *Vansittart, Study of a Diplomat* pp. 1-41.

70 Norman Rose: *Vansittart, Study of a Diplomat* p. 103.

71 *DNB;* Keith Jeffery *MI6* p. 177.

72 *DNB*

73 *DNB*

74 Nadia Benois: *Klop* p. 186.

75 AA 6A WTB Band 2 File R122211

76 William L. Shirer: *The Rise and Fall of the Third Reich* pp. 209-210.

77 TNA FO 372/965 T9306

78 TNA FO 371/16751 C10679

79 Harold Nicolson: *Diaries & Letters 1930-39* p. 121.

80 Anna Sebba: *Enid Bagnold, The Authorised Biography* pp. 112-113.

81 Kurt von Stuttenheim: *Die Majestät des Gewissens* pp. 53-56.

82 Harold Nicolson: *Diaries and Letters 1930-39* pp. 121, 152, 266.

83 Kurt von Stutterheim: *Die Majestät des Gewissens* p. 61.

84 Nadia Benois: *Klop* pp. 201-202.

85 TNA KV 4/111

86 Fritz Hesse: *Das Spiel um Deutschland* p. 37.

87 Fritz Hesse: *Das Spiel um Deutschland* p. 37.

88 Peter Ustinov: *Dear Me* p. 82 & 102.

89 TNA HO 334/139 AZ6678

90 Peter Ustinov: *Dear Me* p. 120.

91 Peter Ustinov: *Dear Me* pp. 95-96.

92 *DNB*

93   Peter Ustinov: *Dear Me* pp. 83-89.

94   Peter Ustinov: *Dear Me* pp. 106.

95   Nadia Benois: *Klop* p. 176.

96   *Daily Mail*, 1 November 1932, 27 June 1936

97   Nadia Benois: *Klop* pp. 182-184, 190-192.

98   TNA KV 2/819

99   Stephen Dorril: *MI6 Fifty Years of Special Operations* pp. 404-412.

100 Bernard Wasserstein: 'The British Government and the German Immigration 1933–1945' (Hirschfeld – *Exiles in Great Britain* p. 63.)

101 Francis L. Carsten: 'German Refugees in Great Britain 1933–1945' (Hirschfeld – *Exiles in Great Britain* pp. 11-13.)

102 John P. Fox: 'Nazi Germany and German Emigration to Great Britain' (Hirschfeld – *Exiles in Great Britain* pp. 48-52.)

103 TNA KV 2/343-344

104 TNA KV 2/390

105 Ian Colvin: *Chief of Intelligence* pp. 60-61.

106 TNA KV 2/390

107 Tom Bower: *The Perfect English Spy* pp. 28-31.

108 Anthony Cave Brown: *Bodyguard of Lies* pp. 140-145.

109 Winston Churchill: *The Gathering Storm* pp. 168-171.

110 CA VNST 1/19

111 Nadia Benois: *Klop* p. 179.

112 Antony Penrose: *Roland Penrose, The Friendly Surrealist* p. 82.

113 TNA KV 2/350-351, HO 213/1941

114 Bob de Graaff: *The Stranded Baron and the Upstart at the Crossroads*.

115 Claud Cockburn: *In Time of Trouble* pp. 103-104, 194-198.

116 Wolfgang zu Putlitz: *The Putlitz Dossier*.

117 Bob de Graaff: *The Stranded Baron and the Upstart at the Crossroads*.

118 TNA KV 4/170

119 John Costello: *Mask of Treachery* pp. 307-309.

120 Miranda Carter, *Anthony Blunt, His Lives* p. 234.

121 Peter Wright: *Spycatcher* pp. 85-86.

122 General Leo Geyr von Schweppenburg: *The Critical Years* pp. 15-16.

123 Peter Ustinov: *Michael Parkinson chat show*, BBC Television.

124 Christopher Andrew: *Defence of the Realm* pp. 201/899

125 John Wheeler-Bennett: *The Nemesis of Power* pp. 410-415.

126 IWM *Payne Best private papers* SPB3

127 Christopher Andrew: *Defence of the Realm* p. 202.

128 TNA KV 4/16

129 TNA FO 1093/107

130 TNA KV 2/915

131 TNA FO 1093/86

132 Christopher Andrew: *Secret Service* pp. 412-417.

133 Anthony Cave Brown: *Bodyguard of Lies* pp. 173-174; James Marshall-Cornwall: *Wars and Rumours of Wars* p. 125.

134 Klemens von Klemperer: *German Resistance Against Hitler* pp. 119-120.

135 TNA KV 4/170

136 TNA KV 4/185 *Liddell Diaries* August–September 1939.

137 Wolfgang zu Putlitz: *The Putlitz Dossier* pp. 184-194.

138 Michael Graf Soltikow: *Ich war mittendrin: Meine Jahre bei Canaris* pp. 45-60, 185-192.

139 TNA FO 371/23057

140 USNA RG226 190/08/05/06 136A Box 4

141 TNA KV 2/1741, KV 2/3643

142 Ben Macintyre: *Double Cross* p. 71.

143 TNA KV 4/185 *Liddell Diaries* September 14, 1939; Christopher Andrew: *Defence of the Realm* p. 242.

144 Keith Jeffery: *MI6* p. 383.

145 Christopher Andrew: *Defence of the Realm* pp. 200-201.

146 *Hansard* September 1, 1939.

147 IWM SPB3 09/51/1

148 Callum MacDonald: *The Venlo Affair.*

149 John Wheeler-Bennett: *Nemesis of Power* pp. 467-469.

150 TNA KV 4/185 *Liddell Diaries,* Oct 11, 1939.

151 Wolfgang zu Putlitz: *The Putlitz Dossier* pp. 197-198.

152 Sigismund Payne Best: *The Venlo Incident* pp. 12-17.

153 TNA KV 2/279

154 CA CHRS 1/30

155 USNA RG263 ZZ 18 Box 112

156   W. J. West: *Truth Betrayed* pp. 189-200.

157   Nicholas Elliott: *Never Judge a Man by his Umbrella* pp. 101-103.

158   TNA FO 1093/202

159   František Moravec: *Master of Spies* pp. 144-145, 181-190; Amort & Jedlicka: *The Canaris Files* pp. 45-48.

160   TNA KV 2/2106

161   Callum MacDonald: *The Venlo Affair.*

162   TNA FO 800/322

163   TNA KV 2/3768

164   John H. Waller: *The Unseen War in Europe* pp. 229-237.

165   TNA KV 2/14

166   TNA KV 2/15

167   Nadia Benois: *Klop* pp. 207-210.

168   TNA KV 2/14

169   TNA KV 2/15

170   TNA KV 2/15

171   TNA KV 2/16

172   Nikolaus Ritter: *Deckname Dr Rantzau* pp. 315-316.

173   TNA KV 2/927

174   TNA KV 2/297

175   TNA KV 2/928

176   TNA KV 2/928

177   TNA KV 2/928

178   TNA KV 2/928

179   *The Times* p. 8 November 11, 1942.

180   Michael Mueller: *Canaris: The Life and Death of Hitler's Spymaster* p. 222.

181   Richard Breitman: *US Intelligence and the Nazis* p. 94.

182   TNA KV 2/268; *Liddell Diaries* 23 January, 12 and 23 February 1943.

183   TNA KV 2/275

184   TNA KV 2/268

185   USNA RG226 Entry 190 Box 392

186   Anthony Cave Brown: *Bodyguard of Lies* p. 314.

187   Allen Dulles: *From Hitler's Doorstep* pp. 206-207, 595.

188   Hugh Trevor-Roper: *The Philby Affair* p. 78.

189 TNA KV4/192: *Liddell Diaries* p. 409.

190 Anthony Cave Brown: *Bodyguard of Lies* p. 315.

191 Genrikh Borovik: *The Philby Files* pp. 226-228.

192 Rufina Philby: *The Private Life of Kim Philby* pp. 90-91.

193 USNA RG 226 Entry 124 Box 13

194 Desmond Bristow: *A Game of Moles* pp. 150-159.

195 Tim Milne: *Kim Philby: The Unknown Story* pp. 130-133.

196 Phillip Knightley: *Philby: The Life and Views of the KGB Masterspy* pp. 107-110.

197 William L. Shirer: *The Rise and Fall of the Third Reich* pp. 1042-1072.

198 CIA online historical note.

199 Richard Breitman: *US Intelligence and the Nazis* pp. 100-101; USNA RG226 Entry 210 Box 304.

200 TNA FO 1093/219

201 Anthony Glees: *The Secrets of the Service* pp. 110-118.

202 Hans Speidel: *Aus unserer Zeit* pp. 109-112.

203 Hans Speidel: *Aus unserer Zeit* pp. 169-171.

204 Reinhard Neebe: *Grossindustrie, Staat und NSDAP* pp. 20-21.

205 Manfred J. Enssle: *Five Theses on German Everyday Life* pp. 5-7.

206 USNA RG319 270/84/1/01 Box 673

207 TNA KV 4/194 *Liddell Diaries* pp. 219-221.

208 Nadia Benois: *Klop* p. 215.

209 Keith Jeffery: *MI6* pp. 570-572.

210 TNA KV 2/197

211 TNA KV 2/198-201

212 TNA KV 2/198-199

213 TNA KV 4/469: *Liddell Diaries* pp. 105-110.

214 TNA KV 2/1457

215 Society of Former Special Agents of the FBI.

216 USNA RG65 230/86/11/3 Box 2

217 TNA FO 1093/206

218 Keith Jeffery: *MI6* pp. 508-509.

219 Nadia Benois: *Klop* p. 215.

220 Walther Schellenberg: *Invasion 1940* p. 256.

221 William L. Shirer: *The Rise and Fall of the Third Reich* p. 991.

222   USNA RG65 230/86/11/3 Box 2

223   TNA KV 2/95

224   USNA RG65 230/86/11/3 Box 2

225   TNA KV 2/95

226   Oliver Hoare: *Camp 020: MI5 and the Nazi Spies* p. 365.

227   Reinhard R. Doerries: *Hitler's Last Chief of Foreign Intelligence* p. 47.

228   TNA KV 2/99

229   TNA KV 2/95

230   Reinhard R. Doerries: *Hitler's Last Chief of Foreign Intelligence* p. 101.

231   USNA RG226 Entry 210 Box 9

232   Reinhard R. Doerries: *Hitler's Last Chief of Foreign Intelligence* pp. 48-55.

233   Gustav Hilger & Alfred G. Meyer: *The Incompatible Allies* pp. 338-340.

234   TNA KV 4/466 *Liddell Diaries* pp. 98, 154-156, 163-166.

235   TNA WO 208/4345

236   Robert Wolfe: *Gustav Hilger: From Hitler's Foreign Office to CIA Consultant.*

237   TNA WO 204/11574 British interrogation of Obergruppenfuhrer Siegfried Kasche, German
       minister to Croatia, conducted 23 June–5 July 1945.

238   USNA RG319 Entry 134B Box 599

239   USNA RG319 Entry 134B Box 599

240   Nadia Benois: *Klop* p. 217.

241   TNA KV 2/94

242   USNA RG319 Entry 134B Box 599

243   For a fuller account see Richard Breitman: *U.S. Intelligence and the Nazis* pp. 203-226 and
       Aarons and Loftus: *Ratlines.*

244   Stephen Dorril: *MI6, Fifty Years of Special Operations* p. 335.

245   TNA KV 2/1495

246   Nigel West and Oleg Tsarev: *The Crown Jewels* pp. 185-186.

247   Nigel West and Oleg Tsarev: *The Crown Jewels* pp. 197-198.

248   Nigel West and Oleg Tsarev: *The Crown Jewels* pp. 191-194.

249   TNA KV 2/1497

250   TNA KV 2/1495

251   TNA KV 2/1591

252   TNA KV 2/1496

253   TNA KV 2/1453

254 TNA KV 2/1629

255 TNA KV 2/1453

256 Arnold M. Silver: *Memories of Oberursel.*

257 Walther Schellenberg: *The Schellenberg Memoirs* pp. 307-308.

258 Stephen Dorril: *MI6 Fifty Years of Operations* pp. 189-190.

259 TNA KV 2/3644

260 TNA KV 2/1592

261 TNA KV 2/1453

262 USNA RG319 Entry 134-B Box 812

263 Arnold M. Silver: *Memories of Oberursel.*

264 Mark Aarons and John Loftus: *Ratlines* p. 50-51.

265 TNA KV 4/467 *Liddell Diaries* p. 74.

266 Richard Breitman: *US Intelligence and the Nazis* p. 146.

267 TNA KV4/467 *Liddell Diaries* p. 78.

268 TNA KV4/467 *Liddell Diaries* p. 100.

269 TNA KV 4/216

270 Keith Jeffery: *MI6 The History of the Secret Intelligence Service* pp. 504-505.

271 TNA KV 2/956-957

272 Nicholas Elliott: *Never Judge a Man by his Umbrella* p. 149.

273 Personal interview, January 2013.

274 Nadia Benois: *Klop* p. 219.

275 Personal property of Igor Ustinov.

276 Mark A. Tittenhofer: *The Rote Drei: Getting Behind the Lucy Myth.*

277 Sándor Radó: *Codename Dora* pp. 130-135.

278 Malcolm Muggeridge: *Chronicles of Wasted Time* vii p. 188.

279 TNA KV 3/349-351

280 TNA KV 2/1647

281 TNA KV 2/2714-5

282 TNA KV 2/3502

283 TNA KV2/2883

284 TNA KV 2/1010

285 Richard J. Aldrich: *The Hidden Hand* p. 97.

286 TNA KV 2/1657

287 František Moravec: *Master of Spies* pp. 186-187.

288 TNA FO 371/39864A

289 Klemens von Klemperer: *German Resistance Against Hitler* p. 193; *Daily Telegraph*, 15 November 2002.

290 TNA KV 2/1649

291 Richard J. Aldrich: *The Hidden Hand* pp. 98-101.

292 TNA KV 2/1647, KV 2/1612

293 Sándor Radó: *Codename Dora* p. 238.

294 Elizabeth Wiskemann: *The Europe I Saw* pp. 42-45, 160-161, 200.

295 TNA KV 2/1611

296 TNA KV 2/1614

297 Hans Rudolf Kurz: *Nachrichtenzentrum Schweiz* pp. 54-57.

298 Constantine Fitzgibbon: *Secret Intelligence in the Twentieth Century* pp. 277-283.

299 TNA KV 2/981

300 *The Manchester Guardian*, 10 April 1948.

301 Personal interview, February 2014.

302 Personal interview, February 2014.

303 TNA KV2 1927

304 Meriel Buchanan: *Ambassador's Daughter* pp. 142-3, 194.

305 H. G. Wells: *H G Wells in Love* pp. 163-4.

306 TNA HO 405/1996

307 TNA KV 2/979

308 Nina Berberova: *Moura* pp. 247-254.

309 Sofka Zinoviev: *Red Princess, A Revolutionary Life*.

310 TNA KV 2/979

311 TNA KV 2/979

312 TNA KV 2/980

313 Nina Berberova: *Moura: The Dangerous Life of the Baroness Budberg* p. 284.

314 Tania Alexander: *A Little of All These* p. 140.

315 TNA KV 4/187 *Liddell Diaries* pp. 709-710.

316 Harold Nicolson: *Diaries and Letters 1939–1945* p. 197.

317 Christopher Andrew: *Secret Service* pp. 464-465; François Kersaudy: *Churchill and De Gaulle* pp. 161-167, 180-182.

318 TNA HW 15/43

319 TNA KV 2/980

320 TNA KV 2/1673

321 TNA KV 2/1674

322 *The Times* 30 October 2004.

323 *The Times* 15 June 2011.

324 TNA KV 2/981

325 Nigel West and Oleg Tsarev: *The Crown Jewels* pp. 151-152.

326 TNA KV 2/981

327 Tania Alexander: *A Little of These* p. 148.

328 *The Sunday Times* London, 2 May 2010.

329 Nadia Benois: *Klop* p. 197.

330 Tania Alexander: *A Little of These* p. 144.

331 Peter Ustinov: *Dear Me* pp. 345-346.

332 TNA FO 372/6337

333 TNA KV 2/2714 and TNA KV 2/2715

334 James Joll: *Europe Since 1870* pp. 440-441.

335 Stewart Steven: *Operation Splinter Factor* gives a full account from the perspective of a CIA plot; Flora Lewis: *The Man Who Disappeared* tells the story from the Fields' perspective.

336 Nigel West: *Historical Dictionary of British Intelligence* p. 556.

337 TNA KV 2/2209

338 TNA KV 4/466 *Liddell Diaries* pp. 201-2.

339 TNA KV 4/466 *Liddell Diaries* pp. 289-90.

340 Nigel West and Oleg Tsarev: *The Crown Jewels* pp. 238-9.

341 Nigel West and Oleg Tsarev: *Triple X, Secrets from the Cambridge Spies* p. 303.

342 Tom Bower: *The Perfect English Spy* p. 122.

343 Nadia Benois: *Klop* pp. 217-221.

344 Owain Hughes: *Everything I Have Always Forgotten* pp. 103-4.

345 TNA FO 1093/551

346 TNA FO 1093/551

347 TNA KV 4/472 *Liddell Diaries* p. 165.

348 TNA FO 1093/349

349 David Aaron Meier: *A Cold War Catastrophe* pp. 25-26, 134.

350 TNA KV 4/473 *Liddell Diaries* p. 2.

351 USNA RG263 230/86/22/06 Box 38

352 TNA KV 2/915

353   L-H 5/2/2

354   TNA FO 371/55671 C11118

355   Bob de Graaff: *The Stranded Baron and the Upstart at the Crossroads.*

356   Otto John: *Zweimal kam ich heim* pp. 251-252.

357   Sefton Delmer: *Black Boomerang* p. 260.

358   TNA KV 2/3715

359   USNA RG 319 270/84/1/01

360   TNA FO 371/109324 (Extracts released 1 October 2013 in response to FoI request)

361   TNA FO 371/109324 (Extracts released 1 October 2013 in response to FoI request)

362   TNA FO 371/109324 (Extracts released 1 October 2013 in response to FoI request)

363   Bob de Graaff: *The Stranded Baron and the Upstart at the Crossroads.*

364   *The Times:* 6 May 1957

365   Nadia Benois: *Klop* pp. 225-230.

366   Hans Speidel: *Aus unserer Zeit* p. 367.

367   Peter Wright: *Spycatcher* pp. 85-87.

368   Peter Ustinov: *Dear Me* p. 250.

369   Personal information, February 2014.

370   Peter Ustinov: *Dear Me* pp. 250-251.

371   Wolfgang zu Putlitz: *The Putlitz Dossier.*

372   Peter Day and Michael Smith: *Daily Telegraph* 4 March 2003.

373   Personal interview, February 2014.

374   Lynda J. Murray: *A Zest for Life* p. 23.

375   Interview with Igor Ustinov, 22 May 2013.

376   Nadia Benois: *Klop* p. 191.

377   Private correspondence.

378   Peter Ustinov: *My Russia* pp. 8-13.

379   Interview with Igor Ustinov, 22 May 2013.

INDEX

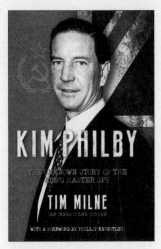

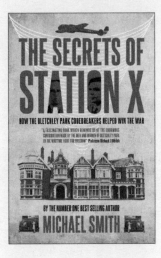